A Bonfire of Inanities
The Bible Dismantled

VOLUME TWO

Mistaken Messiahs

A Bonfire of Inanities
The Bible Dismantled

VOLUME TWO

Mistaken Messiahs

THE REAL TRUTH
ABOUT JESUS AND
THE EARLY HISTORY
OF CHRISTIANITY

Paul McGrane

SINGULAR BOOKS

First published in 2023

Singular Books
www.paulmcgrane.co.uk
All rights reserved

The right of Paul McGrane to be identified as the author of this work has been asserted in accordance with Section 77 of the Copyright, Designs and Patents Act, 1988. No part of this publication may be copied, reproduced, stored in a retrieval system, or transmitted, in any form or by any means without the prior permission of the publisher, nor be otherwise circulated in any form of binding or cover other than that in which it is published and without a similar condition being imposed on the subsequent purchaser.

Thanks to Joey Everett for the maps

Text design by Ellipsis, Glasgow

A CIP record for this book is available from the British Library

ISBN 978-1-7393926-2-8 (paperback)
ISBN 978-1-7393926-3-5 (ebook)

1 3 5 7 9 8 6 4 2

For my extended family
Tina, Vix and Dave, and their children, Max, Orla, Jack, Serenna, Harry, Sam and Wren

The difficulty lies, not in the new ideas, but in escaping from the old ones, which ramify, for those brought up as most of us have been, into every corner of our minds
—J. M. Keynes

Not deep the poet sees, but wide.
—Matthew Arnold

CONTENTS

Maps	x
Foreword	xiii
Preface	xvii
1 Overview	1
2 Jewish Origins	23
3 Christian Origins	64
4 The Jesus Fallacy	130
5 The Pauline Fallacy	204
6 The New Paradigm	286
Select Bibliography	301

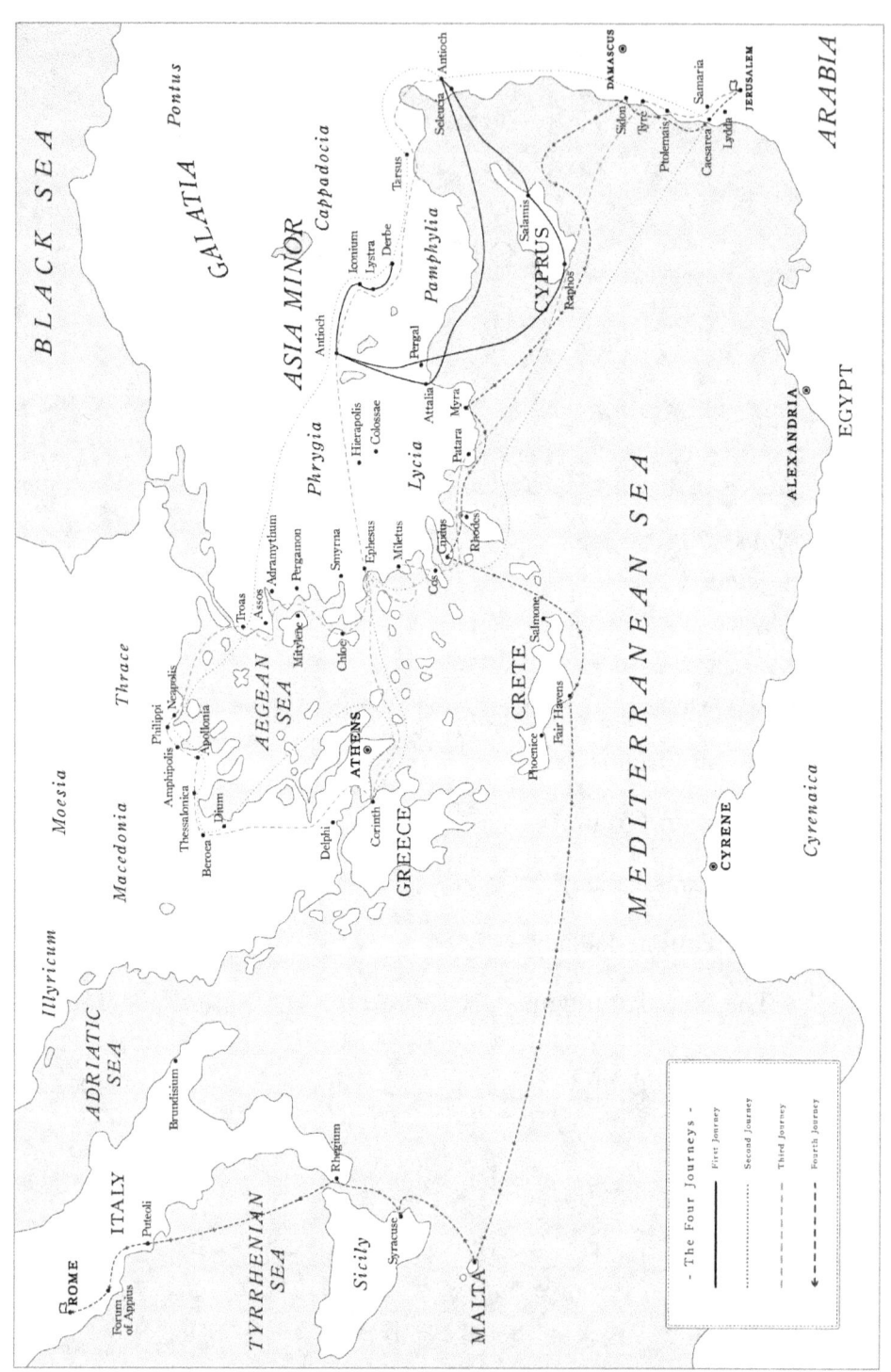

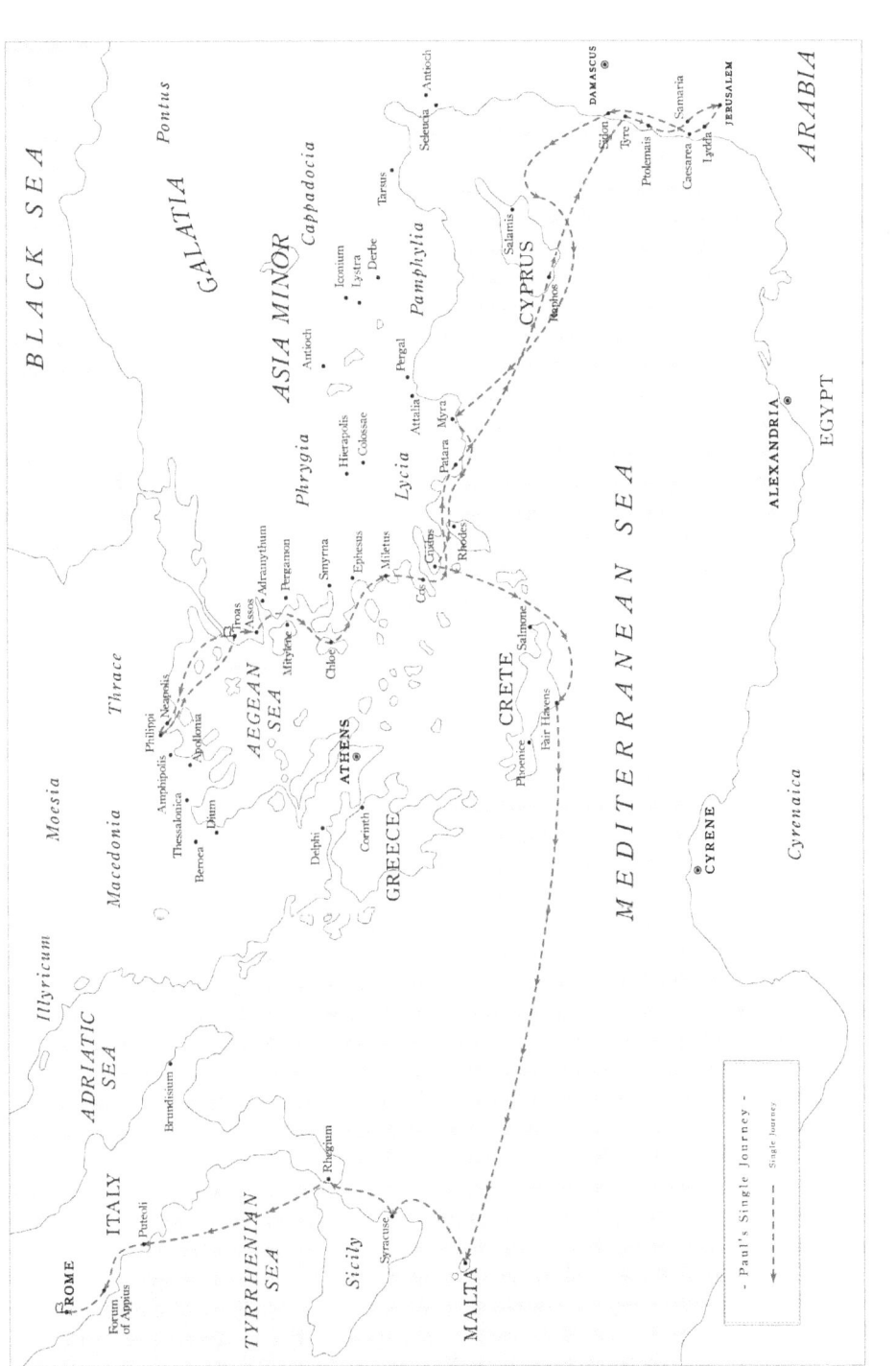

FOREWORD

A Bonfire of Inanities: The Bible Dismantled

As a teenager over half a century ago, I had a brief flirtation with evangelical Christianity: the apparent certainties on offer were attractive then to the self-conscious, uncertain youth that I was. The flirtation ended very quickly during my undergraduate years, to be replaced with the atheism that I have held ever since, but the experience left me with a lifelong interest in religious faith. I retired fifteen years ago and have spent much of the time since then in revisiting Christianity from a rationalist point of view. At the heart of my approach has been what is known as 'textual criticism': a critical study of writings emphasising a close reading and analysis of the text. Specific techniques include the identification of bias resulting from authorial belief and intent; the identification of possible errors in scribal transcription and mistranslation; and the comparison of different versions of events in different texts. All of these possibilities exist in abundance in the Bible. My own training, experience and qualification is in modern literary texts, but I decided to apply that training in critical analysis to the Bible and other contemporary texts.

I took First Class Honours in my undergraduate degree at Ulster University, and I subsequently conducted three years' research in an archive of original manuscripts in Duke Humphrey's Reading Room at the Bodleian Library at Oxford University, before attaining my Doctorate (DPhil) from the latter. I have subsequently published peer-reviewed articles in respected academic journals. My degrees and my research have been in English literature, specialising in the Victorian period. In the academic world this does not qualify me to write about the early history of Judaism and Christianity, because in that world there are strict and rigid demarcation lines between academic disciplines. There is, however, a growing recognition that those divisions get in the way of real knowledge. In the case of my own research, my stance is that someone like me, trained in textual analysis and practised in working with sometimes chaotic manuscript sources, can have something to bring to the party when studying ancient scriptural texts. Of course, I am dependent on the linguistic, archaeological and historical work of experts in the field – but with my objectivity, born of a different academic discipline, combined with a lack of supernatural preconceptions – I may be able to offer new insights into the interpretation and meaning of those scriptural texts.

I believe that my researches over the last couple of decades have uncovered a revolutionary new understanding of the roots of Judaism and Christianity. In 2017, I published a book called *The Christian Fallacy* in which I set out my initial findings. This attracted little attention and only a few readers, but undeterred, I continued my research, revised and much enlarged my previous book, and this trilogy is the end result. [That first book now forms the essence of Volume II although some of those original arguments, relating to the Book of Revelation and Simon Magus, can now be found in Volume III.] The trilogy offers, for the first time, a complete, rationalistic re-interpretation of the Bible, from Genesis to Revelation, and relates it to other contemporary texts, religious and secular, and to contemporary events and people. *Volume I: Ancestral Tales* analyses the various source texts that make up the so-called Books of Moses in the Old Testament, and in conjunction with the non-biblical record – notably the Egyptian one – is able to unravel the true roots of Jewish belief. *Volume II: Mistaken Messiahs* traces how Jewish Messianic belief finds its way into the New Testament and Christianity and identifies historical figures behind Jesus and the Apostles. *Volume III: 'Apocalypse Postponed'* then focuses on the Christian belief in imminent apocalypse and traces how thoroughgoing misunderstanding of the relevant texts has led to two millennia of fallacious expectation.

On 7 February 1497 in Florence, the religious extremist Friar Girolamo Savonarola, held the first of his 'bonfires of the vanities' on which thousands of objects, condemned by religious authorities as 'occasions of sin', were consigned to the flames. It is high time we rationalists had our own bonfire on which to consign the sheer inanities of religious belief. This trilogy is a metaphorical bonfire of biblical fallacies. Each volume in the trilogy has been written to stand alone, but there is a natural sequence to the arguments developed which is facilitated if they are read in order:

Vol I	Ancestral Tales
Vol II	Mistaken Messiahs
Vol III	Apocalypse Postponed[1]

There has never been anything like this – in scope, in approach,

---

[1] This volume in particular is very much a sequel to Volume II, adding to and building on the arguments found there. It begins with a summary of Volume II but, if at all possible, I would urge that they be read consecutively.

and in findings. It may be possible to continue in Jewish or Christian belief in the light of these three volumes, but it would be a very different kind of religious faith from the one normally espoused.

PREFACE

Having examined the roots of Judaism in Volume I, I now turn my attention to the way in which Christianity emerged as a sect out of Judaism. More specifically, this volume will present what I term a 'New Paradigm' for the origins of the Messianic concept that characterizes Christianity. The arguments I present, therefore, will often be fresh and new. But of course, I would be the first to acknowledge that I stand on the shoulders of giants – scholars who over the last two centuries have begun to free biblical research from the shackles of religious belief. I hope that I have paid tribute to them as appropriate as I build upon their arguments and insights as this present volume proceeds. But there is an important caveat to this. As you have every right to expect as a reader, I have read widely in the relevant literature on the subjects that concern this volume. But it must be said – and I shall win no friends here in the biblical scholarship community – that much New Testament scholarship can only be described as a pseudoscience. Its erudition is often massive and the result of extraordinary immersion in ancient languages and texts. But it is written out of a paradigm that in some way or another accepts the essential truths of the Christian religion. And if you set out in any scholarship with a set of beliefs that you hold to be inviolable, then you are bound to interpret your results in a biased way. It is a simple fact that the only people, by and large, who choose in life to be biblical scholars are people with an *a priori* belief in the supernatural origin or imprimatur of the texts they study. Those texts are, for them, not just ancient texts to be interpreted in the same way as ancient Latin and Greek classics; they are 'scripture' to be reverenced and interpreted in the light of Christian credo. It is true that over time, partly because of their studies, some of these scholars lose part or all their 'faith' in scripture. But by then, their careers are so committed to educational institutions that require such faith, it becomes difficult if not impossible to speak and write freely. Put simply, if your livelihood depends upon teaching the New Testament to theology students, you are not likely to rock the boat by saying (as I do) that Jesus Christ was a 2nd Century fiction.

So, although I benefit hugely from the scholarship of the biblical academic community, I do not find in their writings many interpretations or conclusions that appeal much to rational common sense. Stand outside the core Christian paradigm and most of what these scholars write is unreadably wrong-headed. For example, I shall examine the influence of the prophet Zechariah on the Gospel stories about Jesus. One such is Jesus' entry into Jerusalem on the back of an ass. There are only three possible interpretations of this story. Either Jesus was fulfilling a miraculous prophecy of His[1] life made centuries before; or He was consciously fulfilling that prophecy as a demonstration to His followers of His awareness of His own divine nature and destiny; or a later writer was creating a fictional life of Jesus and raiding

---

[1] I will use the customary honorific initial capital for all references to supposedly divine personages, not because I subscribe to their divinity but because it looks strange not to.

the Old Testament for inspiration. The first and second interpretations are the only ones countenanced by most biblical scholars. I have read many scholarly articles by academics, not just from American evangelical theological colleges but mainstream, respected universities both sides of the Atlantic, that espouse these supernatural interpretations. As I shall argue in my book, the third alternative is the only one that makes rational sense. The Gospel writers were creatively constructing fictions from prior scriptural and other texts. And I shall supply plenty of evidence that, given the allegorical habits of Judaeo-Christian writers, this explanation becomes a near certainty. I am grateful to other scholars for identifying all the possible influences of Zechariah on the writers of the Gospels – it has saved me many hours – but I must be excused if I find them almost universally naive about the implications of such influences for the truth about Christianity.[2]

In researching the matters raised in this volume, I have been often guided by three very straightforward principles. The first is the relatively simple philosophical concept of **Occam's Razor**. There are many different versions and expressions of this, but in essence the *Razor* states that among competing hypotheses the hypothesis with the least assumptions is *probably* the right one. It cautions us that whenever we find 'multiplied entities' to explain something, the chances rise that the explanation is false. I am not suggesting that the *Razor* is infallible, nor am I denying that judgements about what is simple and what is complex will have a considerable degree of subjectivity. But all other things being equal, it is a matter of common observation that if an explanation of something

---

[2] It never ceases to amaze me that otherwise scholarly institutions around the world continue to run teaching programmes on theology. It cannot be said too many times: theology is a pseudoscience, based on a closed set of beliefs rather than open scientific enquiry, and as such has no place in any teaching or research institution that is in receipt of public funds.

requires one to believe a lot of unlikely things, it will *probably* turn out to be wrong. Any multiplication of entities *probably* indicates falsity. Readers of Volume 1 will know that the early books of the Old Testament are littered with duplication of the same events, attributed to different mythical characters. As we shall see, the New Testament is also full of such multiplicities of events and people. The same names turn up again and again; the same incidents seem to get recounted twice; the same phrases recur. It is a central argument of this book that these multiplying entities disguise, either by intention or accident, a much simpler reality that has been obscured by the creation of layers of narrative that conveniently 'explain' some very inconvenient facts. (On this basis of course, the traditional Christian interpretation fails the *Razor* test because it makes the biggest assumption of all – that there is a God, and that the Bible is His Word. But the *Razor* also works against a whole range of other paradigms that require identifications, correspondences and harmonisations that just multiply the assumptions).

The second principle is best summed up by this phrase, known as the Sagan Standard, after the cosmologist Carl Sagan, who first coined it:

> Extraordinary claims require extraordinary evidence.

'Extra-Ordinary' in the present context is a synonym for 'Super-Natural'. Belief in God and in a Messiah both fall into this category. No one can disprove such beliefs, but it is surely reasonable to request that those who promulgate them should offer commensurate evidence. There is nothing in documented human experience to parallel many of the events described in the Bible – for example, people rising from the dead, or instantaneously being transported over huge distances – let alone the sort of apocalyptic future events described in the Book of Revelation. In the absence of 'extraordinary' evidence, and in the presence of the sort of 'ordinary' evidence that I shall present in this volume, the stance I shall take will be based on rational explanation.

For the third principle, I have been guided by an early Victorian poet, Matthew Arnold, who had an unwavering commitment to the human critical faculty, and faced up to where that led – the existential crisis of faith that he and his generation were the first really to experience:

> Not deep the poet sees, but wide.[3]

I am no poet, but I do think that the truth about the real roots of Christianity lies not in esoteric theories or new discoveries, but in seeing the wood for the trees: no single element of my solution can be 'proved' beyond a shadow of a doubt, but taken as a whole, the paradigm offered in the following pages provides a better overall fit with what we know than any other. The reason why there are so many conflicting theories about Jesus is because the evidence is so contradictory. Focus on any specific issue, and the scope for *deep* disagreement is endless. But accept for the moment that my New Paradigm is correct, and it will become apparent how it manages to be *wide* enough to encompass more limited theories and to provide a contextual framework in which they all then find their natural place. This New Paradigm is the basis on which I invite the reader to judge this book.

The reader will require little if anything in terms of prior knowledge or reference material. I have written for a perceived audience of intelligent, educated and enquiring readers who have hitherto expended little or no energy in relation to

---
[3] Matthew Arnold, from *Resignation*, 1849.

matters of this kind and therefore need a reasonable amount of background explanation. Readers who are keen enquirers after the truth of these matters may find some of this unnecessary, but I hope I have been able to reach a reasonable balance between explication and length. The two main texts I have used are the Bible itself and the works of the Jewish historian Josephus.[4] The reader will certainly find it convenient to have these to hand, particularly when our investigations delve deeply into key texts, but I have endeavoured throughout to quote relevant passages in full, so in theory this should not be strictly necessary. I have used the King James Authorised Version of the Bible. It is the version that pervades English literature and remains unsurpassed as English prose translation; for me at least, it just feels comfortable and familiar. The Authorised Version and Whiston's translation of Josephus are, in Britain at least, the commonest texts available to most households. They are also readily available (and free) on the internet. However, my arguments rarely depend on matters of contentious translation, and where they might I have explained in full, so any translations will do for the purpose. Those who prefer more modern translations may wish to have their favoured versions by their side as they read.

As with the other books in the trilogy, *Mistaken Messiahs* is based on rational research and mainstream sources and materials. It is emphatically not based on esoteric ideas, or some spectacular new discovery of documents, inscriptions or archaeological artefacts. It does not require the reader to become an expert on the Dead Sea Scrolls, or, indeed, on the Bible as a whole. It does not rely on arcane formulae, numerological calculations, celestial observations, parallels with

---

[4] Readers of Volume 1 will be familiar with Josephus. There, we relied on him for his preservation of the writings of the Egyptian historian Manetho; here, it will be Josephus's own accounts of contemporary events in 1st century AD Judæa that will be of interest.

other religions or esoteric associations with other cults. Nor is it the result of divine revelation, prophetic dreaming or deep psychological probing. As one might expect from a writer whose training is in literary criticism, it is simply based on detailed, and in some cases radical, critical re-examination of biblical texts, trying to put aside two millennia of interpretation founded on expectations of divinely inspired harmony and coherence. I think the answer has been staring us in the face all along. To find it, we just need to sweep aside those 2,000 years of credulous, uncritical interpretation, read the key texts afresh with an eye to who wrote them and with what agenda, and then ask ourselves: what is the most likely explanation of it all?

Most people in Britain today take a relaxed view about Christianity. This probably has a lot to do with the pragmatic nature of the British psyche and the nature of the established Anglican Church in particular. That church was founded on pragmatism, harmonisation and compromise, and so it remains to this day. At the time of writing, diehard conservatives are fighting a rather pathetic and forlorn rearguard action to prevent such modern innovations as homosexuality among the clergy and the ordination of female bishops; but there seems little doubt that these and other compromises will eventually be reached, and the Anglican church will continue to accommodate itself in an evolutionary fashion with changing moralities and beliefs. Not so the Catholic Church, or the vast number of fundamentalist and evangelical churches that continue to find adherents into the 21st century, particularly in the United States of America. These continue to encourage believers to swell the population of a world already unable to feed itself, and to preach intolerance of anybody that does not adhere to their own distorted, infantile and ugly take on reality. But in Britain at least, these attract a minority; many people still put 'C of E' on census forms, but actual church-going continues to decline and, although many, perhaps most, people seem to retain a vague belief in some supernatural meaning to life, there are probably few British people who could subscribe wholeheartedly to the Anglican creed. In my experience, when asked, they say something like: *'I think Jesus probably existed; of course, he wasn't the Son of God or anything like that, but he was a good man, and we should all try to live by what he taught.'* Some also argue more positively, though not in my view convincingly, that we need to retain belief of this sort as a foundation for morality in society.

It is, therefore, almost a convention that in books like this the author should reassure his readers that he is not trying to destroy individual Christian faith; that the Christ of faith and the Jesus of history need not be dependent one on the other. And it is true that I subscribe genuinely to the rights of individuals to believe anything they like, as long as they do not try to impose those beliefs on others. But in the modern world, with fundamentalist Christians and jihadist Muslims squaring up to each other for some sort of cataclysmic, apocalyptic endgame, I do not think I have the luxury of prevarication. So, at the outset, I must declare that not only do I not believe in the person Christians call 'Jesus', or in the teachings of any of the myriad varieties of Christianity, I do not even believe there is a God: I am an atheist or, more positively as some prefer, a humanist. I cannot prove that there is no God – but I cannot prove that there is no Santa Claus either, and the odds on me being wrong are about equal in either case.

Furthermore, I believe that religion, including all varieties of Judaism and Christianity, has been a pernicious influence on civilisation. Looking over the long, appalling history of persecution, murder, war and genocide, all conducted in the name of religion, I find the way in which people still cling to the ludicrous beliefs taught by all the world's religions to be both baffling and depressing. Are we never to be free of the repulsive ideas of pre-scientific religious founders whose personal delusions, often contrary to all humane conscience and human sympathy, continue as dogma to influence the thoughts and actions of millions of people? More specifically, are we really to believe that the psychotic visions of people like the Apostle Paul on the road to Damascus 2,000 years ago are the way in which an omnipotent and loving God would choose to reveal Himself to His creation? And do the people who daily preach hatred of their fellow creatures, and take up arms against them purely because they believe their deity wishes it, ever stop and wonder whether any deity that requires such absurdities and cruelties is worthy of the worship He seems to demand?

However, I did not write this book (and the other volumes in the trilogy) just to debunk Christianity from an atheist standpoint. I wrote it because I wanted to understand for myself how Christian beliefs came about, and having reached that understanding, I wanted to share it with anyone else who takes an interest in these things. Those like me who find the traditional Christian narrative unbelievable are still entitled to look for alternative explanations for a religion that has dominated world history for 2,000 years. The western culture in which I have lived out my seven decades is founded on Christian beliefs and if, as an atheist, I find those beliefs untenable, then I can think of no more important quest than the one embarked upon in this trilogy. That search would be worthwhile for the intellectual fascination of historical enquiry alone, but if this book contributes in any way to a decrease in supernatural belief – and more particularly, fundamentalist belief – in the world of the 21st century, I am not ashamed or embarrassed to say that, personally, I shall be delighted.

CHAPTER 1

Overview

You may ask why we need yet another book about the Christian Messiah, Jesus. After all, the British Library main catalogue lists nearly 20,000 volumes with 'Jesus' in the title, and this must just scrape the surface of books that have Jesus and the Christian religion as their subject. Indeed, in recent decades[1] the number of books appearing has increased exponentially and is now supported by an avalanche of self-publication and internet-based interest groups, all pursuing the subject of Christian belief from every conceivable angle. This is powerful testimony to the fact that, in an age of scepticism and falling church attendance, people are as fascinated as ever by the story of Jesus and the origins of Christianity. The sceptical interest has also been fuelled in more recent times by the overt decision by a group of atheist writers and thinkers – people like Richard Dawkins, Christopher Hitchens, Sam Harris and Daniel Dennett – to come out of the closet and proclaim not just the case for atheism, but the proposition that mankind and civilization

---

1 Particularly following publication of Richard Dawkins' *The God Delusion*. For full details of this and all books referred to in footnotes, please see the Select Bibliography at the end of this book.

would be better off if we abandoned belief in the supernatural entirely. For western civilization, based on Christianity since Constantine adopted it for the Roman Empire, the issue of belief in God is inextricably bound up with the parallel issue of belief in Christianity.

Surely then, there can be nothing new to say after over two millennia of Christian belief, biblical interpretation and theological enquiry? I have the temerity to think there is. Most books about Christianity are, of course, written by committed Christians of one variety or another; that is, their authors subscribe to the belief that Jesus was the 'Son of God', the divine intersecting with the human in a unique event of eternal significance to mankind. Whatever they have to say about Jesus in particular is written out of the paradigm promulgated by the Christian church: that Jesus was a Jew, born at or around the beginning of the Christian era; that He began his ministry at about 30 years of age by being recognized and baptized by John the Baptist; that He was crucified three years after that; but that His new religion was spread to the Gentiles by His followers, chief of whom were Peter and Paul. But for the last two centuries an increasing number of writers about Jesus have taken a sceptical stance – sceptical certainly about His divine status, but more recently, sceptical about His actual existence as a historical figure. This book is written from such a sceptical point of view. I believe, along with very many people, that every part of the traditional story of Jesus is historically suspect. But for me, this purely negative assertion is not enough. The recent profusion of books attacking Christianity do little or nothing to explain how, nevertheless, the story of Jesus, enshrined in a religion called Christianity, came to dominate western civilization for 2,000 years. The Gospels may be fiction – and I shall argue that they are – but their writers claimed to be conveying truth. Were they liars, or perhaps deluded, or were they themselves misled? What was really going on in the first half of the first century AD? It is to questions like these that this book seeks to find answers.

Christianity is a religion founded on assertions about historical events in the first century AD. But these assertions are largely without supporting evidence from outside of the Bible, and, in places, conflict with what we do know about what was happening at the time. This will surprise many. Christians are often taught by their leaders that their faith is supported by the findings of historians and archaeologists, and the media often run stories about new 'evidence' – new archaeological finds, new manuscripts – that seems to bear out the historical truth of the Bible. But in all the key essentials, the idea that the story of Christianity has any basis in historical fact is misguided and wrong. For this reason, there are a plethora of theories to compete with the traditional Christian account and an increasing supply of books that offer alternative views – that, for example, Jesus was a revolutionary,[2] or a pagan philosopher[3], or even a magic mushroom.[4] But the fact that Jesus can (arguably) be demonstrated plausibly to be so many quite different things surely points to the truth – that the stories about him in the Bible are drawn from and influenced by most if not all these different versions and more, and that his composite nature results from fictional mythmaking rather than historical reality. As I shall show, the Jesus of the

---

[2] There are a multitude of books taking this line – notably Eisenman's *James, the Brother of Jesus*. Robert Eisenman is an American biblical scholar and this seminal work has been massively influential among sceptics and conspiracy theorists, and it is indispensable reading for anyone seeking to untangle the web of disinformation that characterizes the four Gospels and the Book of the Acts of the Apostles.

[3] Notably, T. Freke & P. Gandy, *The Jesus Mysteries*.

[4] Notoriously, John Allegro's *The Sacred Mushroom and the Cross*.

Gospels was invented by early Christian writers to give flesh-and-blood reality to a heavenly figure about whom they knew next to nothing.

Very few books offer a comprehensive and satisfying answer to the question 'Who exactly was Jesus and how does that relate to what Christians came to believe after his death.' In this Volume I have set out to do just that. I will develop in the following pages a New Paradigm – a new framework for understanding the origins of Christianity – that broadly accepts the validity of many of the various competing theories about Jesus but transcends them and takes the argument a step further into a wholly new and original understanding of how Christianity came about. Christianity as we know it emerged gradually from the ferment of Messianic and apocalyptic[5] Jewish religious sects that arose in the near east in the first century of the Christian era. It was originally a Jewish sect, differing from the others only in its distinctive beliefs about 'Jesus Christ'. The original Jewish adherents of the sect were accepted by other Jews as Jewish and continued to participate in the Jewish way of life. Many attempts have been made to identify the original Christian sect with other sects known from that time and, particularly (following the discovery of the Dead Sea Scrolls in the mid-twentieth century), with the Essene sect that is believed by many scholars to be the source of most of those documents. But there is no reason why any such identification should turn out to be true; there were so many versions of Judaism at this time that the Christian sect could, in principle, be distinct and separate from all the others of which we have knowledge. To avoid prejudging this or any other issue that will be the subject of this book, I have called the sect with

---

[5] i.e. relating to the 'End of Days'. Apocalyptic prophecy will be the subject of Volume III.

which we are here concerned, the 'Jesus Movement', because it was belief in the specialness of Jesus that set it apart from its rivals.

The New Paradigm will provide a revised chronology for events in the first half of the first century AD; identify who the key players really were at the time, including the historical figure of Jesus himself; and show how the religion we call Christianity evolved from competing understandings of what the Jesus Movement was all about. Most important of all, I believe it will provide an account of people and events that is not just intellectually plausible, but psychologically satisfying. So many other theories of who Jesus was fail that crucial test: they rely upon an acceptance that people would have behaved in a way that seems implausible in the real world of the first, or indeed any, century. Of course, it is hard – verging on impossible – for us today to recreate for ourselves the mindset of a Jew or Gentile living in first-century Palestine under Roman occupation. But these were human beings, nonetheless, and their beliefs, motivations and actions should be broadly comprehensible to us; any interpretation of what happened then needs to convince by an overall coherence, consistency and – at the end of the day – a simple likelihood that *this* is what happened.

Who exactly was the historical Jesus? What did he believe and teach? How does this relate to the actions and teachings of the early disciples and Apostles, who together laid the foundations for Christian belief as we know it today? For me, the traditional Christian answers to these questions are unsustainable; the Christian narrative, as set out in the Bible and subsequently mediated by Church doctrines, is simply unbelievable. I say this, not because of the supernatural elements, although many readers may feel this is enough, but because even putting rational scepticism to one side, the Bible itself is too full of internal inconsistencies (which we shall look at later) to be accepted as, in any real sense, the 'Word of God'. This is hardly a new perception. Theologians have wrestled with all the inconsistencies since the earliest days of the Church. However, in doing so they have been constrained by their belief in what is known as 'scriptural inerrancy': the upfront conviction that, as the Word of God, Scripture is infallible and therefore by definition cannot be mistaken, inaccurate or contradictory. God is perfect and therefore His Holy Word must be perfect too. If Scripture appears imperfect, the mistakes derive from man's imperfect understanding.

I do not start from this perspective which requires a step of faith I see no reason to take. Just because the Bible (or to be more precise, the Christian church, based on one or two of the individual documents that comprise the Bible) *claims* to be the Word of God is no reason to accept that it *is* so. The world is full of other holy texts making similar claims, so why believe just this one? By not making that step of faith, one is free to seek explanations, unfettered by a need to find unerring consistency or conformity with other sources of historical knowledge. And so, what the Christian Church regards as seeking the truth through harmonization of inconsistencies, and explication of errors, I regard as so much special pleading for what, in my opinion, is the long-lost cause of 'scriptural inerrancy'. What the Church regards as fulfilled prophecy from the Old Testament, I regard as New Testament fictionalizing based on texts wrenched out of context. Christian apologists have had two millennia in which to smooth away all the difficulties, and the faith of millions today, if not based purely on faith in the teachings of one church or another, is based on these explanations.

For me, this is all incredible at best and dishonest at worst. I am not alone, of course. As I will show in this book, there have been many scholars over the last couple of centuries at least who, looking at the evidence with an open mind and a rational outlook, have reached a similar sceptical view. Most such sceptical scholars are reasonably united in the view that, whoever and whatever Jesus was (or wasn't), he did not actually found the *religion* we know today as Christianity. Opinions vary widely about exactly what Jesus taught, but it does seem clear that early Christianity, as an organized religion, was founded not by Jesus but after his death by others, based particularly on the writings of the Apostle Paul. Paul's theology seems to have originated with visions he claims to have had, initially at the time of his conversion and on an unknown number of occasions subsequently. These led him to believe that someone he calls 'Jesus', or 'the Lord', has become a human sacrifice acceptable to God for the remission of the sins (i.e. 'salvation') of all those that believe in him. The degree to which Paul saw Jesus as divine and how this divinity related to God is a matter of theological debate: the doctrine of the Holy Trinity – God the Father, God the Son and God the Holy Spirit (or Holy Ghost) – was developed by the Church over succeeding centuries. But Paul taught that the remission of sins of all believers was freely available to all that placed their faith in Jesus, Jew and Gentile alike, and that as a result God was offering a new Covenant with mankind that replaced the need for man to follow any prescribed code of conduct. In fact, Paul does seem to say that faith in Jesus is the only thing necessary for salvation – that there is nothing that man can do to affect things. This point – the dichotomy between the 'works' of man and 'faith' in Jesus alone – very rapidly became a key point of theological debate for the early Church; it was, more than any other, the issue on which the Reformation turned, and it remains so to this day.

The implications of salvation by faith alone are various:

1. If man can have no effect on his future eternal fate by his own efforts, what is the implication for individual free will? A God who is omniscient must have known at the beginning of time who would be 'saved' and who would not be; in some sense[6] at least, therefore, He must have 'predestined' some people to eternal damnation, about which they could do nothing at all. This is often called Calvinism, and acceptance of this idea characterizes many extreme Protestant sects to this day; for them, salvation from this terrible fate lies in strict adherence to their own theological interpretation of the Bible.
2. A less extreme view of the matter is that free will does exist, but predestination is also somehow true. C. S. Lewis, for example, called this an 'antinomy'. The reconciliation of this antinomy is beyond our human understanding, but we can trust that God has it all sorted out. This somewhat muddled compromise characterizes most mainstream Protestant groups, including, for example, the Anglican Church.
3. The Catholic Church, however, has never really accepted predestination, at least without severe qualification. It solves the problem through a range of other ideas: notably the existence of purgatory where sins can be expiated over time, and an ordained priesthood who mediate between man's sinful behaviour and the provision of God's mercy made possible by the sacrifice of Jesus. These ideas are not to be found in Paul's writings (or, arguably, anywhere else in the Bible) but were developed over the first few centuries and are the

---

[6] The degree to which God's foreknowledge implies predestination was a key issue between Lutheran Churches and Calvinist Reformed Churches, but the distinctions between extreme Protestant sects need not concern us here.

reason why Paul's theology is less prominent in Catholic dogma than in Protestant.

4. For others, the key point is that Jesus has freed mankind from all external laws and man is, therefore, now free to live according to his conscience – or the internal guidance of God within the individual believer. This manifested itself from the beginning in the plethora of 'Gnostic' sects that arose and flourished from the second century onwards. We shall look more closely at these later. In the modern era, the Quaker movement is probably the best example of this line of thinking.

We shall see that this faith/work dichotomy has its roots in the more parochial concerns of the early Jesus Movement, but Paul's interpretation of it lies at the heart of all these later developments in Christianity. It is an extraordinary fact that if one is looking for a clear statement of Christian theology on this matter – or indeed any other – one would be hard put to find it in any of the Gospel accounts of Jesus' life. It was Paul who developed the theology of Christianity in his letters to various early churches, and it is to Paul that theologians look for answers to the key issues of Christianity as an organized religion. This is downplayed to some extent by all versions of Christianity, although especially by the Catholic Church, which likes to explain away those of Paul's teachings that seem to contradict Church teachings. Paul is more prominent in Protestant theology; in many ways, Paul was rediscovered by the leaders of the Reformation. But nevertheless, he is still traditionally regarded by 'reformed' churches as simply explaining and promulgating what Jesus originally taught. And if this book is to grapple with the puzzle of the historical Jesus, it must inevitably, therefore, also deal with similar questions about Paul: who *he* was and what *he* taught.

Those who, like me, reject the standard Christian narrative broadly take one of two views about Jesus himself. One view, and probably the most prevalent among those who have no active Christian faith but have never delved into the evidence, is that Jesus *was* a historical person, but that he was *not* the 'Son of God'. In this view, Jesus is seen as variously, a teacher, a prophet, a 'good man', a rebel, a revolutionary, a Pharisaic rabbi, and an earthly Messiah. There are many scholarly and popular accounts of Jesus that champion one or another of these pictures of him. On this view, the Christian religion as we now know it, was created after Jesus' death by the Apostle Paul from personal 'visions' and 'transports' that he experienced over several years, combined by him with Old Testament passages and ideas from classical philosophy and the various Mystery religions popular in the Roman Empire at the time.

A major problem for me with all these sceptical 'Jesus as mortal man' theories is that they fly in the face of human psychology. They require that Paul should have promulgated the idea of Jesus as Son of God, against overwhelming evidence that he was not. The Gospels mention Jesus having brothers and sisters. The Catholic Church regards these as 'cousins', which seems to me to be a classic piece of harmonization. But even accepting this, Paul, undoubtedly knew and met with members of Jesus' family and others who would have known Jesus from childhood. He must have explained to them his visions of Jesus as Son of God, who died for the remission of the sins of all that believe in Him. I just cannot conceive the circumstances in which this would not have led to derision from people who knew the mortal Jesus well. How could Paul have sustained his own self-belief, let alone convince others, in the face of such first-hand denial?[7] If Jesus lived and had family and friends in the first century AD, and if he was a mere human, it is hard to avoid the conclusion that Paul was dishonest; that he knew his religion to be nonsense (because everyone told him it was) but he promulgated it nevertheless. And this leads then to the inevitable idea that his motives must have been material – either power or money or both.

But there is also a second view about Jesus – probably less popular, but growing in its adherents as rational enquiry into scriptural texts continues and as more ancient texts are discovered – that so far from being a mortal man, Jesus in fact *never actually existed at all*. This is the 'mythicist stance'. In this view Jesus was a mythical character, a Jewish equivalent to the many other gods of the ancient world who were said to have died and been reborn for the benefit of nature and mankind. This mythical view has the advantage of exonerating Paul. It implies that Paul was essentially honest about the visions he saw and what he came to believe as a result; he may have been delusional, or even psychotic, but in matters of faith when he said he 'did not lie' he was being truthful to his subjective experience, and no one could challenge or question his right to that experience. In this book I shall argue that there *was* a historical figure called Jesus, but he lived so long before the Christian era that, early Christians felt themselves able to make up stories about him.

I should emphasize again here that I do not set out in this book to prove that Jesus Christ is a fictional character: I certainly take that view, but it is just my starting point. The full evidence for the mythicist stance would require a volume on its own because that stance cannot, in the final analysis,

---

7 I am reminded of the scene in Monty Python's *Life of Brian*, in which Brian's mother (played by the wonderful but now sadly deceased Terry Jones), exasperated by the crowds clamouring after her son, declaims from her balcony: "He's not the Messiah; he's a very naughty boy!"

be *proved* like a mathematical equation – it can only be *demonstrated* with sufficient evidence that the likelihood of it being true becomes overwhelming.[8] The demonstration requires a verse-by-verse analysis of the Gospels, showing in each case the source of Gospel texts in the Old Testament and other classical writings. Other scholars have already done this brilliantly and comprehensively, and I pay tribute to their labours in my book. But if the mythicist stance *is* correct, and the Gospels are creative fictions concocted from other texts, what are its implications for the rest of the New Testament – notably, the events and characters that appear in the Book of Acts, the Epistles of Paul and the Revelation of John? And if Jesus did not exist in the first century AD, as the mythicist stance implies, that leaves a huge hole in our history of the times: what are the implications for the chronology of events? This volume will, of course, summarize the mythicist argument and provide sufficient evidence to convince an unbiased reader, but as a necessary preliminary to its real subject – an exploration of these wider implications. Inevitably perhaps, readers who are not already aware of the mythicist case may find this a stumbling block to the rest of my book. It is a problem that it would be hard for me to address without just repeating the work of others. But perhaps a few words here might be helpful.

It is a matter of fact, not conjecture or theory, that every event and statement of any significance at all in the Gospels can be parallelled in other earlier texts, particularly Jewish religious writings both in and out of the Old Testament. This is a matter of fact because the parallels are clear to see and have been demonstrated exhaustively. The only issue at stake,

---

8 A good example would be the *theory* of evolution. Creationists love to stress that it is *only* a theory. But scientists understand what constitutes proof. That is why, despite overwhelming evidence to show that it is true, they still call it a theory.

therefore, is how one interprets this fact. Christians would say that in the case of Old Testament parallels we are dealing with supernatural, prophetic texts (and presumably in non-canonical texts, just coincidence). The Sagan Standard rules this out. I see no reason to jump to the extraordinary conclusion if there are ordinary explanations that are satisfactory. Some have argued that Jesus did exist, but He spent his life consciously or unconsciously conforming to these prior texts. But for me at least, this explanation just does not work. For fulfilment, many of the texts require events that would have been outside His control; for Him to be unconscious of the prophecies seems hardly credible either, given who He claimed to be. And if Jesus were conforming to prophecy consciously, that would surely be the actions of a charlatan rather than a genuine Messiah. In my view, the only rational explanation that is psychologically credible is that Jesus was a fictional character concocted from Messianic prophecy, or at the very least, if He did exist in first century Judæa, the stories about him in the Gospels are later fictions. The reason we can believe this to be the case is that we know for another fact that this was exactly the sort of thing that religious writers were doing at the time. The techniques were known as *Midrash* and *Pesher* and involved convoluted and far-fetched allegorical interpretation of unrelated scriptural texts. We shall look closely at this practice later, but if you find that unlikely, listen to a few Christian church sermons and you will find that the technique is alive and well today.

Many people regard books such as this one as pointless. Ironically, this view can be held by both sceptics and traditional believers alike. On the one hand, believers argue that it is all beside the point. Whoever or whatever Jesus was is unimportant; it is the Jesus of faith that matters – the Jesus that teaches us how to live and gives us the promise of everlasting life. Yet Christianity makes the unique claim that Jesus was not only God, but that he walked amongst us and died a grisly death for us. It is founded on this historical claim, and must surely therefore be open to rational, historical enquiry. On the other hand, sceptics who take the extreme view argue that we can never know the truth of these things, they all happened so long ago, and the evidence we have is so fragmentary, contradictory and compromised by bias and forgery, that it is useless to try. Yet in my view, the Bible is full of clues to the puzzle of the historical Jesus. Those clues alone can never produce historical certainty, but we *can* search for a hypothesis that best fits the evidence and clues that we have.

To do this we need to treat all the evidence on an equal basis. Each document (irrespective of whether it has been sanctioned as part of the Bible or not) must be examined in the same way, using basic textual critical techniques. This means that we must, wherever possible, identify for each text who wrote it and, more important, why; identify that is, what political, personal and religious biases influenced the original writer and, as important, may also have influenced subsequent editors. We can never assume that what we read today is precisely what the original author or authors wrote. In my view this requires careful textual study but also a broad grasp of historical context. There is so much in the written record that is inconsistent and contradictory that, unless one stands back to see the whole picture, one can too easily be drawn off into seductive error. The history of post-Reformation, sectarian Christianity shows how easy it is to go down that path. The smallest textual ambiguity can lead to schism and eventually a proliferation of sects, each conveniently overlooking the interpretation that other sects regard as fundamental. We must examine the relevant details and then step back and grasp the whole. Given the inconsistencies and ambiguities, no overall interpretation will fit every detail. But some will feel more reasonable, coherent and likely than others.

The following chapters will, therefore, offer the New Paradigm for the foundation of Christianity. It will trace how longstanding Jewish ideas about God and his interactions with humanity underwent unparalleled distortion during the upheavals in Palestine in the first century AD to emerge unrecognisable as the Christian religion. Jewish concepts of the historic role of the Jewish people as the priestly nation to the world somehow emerged as a religion in which the Jews had no role at all. Related beliefs about how the world would end, and the prophetic and Messianic figures that would herald those events, emerged as the novel concept of a son of God whose death redeems the world. And I shall argue that we can trace almost exactly how this happened from texts that survive from those times – not obscure, recently discovered manuscripts of ambiguous meaning, but mainstream texts that survive in the very Bibles that adorn bookshelves in virtually every home in western civilization. The problem is that it is ridiculously hard to read those texts outside the dominant Christian paradigm. The simplest words trip us up. We see words and phrases like 'Christ', 'Lord' or 'Lamb of God' and we interpret their meanings in ways that the Jews who wrote them would find extraordinarily perverse. As we shall also see, those Jews were capable of bizarre and perverse interpretations of their own, and their propensity to do so perhaps created the environment within which later Christian distortions became possible. But if we can step outside the dominant Christian paradigm and look on these texts with fresh eyes and an unbiased, rational perspective, we shall see that, quite amazingly, the historical truth *can* be recovered, and that truth will indeed set us free.

I shall now set out briefly the key points of my New

Paradigm without at this stage offering much if anything in the way of evidence. I shall do so for two reasons. First, because in order to orientate the reader and prepare them for some of the detailed arguments, the next couple of chapters will set out a great deal of background material; if the reader has in mind the bare outline of the argument to come, they are more likely to understand the relevance of this background and to bear with it. And second, because the evidence that I do present at last in Chapters Four and Five is, at places, intricate and difficult, and I believe the reader will be assisted through it if they have some outline in their head of where it is all heading. Please, therefore, read the following pages in this light. I do not expect the reader to be convinced at this stage – merely intrigued enough to continue.

Given all that I have said above, it may be a surprise to the reader that I shall argue that there *was* indeed a historical person called Jesus. Like many other ancient myths of gods and heroes, the Christian myth does have its roots in somebody real, but that person did not live in the time that Christians believe he did, and because they knew truly little about him, all the stories in the Bible about him are just that – stories. I shall show that this Jesus did not live in the first century AD as portrayed in the Bible, but in fact lived half a millennium *before* the Christian era in the sixth century BC. He was an important figure in Jewish history: the first High Priest of the new Jerusalem Temple, built after the Jewish return from captivity in Babylon. He is mentioned in several places in the Old Testament and, in particular, in the Book of Zechariah. Here the prophet Zechariah describes a sequence of heavenly visions given to him by God, and in these Jesus figures as a Messianic[9] figure, raised by God from the dead

---

[9] 'Messianic' refers to the Hebrew concept of the 'Messiah' meaning saviour or

Overview

and the clutches of Satan, cleansed and designated to be the judge of mankind at the 'End of Days', when God establishes at last his Kingdom on Earth. The Jesus Movement of the first century AD was not founded by the *Jesus* of the Gospels, but by two Jewish leaders of the time who believed that the Last Days had arrived, and that God was about to establish His Kingdom; they believed that this new era would be ushered in by the return to Earth in glory of Zechariah's Jesus, as God's anointed judge of mankind. There was no human being as described by the Gospels and called Jesus living in first-century Judæa, and all the stories about that figure in the Gospels are pure fiction.

To avoid confusion, I shall hereafter distinguish between the two characters called Jesus using italics. The Jesus described in the Gospels and on whose fictional existence Christianity is based, I shall refer to as *Jesus* in italics. The historical sixth-century High Priest, described in Zechariah, I shall refer to as Jesus without italics.

The first of the two Jewish leaders who expected Jesus (not *Jesus*) to return to Earth was another key figure in Jewish history: Judas the Galilean. He is a well-attested, historical Jewish leader who operated in Galilee like *Jesus* and introduced a new Jewish 'Philosophy'[10] to Judæa in the early years of the Christian era. Until then, there had been three such Philosophies: the Pharisees, the Sadducees and the Essenes. We know of the first two from the Bible; the Essenes do not figure there, but together with the other two Philosophies, they are described in detail in other accounts of the first century AD. The new Fourth Philosophy of Judas the Galilean, as

---

    liberator. We shall examine the term more closely later.

10 The word 'Philosophy' – perhaps a little strange in this context – is that used by Whiston in his translation of Josephus; its meaning is something more like 'sectarian set of beliefs' and we shall examine those beliefs in detail later in this book.

with the other three, was both political and religious. Judas believed that God wants to be wrestled with – He helps those who help themselves – and, specifically, that living in the Last Days, the 'End of Days' would be ushered in when Jews themselves rose against their Roman oppressors; then, and only then, would God finally intervene and establish his Kingdom.[11] Some scholars have sought to find the roots of Christianity in one or other of the three 'old' Jewish Philosophies but because *Jesus* is portrayed in the Gospels as an apolitical, peaceful preacher, and also because the Gospels are confused about chronology, scholars have failed to recognize that this new Philosophy, arising at the time *Jesus* was supposed to have lived, and in the same geographical area as *Jesus*, is in fact identical with the Jesus Movement. It must be emphasized that Judas was not *Jesus*; Judas believed he was living in the Last Days and preached the imminent return of Zechariah's Jesus. As long as the political nature of Judas' Movement and the religious nature of the Jesus Movement are looked at in isolation, their identity is obscured. But as soon as one realizes that in both movements the religious expectation of Jesus' Messianic return, and the political expectation of a new Kingdom of God, are inextricably entwined, the true nature and unity of both is revealed.

The second of the two leaders of the Jesus Movement is the character we now call John the Baptist (or John the Baptiser, or just the Baptist). Unlike the *Jesus* of the Gospels, he seems to be, as much as Judas the Galilean, a historical character, independently attested outside of the Bible. It has always been a mystery (to me at least) why John, having recognized *Jesus* as the true Messiah in the Gospel accounts, did not abandon

---

[11] This idea survives today among Christian fundamentalists in the USA, who through political action seek to bring about the End Time events. It is a chilling prospect.

his own ministry and follow *Jesus*. The story as we have it in the Gospels makes no sense at all. And indeed, we know that John's followers did represent a separate and distinct strand of early Christianity for decades – perhaps even centuries – after *Jesus* was supposed to have lived. It will be my contention in this book that John the Baptist founded the Jesus Movement alongside Judas; he seems to have represented the religious side of the movement and Judas the political side. He, like Paul, had visions that led him to believe that he was living in the Last Days before God brought about His Kingdom, and he saw himself as the last prophet preparing the way for that event. I will argue that after the failure of Judas' political activities and his death, the Jesus Movement split into two. The section that still agitated for political change was led by members of Judas' family, based in Jerusalem itself; the section that became disillusioned with political activity and was content to await God's imminent intervention was led by John the Baptist, who continued his religious activities in the Arabian Wilderness to the east of the river Jordan.

But the story does not end there. If the Jesus Movement had been nothing more than that, it would have remained a footnote at best in histories of the near east in the first century AD. There are two other key characters in the story of Christian origins: the 'Apostles', Peter and Paul. Peter is depicted in the Bible as accepting the admission of Gentiles to the Jesus Movement, in a vision sometime after *Jesus*' death. Many scholars today would reject this. Whoever Peter was, he led a Jewish Movement, based in Judæa, focused on a Jewish Messiah and a Jewish destiny as the priests of the new Kingdom of God. Most scholars would also agree that it was, in fact, the Apostle called Paul who turned the Jewish Jesus Movement into a religion for Gentiles called Christianity. The puzzle here is that nowhere in Paul's writings does he show the slightest knowledge of, or even interest in, the facts of the life of *Jesus*. His sole concern is the death and resurrection of Jesus: entirely consistent with the New Paradigm put forward in this book, that Jesus was an Old Testament High Priest anointed by God to be the judge of mankind at the End of Days.

I shall also tackle the knotty problem of Paul's relationship with the Jewish church in Jerusalem. The biblical evidence is famously contradictory. In this book, I shall show how the contradictions can be reconciled by the adoption of a new chronology for the key events in the first half of the first century AD. As soon as one abandons the idea that *Jesus* lived at that time, one is free to look at the evidence afresh, and then it becomes clear that, either deliberately or by accident or by a combination of both, the need to accommodate a *Jesus* living in the first thirty or so years of the Christian era has the result of shifting all the events of early Christianity forward in time by a decade or so. By taking *Jesus* out of the 1st century picture, not only is the way open to make the identification of the *Jesus* and Judas movements, but also to shift the activities of Paul back in time by a decade. Dating Paul's life is traditionally done through references to historical persons and events in the Book of Acts. But like many scholars, I believe the writer of Acts was ransacking the Jewish historian Josephus for this material and, therefore, as with the Gospels and the life of *Jesus*, this is all just storytelling. By a careful rereading of the key texts in the New Testament, I will show that Paul and all the early founders of the Jesus Movement were either dead or in prison (and certainly removed from the Judæan scene) by the mid-forties. This means that when the Gospels came to be written, an awfully long time had passed. Matthew, Mark, Luke and John were writing ancient history based on virtually no evidence at all.

But now it is time to abandon assertion, backtrack the argument and, as promised, set out some key background material, essential if we are to unravel the truth about Jesus and the origins of the religion founded in his name. First it will be necessary to cover some background for the general reader. Knowledge of the Bible in Britain, regardless of intelligence or education, is extremely low. I recognize that the situation may be different in other countries and in the United States of America in particular, where fundamentalism seems to be deep rooted, and knowledge of the Bible and belief in it as the inerrant Word of God is much more prevalent. But, because I want an audience on both sides of the Atlantic, I have written this book with an average British audience in mind and hope that better-read Americans will forgive any overkill. This means that I cannot take it for granted that the reader will be familiar with the basics of Jewish history as set out in the Bible, or of the stories of *Jesus* and the Apostles as set out in the New Testament. This is even truer of the period between the Old and New Testaments, when historical events of major importance took place.

In addition, a further problem is that, even given a good understanding of the traditional Christian story, most people are largely unaware of the brilliant and massive scholarly endeavour of the last two centuries to peel back two millennia of dogmatic and rigid interpretation, and to view the texts on which Christianity is based with an unbiased eye. The interpretation I offer in this book is grounded in the scholarly work that has gone before me. In its key features, where I have broken new ground, it is I think both startling and innovative, but to understand its innovation the reader will need to have a basic grasp of where scholarship has reached today. For these reasons, I feel it is necessary also to bring the reader up to speed, not only with the traditional Christian story, but also with the scholarly research of the last 200 years. Some readers may be tempted to pass this by, but I would encourage them not to do so. Inevitably, I could not précis so much in so few pages; selection was unavoidable, and I was guided by the need to provide information and interpretation that most facilitated understanding of my innovative arguments. I hope the result is genuinely an integral part of the overall argument of the book.

CHAPTER 2

Jewish Origins

THE OLD TESTAMENT (AND OTHER SOURCES)

The main (but not the sole) source of our knowledge about the origins of the Jewish people is of course their own scriptures, which are preserved for Gentiles in the Christian Bible. The Bible is divided into two: the Old and New Testaments. The Old Testament is, in essence, the Jewish scriptures, but it is so named in Christian Bibles to reflect Christianity's own understanding of itself as the result of a *New* 'Covenant' between God and Christian believers, to replace the 'Old' Jewish covenants between God and his creation. For obvious reasons, the Jews accept no part of the New Testament as scripture. All versions of the Old Testament, Jewish and Christian alike, include the same first five texts, known as Books – those that Jews call the Torah and Christians the Pentateuch. Christians call these Books Genesis, Exodus, Leviticus, Numbers and Deuteronomy. They relate the 'history' of the Jewish people, from stories about how God created the world through to the death of the great Jewish leader, Moses. The first volume in this trilogy – *Ancestral Tales* – subjects the Pentateuch to textual analysis. All Christian and Jewish Bibles also contain further 'historical' texts, known as the Books of Joshua, Judges,

Samuel, Kings and Chronicles, which cover the subsequent period from the time of Moses up to the traumatic conquest of the Jewish capital city, Jerusalem, by the Babylonians. The extent to which the narrative up to this point can be regarded as real history rather than mythology is a moot point. The Babylonian conquest is certainly a historical fact and, as we shall see, can be precisely dated. But everything leading up to that point is shifting sand. Fundamentalists, of course, regard even the earliest stories – about Adam and Eve in the Garden of Eden, for example – as genuine historical fact. But most reputable scholars would regard all these stories as belonging to the realm of myth; that there might be some historical basis for some elements, perhaps approachable through archaeology and comparison with other ancient records, is explored in *Ancestral Tales*, but the precise historical truth of these stories of pre-literate times is now largely unrecoverable. These 'mythical' Books make up about half the Old Testament.

The other half of the Old Testament is different in nature. These texts do not, except in passing, purport to describe history. They fall broadly into two types: the often-obscure writings of the prophets,[1] and 'wisdom' Books like Psalms, which the Jews simply called 'writings'. With these texts, it becomes difficult to talk about such concepts as 'inspiration' and 'inerrancy', because not only is there is no agreement between Jews and Christians about which texts are sacred, but the different versions of Christianity cannot even agree among themselves. The inclusion or exclusion of Books in the Bible is known as the 'canon', and the process by which the different canons evolved is long and complex. The Jewish canon today comprises only twenty-four different texts in all, comprising *Torah* (teaching), *Nevi'im* (prophets) and

---

[1] Volume III – *Apocalypse Postponed* – will deal in some detail with the Books of the Prophets in the context of their apocalyptic content.

Ketuvim (writings) – known by the acronym *Tanakh*. But this evolved only over time. Certainly, by about the fifth century BC, all Jews regarded the five Books of the Torah as authoritative, and over the next few centuries the prophets came to have a similar status, although without the same level of respect as the Torah. But beyond that, for centuries the Jewish scriptures were fluid, with different sects regarding different Books as canonical until the current twenty-four emerged as victors.

All of these twenty-four Books can also be found in the Christian Old Testament. But these are less than half of the Books that different versions of Christianity have over the years called upon for service in their own Old Testament canons. What constitutes the Christian 'canon' depends totally on which version of Christianity one chooses to believe. Various church councils in the first few centuries AD struggled to determine these issues – for both Testaments. The key issue for the Old Testament was whether to restrict the canon to just the twenty-four Books of the Jewish Bible, or to expand it to include the rest. The answer to that question depended on whether you were a Roman Catholic, in which case you recognized forty-six Old Testament Books (twenty-two more than the Jewish *Tanakh*), or a member of the Eastern Orthodox Church, which recognized the full set of fifty-one Books (twenty-seven more than the *Tanakh*). Either way, these 'expanded' Old Testaments lasted until the Reformation; as long as access to the Bible was restricted to clergy who could read Latin and/or Greek, and it was the Church that defined dogma rather than the written texts, it was hardly an issue. But in the sixteenth century, the Protestant reformers, who wanted to be guided solely by what they believed was the *written* Word of God, reopened the debate, and playing it safe restricted the canon for their own congregations back to the short list of the Jewish twenty-four Books. The

King James Authorised Version, reflecting the peculiarly British compromise that became the Anglican Church, recognized thirty-nine Books – midway between twenty-four and forty-six.

Each of these religions would claim that 'their' Old Testament is correct. One must ask: if the Bible is the inspired Word of God, then exactly which version are we talking about, and by what criteria are Books included or excluded, except in conformity with a preconceived orthodoxy? Which scriptures exactly are we to recognize as inspired by God, when even Christians cannot agree amongst themselves? Christians like to assert that the theological scholars over the centuries who determined the various canons were guided in their deliberations by God, but then, one would have thought that such a basic thing as which texts to include would have been something God would have wanted to make explicit?

And the problems do not stop there. The issue of translation adds another layer of complexity. The scriptures were first translated from the original Hebrew into Greek around two centuries before the Christian era, as Jews living outside Palestine in the Greek world and non-Jews needed a text they could understand. The legend is that there were seventy translators and, miraculously, they all arrived independently at the same translation, known as the Septuagint (after the Latin for seventy). This, of course, points to the other major difficulty facing those that wish to regard these scriptures as the inerrant Word of God. To believe that, you not only have to accept that God has not exactly made it clear which texts He endorses, but also that He in some sense inspires their translators as well. But which translations, into which languages, by which translators?

As the Christian era progressed, the increasing numbers of Gentile converts created a growing need for translations into Latin, which were soon forthcoming and, after a process of selection, 'authorized' Latin translations became the standard used in churches, until the Reformation ushered in demand for translations into all the vernacular languages of Christendom. For many Catholics, the most authentic texts are still these Latin translations; for many Protestants on the other hand, God speaks most authentically through the post-Reformation English of the King James Authorised Version of the Bible.[2] Americans on the other hand often prefer a slightly more modern Revised Standard Version. Attempts in the twentieth century to introduce even more modern versions have met with much resistance from traditionalists, who seem to prefer the more 'poetic' language of the older versions. Are we to believe then that God too prefers poetry to prose? One would have thought that in matters concerning the eternal destiny of human souls, the exactitudes of prose might be preferable to the deliberate ambiguities of poetry – but perhaps not? Why God should have chosen these translations is a mystery that many of today's faithful seem never to question. But then, as the Bible reassures us, God's ways to men are indeed mysterious. Perhaps the precise words do not matter. Perhaps what is important is the 'Truth' they convey. But since every version of Christianity perceives that Truth differently and choose 'their' translations accordingly, this does not really solve the problem.

Protestant Christian Bibles immediately follow the Old Testament with the New Testament, thus silently jumping over centuries of Jewish experience, and ignoring a wealth of Jewish religious literature produced in this 'intertestamental' period. As we shall see here and in Volume III, much of this

---

[2] In the 19th century, Joseph Smith, the founder of the Mormon faith, claimed that the *Book of Mormon* was also inspired of God, and it too is written in Authorised Version English. Indeed, some Protestant sects today regard the King James Authorised Version as not merely to be preferred, but as the only translation actually inspired by God.

literature was 'apocalyptic' in character – looking forward to the time when God would bring history to an end, judge all mankind and institute a new Kingdom of God on Earth. This literature is important to understanding the development of Jewish ideas about life after death, atonement for sin and eternal salvation. It also contains texts that cover the history of the Jewish people during these centuries: this chronological gap is filled by four Books called Maccabees, which are included as scripture in Catholic Bibles as the Apocrypha but omitted by Protestant Bibles. This neglect is a pity because these Books describe a thrilling and important period in Jewish history when, in the second century BC, the Jewish people, led by the Maccabee family, rose up against their Hellenic oppressors and regained their independence from the wider Hellenic world. All Jews know these stories and celebrate them every year in the Hanukkah festival, which roughly coincides with Christmas. But most Protestants know little or nothing of the events they describe and seem hardly to realize the existence of a gap in the Jewish story.

For Christians, events in Jewish history are of interest only as a sort of overture to the main theme of the birth, death and resurrection of *Jesus*. But to understand what happened in the first century AD, it is vital also to understand its roots in the Maccabee period. And, in fact, we know a lot about this period because two other important documentary sources for Jewish history bear directly upon it: Josephus[3] and the Dead Sea Scrolls. Josephus was the first century AD author of (*inter alia*) two books of Jewish history. The first, *The Wars of the Jews*, begins with the Maccabee period and ends with the major Jewish uprising against Rome in the sixties. The second is a monumental work called *The Antiquities*

---

3 See Select Bibliography.

of the Jews. In this, he outlines for a non-Jewish audience the entire history of the Jewish people, from the creation of the world right through to the middle of the first century AD. Both Books follow the narratives provided by the Old Testament and the Apocrypha Books of Maccabees. The Dead Sea Scrolls seem to have been the writings of a Jewish sect. Hidden in caves in the Judæan desert, and first discovered only in 1949, they were regarded by the first scholars entrusted with their interpretation as dating from Maccabean times. But since then they have also controversially been dated to the time of *Jesus*. We shall look at both Josephus and the Scrolls in more detail later in this book.

FROM EDEN TO EXILE: JEWISH MYTH

From all these sources we can piece together a chronological account of the Jewish people and their religious beliefs, as they themselves tell the story: from the Creation, through the Babylonian captivity, the era of the Maccabees and down to the destruction of Jerusalem and the scattering of the Jewish people by forces of the Roman Empire in the second century. Many modern readers will be unaware of the later more historical events, but while previous generations would have required little reminder of the earlier mythic narrative, in the modern age this cannot be relied upon either. And even those with a fair memory of Sunday School and Scripture classes may find it helpful to have their memories of the key Bible stories placed into a chronological and historical context. Some readers may find this background material unnecessary, but for most general readers, I think, much of it will be unfamiliar territory with an interest all of its own, in addition to its role as preparation for the argument to come.

The Bible begins with stories of the creation of the world

and of humanity. I say 'stories' plural because, in fact, the early chapters of the Book of Genesis are cobbled together from two different sources.[4] After creating everything else in five days, on the sixth day God creates mankind.[5] But then, a few verses later,[6] he seems to do it all again: he creates Adam and Eve and places them in the Garden of Eden. Scholars have long recognized that this confusion results from the writer of Genesis (traditionally Moses, but highly unlikely) drawing on two different, pre-existing near-eastern narratives.[7] It must be hard for fundamentalists to hold to their view of Genesis as directly inspired by God in the face of this sort of obvious evidence, but they are well-practised in this sort of harmonization. The story tells us that Adam and Eve lived in a state of innocence in Eden. Their lives were lived in complete accord with God's Will.[8] God's Will for Adam and Eve was simple: they could do what they wanted except for one thing – eat the fruit of the tree of the knowledge of good and evil. Eve persuaded Adam that they should do just that and, in this way, sin entered the world and mankind was thrust out of Eden. Christians regard the sin of Adam and Eve as 'original sin'. The corruption from this has tainted the whole of mankind ever since. God had to sacrifice his son, Jesus Christ, on the cross as an acceptable atonement for the inescapable sinfulness of mankind. Jews,

---

[4] As I demonstrated in detail in Volume I: *Ancestral Tales*.

[5] Genesis 1:26-7.

[6] Genesis 2:7-25.

[7] The two sources, known as E and J, are described in detail in Volume 1.

[8] Not to do so – to act against God's wishes – was (and is) the sole definition of 'sin'. There is a common misapprehension that sin is a human moral concept, but while the two may well overlap in places, the concept of sin, as opposed to morality, requires belief in a deity who issues commandments to his Creation. Similarly with 'righteousness', which is defined as living in accordance with God's Will – the opposite of sin.

however, have a different perspective. We shall explore this later, but, in essence, the Christian concept of a divine sacrifice is entirely alien to Jewish belief. Sin for the Jew is a serious matter, but the forgiveness of God is dependent on repentance rather than sacrifice; the latter was required only at the Jerusalem Temple and only as part of religious ritual. There has been no temple in Jerusalem and therefore no Jewish sacrifices for 2,000 years, but this causes Jewish people no great anxiety about God's forgiveness.

Succeeding generations of men and women (incestuously descended from Adam and Eve, presumably, or perhaps from the 'first' Creation story?) gradually populated the planet, but sin became prevalent to such an extent that, finally, God decided he had had enough and resolved to wipe out his Creation with a great flood.[9] However, in the end he allowed one family, that of Noah, to survive by the expedient of building an ark – a huge boat that also carried breeding pairs of every animal species. After the flood, God made a formal agreement with Noah – known as the Noahic Covenant – in which God promised not to destroy all life ever again. (The symbol of this covenant was to be God's bow[10] in the sky – a sweet, prehistoric explanation for rainbows, but surely not to be taken literally by anyone nowadays, although with fundamentalists you can never tell). The Covenant, crucially for our investigations as we shall see, was far from unilateral. In return for his promise to refrain from 'humanicide' (not to

---

9 Angry actions like these by God occur throughout the Old Testament and are clearly difficult to reconcile with the loving, fatherly God of the New Testament. As we shall see, the Gnostics of the early centuries AD solved it by hypothesizing two gods – the benevolent ultimate Creator, and the harsh 'Demi-urge' (or semi-God) who rules the Earth.

10 Gods in antiquity were often pictured as immortal warriors with bows and arrows, spears, chariots and other accoutrements of war. The Jews pictured their God in a similar way when they envisioned apocalyptic events at the end of time.

mention all other animal and plant life) in the future, God required mankind generally (not just Jews, who at this stage in the story had yet to emerge on the stage) to obey a set of simple divine commandments. The key requirements of this were: to establish courts of justice; not to commit blasphemy; not to commit idolatry; not to commit incest and adultery; not to commit bloodshed; and not to commit robbery. All pretty reasonable, in fact. For those familiar with the dietary and behavioural restrictions placed by God on Jews, it may come as a surprise that this Covenant contained no such requirements except for one, which was not to eat flesh cut from a living animal. This Covenant is important to the argument of this volume because it was still regarded by Jews as in force for mankind in general by the first century, when *Jesus* is supposed to have lived.

These Jewish stories of the Creation, Adam and Eve in the Garden of Eden, and Noah's Ark and the Flood, as their usual initial capitals suggest, are embedded deep in the Christian tradition and transferred directly, therefore, into the central myths of western civilization. In fact, of course, the writers of all these stories in the Bible did not invent them: they re-told stories that were already current in the myths of all the early civilizations of the Near and Middle East.[11] Civilization – however one defines that slippery term – arose first in these arid lands, at places where water was most abundant, notably in the fertile crescent of Mesopotamia, and a little later around the fertile flood plains of the Nile. In the swamplands between the Tigris and Euphrates rivers, and around the Nile floodplain, agriculture for the first time in history was sufficiently abundant to generate the surpluses necessary to support human division of labour. When aristocratic and priestly classes thus arose with the

---

11 See Volume I: *Ancestral Tales*.

'leisure' time necessary for speculation about human origins and the nature of the gods, it was inevitable, therefore, that life-giving water was at the heart of those speculations. As Genesis puts it right at the start:

> And the earth was without form, and void: and darkness was upon the face of the deep. And the spirit of God moved upon the face of the waters.[12]

Everything begins with water. And when God decides to destroy what he has made, he does it with water. Early Near and Middle Eastern myths abound with stories of the primeval waters and massive, catastrophic inundations of water. Every time an archaeologist discovers evidence of those inundations in lands associated with the Bible, fundamentalists regard it as evidence of the truth of the Bible. The only truth is that for people whose very daily existence depended on beneficent rivers, stories about the gods and water were inevitable and ubiquitous, and the Bible accounts are just that – the versions of those stories that the Jewish people wove into their own racial myths.

Sometime later in the biblical narrative, God decided that he would appoint one nation of mankind as special; its people would become his chosen representatives on Earth. That chosen nation was to comprise the descendants of a man called Abraham and they became known as the Israelites and, ultimately, the Jews. And it is the nature of the Jewish God, and the beliefs the Jews came to hold about him over time, which began to separate the Jewish racial myth from those of the peoples around them.[13] Adam and Eve and Noah are recognizable figures with parallels in other myths

---

12 Genesis 1:2.
13 Volume 1 traces how and when the Jewish religion emerged following the Exodus.

and stories at the time, but from Abraham onwards something distinctive, and in many ways unique, began to evolve: the monotheistic concept that the Jewish God was the only God. Again, fundamentalists will take exception to the word 'evolve', not because they do not accept biological evolution (although, of course, they do not) but because their Christianized version of the Jewish myth has monotheism central to the biblical story from the outset. So, it is worthwhile to pause at this point and consider what we mean by monotheism, and how it is actually presented in the early Books of the Bible.

In the civilizations that preceded and surrounded that of the Jews, the norm was some form of ancestor reverence/worship combined with pantheism – belief in many gods. And because these gods were personifications of natural forces – the sun, the wind and the rain (known as 'animism') – it was relatively easy for different races to recognize that although they might have different names for their gods, they were all essentially the same gods. This is known as 'syncretism' and will be familiar from classical Greece and Rome, where, for example, Ares is the Greek god of war and Mars is the Roman equivalent. In the myths about these various gods, they behaved like humans; they married, had offspring and warred between themselves and between generations. And as in human societies, there was always a hierarchy among the pantheon of gods and a chief God who sat at the top of the immortal pile: a father/husband of the gods who also won all the heavenly wars. The lesser gods may have had some considerable degrees of freedom – either to rain pestilence down on poor hapless mortals, or to favour them with good fortune and abundant harvests – but ultimately, they were all responsible to the chief God. And the chief God was regarded as unique to its people: the chief God of a people was *their* God, intimately involved in the establishment of *their* race, and symbolic of *their* uniqueness and superiority to other races, cultures and religions.

In the fourteenth century BC, the Egyptian Pharaoh Akhenaton built on his father's introduction of a new chief God to the Egyptian pantheon: the sun disc, or the Aton. Many have seen this as a prefiguring of Jewish monotheism, and in Volume 1 I have explored this idea. My own view is that the influences probably worked in both directions: the ancestors of the Jews were located in the Nile Delta region and that was where Akhenaton chose to establish his centre of power. In any case, Akhenaton's innovations were less to do with religious conviction and more to do with political power. By replacing the Egyptian pantheon with a single God, he was able to elevate himself and his wife Nefertiti to the roles of demi-gods and thus, at one stroke, transfer the power of the priesthood to the throne. The rivalry between secular and religious power is a theme that runs throughout Judaism and the religions – Christianity and Islam – that flow from it. Islamic jihad derives from the Muslim belief in theocratic totalitarianism, but the cult of the Aton was probably just an extreme form of chief God for state worship.

So, the distinction between pantheism and monotheism was never a rigid one in the Near and Middle East, and it is inherently unlikely that the evolution of Jewish religious belief was any different. Certainly, the early Jews would pray to ancestors, and although Jews regarded themselves from Abraham onwards as 'the people of Yahweh',[14] in the beginning this was no more than a statement that Yahweh was *their* chief God, the embodiment of all that was distinctive

---

14 In fact, the early biblical stories have two names for God. The other is 'El', meaning 'mighty' and was adopted from an existing Canaanite deity of that name. See Volume I.

about them as a people. Abraham would have accepted the existence of many other gods – the chief gods of other peoples and the lesser gods subordinate to Yahweh. We know the names of some of these lesser Jewish gods – for example, *Milkom* and *Chemosh* – and the gods of other peoples are often referred to as 'Baals'.[15] Yahweh in these early days,[16] like all the other state gods of the time, had a female consort/wife, who was called Asherah or Ashtoreth – a Jewish version of a Canaanite goddess called Astarte who was roughly equivalent to the classical Greek Aphrodite. Ironically, we know she was worshipped because as Jewish monotheism developed Jewish worship of her became anathema and several Old Testament passages rage against her cult.[17] All this, of course, runs directly counter to the Jewish story as it is presented in churches, but scholars have been teasing out this sort of inconvenient truth for many years now. And while the idea that God the Father had a wife as well as a son may have outraged the fundamentalists, at least in recent times it has delighted a generation of feminist believers in the supernatural.

Notwithstanding all this, at some point in Jewish history Jewish religious belief did head off in a new direction, totally at odds with the ideas of those around them. This was not full-blown monotheism at first; remember, we are tracing an evolving concept here. But Yahweh did start to be regarded by the Jews as qualitatively different, both to other gods that Jews might worship and other chief gods of surrounding peoples. The change was associated with a growing recognition that physical representation of gods – what the Bible

---

[15] Baal was a Canaanite storm God.

[16] I am avoiding dates at this stage because we are still discussing myth and there is no consensus among scholars about dates – just about the general evolution of monotheism.

[17] See Judges 2:13-14; 10:6-7 and I Kings 11:5, 33.

calls false idols – were distinct from the reality of the god itself. Other people might worship idols, but the Jews worshipped an unseen God. And over a period of centuries the distinctive monotheism that we associate with Jewish belief gradually emerged. At the end of that process, Yahweh was seen not just as the chief God of the Jewish pantheon, not even just a more powerful chief God than other chief gods, but the only true God. And the Jewish people alone were to be His priests on earth. Other gods became rationalized as other supernatural beings – angelic and demonic beings that appear throughout the Bible in the various stories of God's interaction with the Jews, including one called Samyel who will turn out to be important to an understanding of the Book of Revelation in Volume III. So, over time, the Jews began to see all other gods and supernatural beings as not just inferior, but false, and their God as the unique creator and ruler of the whole earth. This monotheism was regarded by the Jews themselves as superior theology to the contemporary worship of ancestors, idols and pantheons; and by classical times[18] it generated much respect for the Jewish religion among many non-Jews: it seemed a more 'sophisticated' religious belief than the polytheistic pantheon of Greek and Roman gods.

I have referred throughout this narrative thus far to 'the Jews'. In the early stories of the Bible, following those about Abraham, they are referred to as Israelites for the following reasons.[19] Abraham had two sons, Isaac and Ishmael, who mythically founded the Jewish and Arab races respectively (we shall have cause to review this idea when we examine the writings of the Apostle Paul). Isaac took the growing

---

18 i.e. ancient Greece and Rome

19 In the paragraphs that follow, I outline the story uncritically, as it appears in the Pentateuch. In Volume I, I dissect the story into its four constituent sources and examine the consequences for its historicity.

Jewish tribe into Egypt and had two sons, twins called Esau and Jacob. It is Jacob who then carried forward Abraham's 'birth-right' and this is recognized by God when (for some reason) He gave Jacob the name 'Israel'. The Jewish nation thereafter was (mythically) split into twelve tribes, all descended from the twelve sons of Jacob/Israel – the Israelites. These tribes over time found themselves in captivity as slaves in Egypt. Up to this point, although they had a special relationship with their God Yahweh, they were relatively passive players on the world stage. Although God had promised them a special destiny as his chosen people, it seems hard to see how this would manifest itself. But then, the next major Jewish hero came along, and his name was Moses. With God's prompting and miraculous help, he led the Israelites to freedom from captivity in Egypt (the Exodus) and eventually, after years of wandering, to the land promised to them by God – Israel.

But Moses did not lead the Israelites into their final destiny in the land of Israel. He died and the leadership was taken over by another great Jewish hero, Joshua, who led the twelve tribes into a series of bloodthirsty battles, in which they annihilated (on God's specific instruction) all the existing peoples of the region (the Conquest). In return for His special favour, in thus protecting the Jewish nation and giving it genocidal victory over its enemies, and as befits a nation specially consecrated to God's service, the Jews now had their own special Covenant with God that, for them, superseded the Noahic Covenant. This was received from God and handed to them during their wanderings by Moses – and is hence known as the Mosaic Covenant. At its heart it had what we now know as the Ten Commandments, which were like some of the requirements of the Noahic Covenant. But in addition, the Jews were required by God to observe a whole raft of extra behavioural and dietary requirements that would mark them out to the rest of mankind – known now as Gentiles – as God's chosen people. These requirements are all set out at great length and not without some degree of imprecision and contradiction in the early Books of the Bible. Two need be noted here.

First, the single Noahic dietary restriction – not to eat flesh cut from a living animal – was considerably extended so that it became difficult for Jews to share a meal with Gentiles, unless the Gentiles were prepared to adopt the same restrictions. This remains true for Jews to this day; readers may be familiar with the requirement for Orthodox Jews to eat only *kosher* food. But then, as now, there was no theoretical restriction on Jews and Gentiles eating together *per se*, as long as the Jewish dietary rules were observed by the Jews at the table. The second major requirement of the Mosaic Covenant was that male Jews were to be circumcised as infants – as again remains true today. Unlike the Sikh turban or the Muslim burka, not a very visible sign of one's Jewish status one might think. But by the first century AD, when, as we shall see, the Roman province of Judæa had become very influenced by the classical Greek and Roman worlds, it did become problematical. Male public nudity in the classical world was a common occurrence – in communal bathing and in sports and games. Circumcision in these circumstances became a very visible emblem of religious and racial affinity. These two elements of the Mosaic Covenant, diet and circumcision, became a contentious issue in the first century AD for Gentile converts to Christianity: did male adult converts need to be circumcised, and could Jewish and Gentile converts eat together at the same table?

Centuries before Christianity, the Jewish people, now established in Israel, needed to determine how they would organize their society. They chose a monarchical model of government (apparently, according to the Bible, because that was the dominant model among their neighbours) and God seems to have unenthusiastically acquiesced. God chose the first king for his people, a man called Saul who turned out to be mentally unstable; not, one would have thought, the finest proof of God's own omniscience. He was succeeded, not by one of his sons, who also had feet of clay, but by a man called David who, although not without fault, is remembered as both a righteous man and a powerful ruler. King David established the main dynastic line. In the future, including in the first century AD, aspirants to the Jewish throne were expected to claim, if not demonstrate, descent from David. This is why the Gospels, which purport to tell the life story of *Jesus*, are so concerned to establish His Davidic lineage. Two of them provide genealogical charts tracing His descent from David; they differ significantly from each other, thus providing Christian commentators endless opportunity for creative harmonization. And as we shall see, some of the Gospels tie themselves in knots trying to get *Jesus* born in Bethlehem, the City of David, when tradition said he was born in Nazareth (itself, as we shall see, a mistake) and one prophecy at least required him to be born in Egypt.

The new Jewish nation also adopted over time a system of shared power, with built in checks and balances. In ancient Israel, the power of the king was limited by two other institutions: prophets and priests. Prophets were people who had direct revelations from God which they were required to pass on to the people. These revelations were concerned with how God viewed the actions of the king and the priests and the people generally. If God's view was favourable, the prophets would foretell great blessings in store; if God's view was unfavourable, the prophets would foretell doom and punishment, either through natural disasters, such as famines and droughts, or alternatively, to be inflicted on the nation by foreign powers who would act as the unknowing agents of a vengeful God. Prophets thus had considerable power to check the activities of kings, who could be threatened with dire consequences to their actions if they were not in accordance with God's Will and/or if they were personally less than righteous. Many Books of the Bible contain the recorded pronouncements of prophets and provided happy hunting grounds for the pious of future generations in search of prophetic messages from God pertaining to their own times.[20] We shall see in this book how by the first century AD, this practice had become an esoteric game, divorced entirely from any sense of historical context or reality.

The third power was held by the priests generally, and particularly in the case of real political power, by the appointed High Priest. These officiated at the Temple in Jerusalem, which was originally built by King Solomon (who succeeded David), as a symbolic 'house' for God. The Mosaic Covenant included a requirement for the Jews as a nation and as individuals to make sacrificial offerings and perform priestly rituals to God. It is important to stress that the temple sacrifices, as with those of other religions even today, had little to do with the concept of atonement for sin. This is a peculiarly Christian paradigm. For the Jews, ritual sacrifice was just the way in which their chief God was worshipped and placated. If conducted correctly, the result would be earthly beneficence, not eternal salvation. This is a vital distinction if we are to unravel the process by which Jewish ritual evolved into Christian dogma, and we shall examine it in more detail presently. But here it helps explain why, in the early days at least, the priests were the weakest of the three powers; their rituals were important, but not essential for salvation from sin; they did not have the direct communication with God that the prophets enjoyed, and kings wielded the real political power.

---

20 Volume III explores these prophets in more detail.

However, in the centuries leading up to and including the time of *Jesus* this situation changed, not because the religious role of the priesthood changed, but because their political role was enhanced. As we move into the period following the Maccabee uprising, at various times the High Priest would wield considerable political power, usually in collusion with the secular power of the time. One reason for this was that by the first century AD, the 'Age of Prophecy' was considered to be over. The great prophets of the Bible had all lived centuries before and it was believed that God no longer communicated with his people in that way. Indeed, it was believed that God's revelation to man was now complete in the Books of the Bible. The first five Books, the *Torah*, were believed to be written by Moses himself; other Books were the recorded utterances of the prophets, and all were believed to varying degrees to be the inspired Word of God. With the disappearance of prophets, both priests and other scriptural interpreters of one kind or another filled the vacuum. In addition, most other nations *did* invest political power in priesthoods; as the Jewish nation became subject to various conquering empires from the east, and then the west, their external rulers tended to expect similar circumstances to pertain in Israel.

FROM EXILE TO EXILE: JEWISH HISTORY

The first of these eastern empires to conquer Israel was that of the Assyrians. Out of this conflict seems to have arisen the disappearance of ten of the twelve tribes, and Jewish history thereafter concerns just two; the biggest and most important, named Judah, gave its name to the Jewish people.[21] But by

---

[21] The unknown fate of the other ten 'lost' tribes will be discussed in a later chapter of this book and is explored more fully in Volume III.

the middle of the first millennium BC, the Assyrian Empire was in decline and the city of Babylon, having gained its independence, was in the process of carving out an empire of its own. The Babylonians conquered Jerusalem in 587 BC. And this event in Jewish history is also the first to which we can assign a confident date, and which brings the Jewish religious myth into contact with wider world history. The Babylonians destroyed the Solomonic Temple and took the ruling classes of the Jewish state into captivity in Babylon for half a century. This was standard practice at the time; without their rulers it was more difficult for a subject nation to revolt against the empire of which they were now a part. The forced Exile ended forty-nine years later in 538 BC, after the fall of Babylon to the Persian king, Cyrus the Great, who gave the Jewish rulers permission to return and rebuild their Temple. This captivity, and subsequent return to Israel is one of the most significant events in Jewish history and culture and had a far-reaching impact on the development of Judaism. It was now much harder for Jews to cling to their traditional understanding of the Mosaic Covenant. Surely the whole point of the Covenant was that God was supposed to protect his chosen people; had the Jews really been so sinful that they deserved this apparent abrogation of the Covenant by God? Over the coming centuries, the pattern was repeated, as succeeding empires in turn conquered or took over the ruling of Israel, and Jews had to rethink their relationship with God: if the Covenant did not protect the Jews from being conquered and downtrodden, what *was* its purpose? This rethink was led by the prophets of these times, who, in desperate soul searching, tried to understand what was required of the Jews by their God; in effect, what was the Jewish destiny?

The thought that naturally occurred to the prophets was that perhaps God was biding his time, just as in the early days of the world, when God had allowed sin to increase until it reached a point where He stepped in and destroyed almost everything with a great Flood. He had promised not to do that again, so this time, it was thought, He must be waiting until the time was right for Him to intervene again – not by destroying the world, but by transforming it at last into a Kingdom of God on Earth, with (of course) a major priestly role for the Jews. Given this new perspective, the continuing tribulations of the Jewish nation were not a matter for despair but for expectant hope; the worse things got, as 'wicked' empires in succession rose and subjugated the Jews, the closer was coming the End of Days, when God would finally and decisively intervene.

One prophet in particular, Isaiah, symbolized this perspective of Jewish national destiny in terms of a 'suffering servant'; the sufferings of the Jewish people in the service of their God were to be welcomed as in some way purifying them for their eternal role as a priestly nation. And at some point the suffering would end, and glorious destiny would await. By the first century AD, the belief that these were indeed the Last Days, and that apocalyptic, divine intervention was imminent, was widespread; it was the force behind a proliferation of new sects, new religious leaders and countless disappointed expectations. Centuries earlier, immediately on the return from Babylonian Exile, the prophets began to look forward to these Last Days and to foretell when and how the Kingdom of God would arrive. Parallel with these *new* prophecies, the devout were finding *old* prophecies that could be reinterpreted by allegory to refer to these Last Days and the End Time.

As I show in detail in Volume III, there is no coherent account in the Bible that describes all the circumstances of the coming of God's New Kingdom, but certain elements recur. First, there would be a resumption of the age of prophecy. Specifically, a last prophet would arise who would prophesy the imminent arrival of the Kingdom of God.[22] He was envisaged to be in the mould of earlier prophets like Elijah. The idea seems to have been widespread in the Semitic lands – the Dead Sea Scrolls speak of it, and the Samaritans believed in a 'Taheb' who would prefigure the Messiah. And then, the second element was the concept of the Messiah, or 'Anointed One' himself. Clearly this concept goes right to the heart of the Christian religion, which sees *Jesus* Christ as the promised Messiah, so it is important that we pause again in this narrative of Jewish history to examine the Messianic concept in more detail. The word 'Messiah' is used often in the Old Testament because in its original form, the Hebrew word *masiah*, it simply means 'anointed'.[23] The use of scented oils on the body was a popular luxury in the Near East – as it is with some westerners today. But then it had religious significance as well; people and objects were anointed with oil as a sign of their dedication to a god. So, when the Jews (and other Near Eastern peoples) chose to have kings, it was only natural that they would use anointment (rather than, say, coronation) as the key symbol in the ceremony by which a king took office. The anointment was carried out by a priest and/or prophet as a sign of the king's special relationship with God, his reception of God's Holy Spirit, and his adoption as 'Son of God'. All fine if the king was worthy of the office and his people continued to be favoured of God and protected by him from other surrounding powers. But as king after king fell short of the religious ideal and Israel was subjugated time and again, by empire after empire, a credibility gap became apparent to even the most optimistic and devout Jew. If belief in eternal Jewish

---

22 Isaiah 61:1; Deuteronomy 18:18.
23 The Greek word for this is *christos* – hence Jesus 'Christ'.

destiny was to be maintained in the face of uncomfortable historic fact, the idea of anointment had to change.

Before the Babylonian Exile, the term 'anointed' was virtually synonymous with 'king' generally, and specifically the successors of David. After the Exile, the term increasingly becomes attached to a concept of a different kind of king: a hoped-for future king who would not have feet of clay but would reign in justice, security and peace.[24] And this concept in turn evolved into something even more dramatic: a Messiah who would be announced by the prophet that would arise at the due time and would then be sent by God himself to deliver His people from subjugation and suffering. This would be a decisive act by the supreme deity, a once-and-for-all intervention by the divine into human history, to put everything right. As this idea evolved, the ancient Jewish scriptures were searched to provide indications and ideas that could be interpreted in this context. The figures of Moses and Joshua provided the key role models for this future king. It was the Exodus from Egypt and the Conquest of the Promised Land under these two heroic leaders, when the Jews had, for a time, ceased to be passive sufferers of whatever history threw at them, and had actively taken control of their own destiny.[25] They had, with God's divine aid, thrown off the bonds of slavery and taken a 'land of milk and honey' for their own; they had created their own state and had been masters of their own fate. The future Messiah would be modelled on this, and having established God's new kingdom on earth, would rule it as His Regent. As indicated above, nowhere in the Jewish scriptures is this set out as fully formulated theology. It can only be pieced together from dozens of passages scattered throughout the Books of the Old Testament. Some of these passages describe attributes of

---

24 Isaiah 9:2-7; 11:1-5; 32:1; Jeremiah 33:14-26; Ezekiel 37:24-28.
25 See Volume I.

the Messiah. The first and most obvious is his military might: he will, it seems, conquer the powers of Jewish oppressors by force of arms.[26] But he will also be wise,[27] gentle and humble.[28]

The concept of Messiah had another tradition associated with it, less strong and obvious, but present nonetheless: that of a second, Priest-Messiah who would stand alongside the King-Messiah described above. This seems a natural development of the concept because High Priests in the temple were also anointed as a symbol of their consecration to God's service. We know that the idea of Messiah-as-priest was part of early Christian theology because the Epistle to the Hebrews in the New Testament describes *Jesus* as a priest as well as a king. In four different places[29] *Jesus* is called a priest 'after the order of Melchizedek'. This phrase in turn is lifted from an Old Testament Psalm where, in a passage which was interpreted as referring to the expected Messiah, the Psalmist declares:

Thou art a priest for ever after the order of Melchizedek.[30]

Melchizedek is a combination of two Hebrew words, *melek* and *sadeq*, meaning 'king' and 'righteous' respectively. Zadok (a version of *sadeq*) was, by some accounts, the first priest of the Jerusalem temple and we shall encounter him again later. But Melchizedek appears in Genesis, where he is described both as 'king of Salem' and also as 'priest of the most high God'.[31] Jewish tradition associated Salem with

---

26 Genesis 49:10; Numbers 24:17; Psalms 2:9; 18:31-42.
27 Isaiah 9:6; 11:2.
28 Isaiah 42:2-3; Zechariah 9:9-10.
29 Hebrews 5:6; 10; 6:20; 7:17.
30 Psalm 110:4.
31 Genesis 14:18.

Jerusalem,[32] so it is significant that in the Genesis story Abraham – the founder of the Jewish race – is described as paying tithes to Melchizedek and receiving a blessing from him. The writer of the New Testament Epistle to the Hebrews certainly thought so; he recounts the story and concludes that, since 'the less is blessed of the better', Melchizedek was superior to Abraham, and thus, *Jesus* is held to be superior even to Abraham, the founder of the Jewish race.

What we seem to have here is some sort of esoteric tradition about this strange character called Melchizedek who appears enigmatically and briefly in Genesis, only to disappear again until he re-emerges in early Christian theology about the Messiah. And this is confirmed by the Dead Sea Scrolls. Whatever date one assigns to them, and whatever sect or group originated them, one of their most distinctive beliefs was that there would be two Messiahs – a King-Messiah and a Priest-Messiah. Christianity rolls these together in the single person of *Jesus,* but for the Scrolls writers, they were in fact to be two distinct characters, as described here by the renowned scholar Geza Vermes in his introduction to his definitive translation of the Scrolls:

> The lay King-Messiah, otherwise known as the 'Branch of David', the 'Messiah of Israel' ... was to usher in ... 'the Kingdom of his people' and 'bring death to the ungodly' and defeat '[the kings of the] nations' ... As befits a priestly sect, however, the Priest-Messiah comes first in the order of precedence; he is also called the 'Messiah of Aaron' ... The King-Messiah was to defer to him and to the priestly authority in general ...[33]

---

32 Psalm 76:2.

33 Geza Vermes, *The Complete Dead Sea Scrolls in English* (London: 1997), p.86.

For the Scrolls sect, therefore, it was the Priest-Messiah rather than the King-Messiah who was to be pre-eminent. I shall argue later that the Jesus Movement was distinct from the Scrolls sect, but there is no reason at all why both movements should not have shared this distinctive belief in twin Messiahs. In fact, I shall show later that the key text for the Jesus Movement was the Old Testament Book of the prophet Zechariah. In that Book, the prophet too envisages twin Messiahs:

> These are the two anointed ones, that stand by the Lord of the whole earth.[34]

The Scrolls sect called the Priest-Messiah 'of Aaron' because Aaron was, according to some scriptural texts, the first High Priest, 'brother' of Moses.[35] Other texts accord primacy to Zadok (perhaps Melchi-Zadok) and as we shall see, this was the name used by the Jesus Movement. For both Zechariah and for the Scrolls sect, the King-Messiah was also called 'Branch'[36] because he was to be a branch of the family tree of King David. All this may seem convoluted and arcane, but an understanding of it at this point is crucial if we are to unravel exactly who Jesus was and what the first Christians believed.

Having determined that God would intervene to end the suffering of the Jews through a Messiah, or more precisely, two Messiahs, the next issue logically to preoccupy the Jewish Prophets was whether God's Kingdom would be for Jews alone or would extend over the whole earth to include Gentiles as well. The envisaged scenario was that the era of

---

34 Zechariah 4:14.
35 I explore the historicity and role of Aaron in Volume I.
36 Zechariah 3:8.

God's Kingdom would be ushered in by an apocalyptic battle in which the wicked would be defeated, judged and consigned to damnation; then those of the Gentile races who were righteous would live in harmony and peace, with the Jewish nation acting as priests to the whole world, centring worship on a new holy city of Jerusalem, from which the world would be ruled. The Jewish destiny thus transmuted from a people whose specialness was their *passive* enjoyment of God's favour, to a people with a God-appointed, vital and *active* role in the new world order.

The idea that the sinful would be damned in some way raised another issue – that of life after death. This had never really been a major issue for the Jews. In common with other early religions, relationship with a god or gods was focused on securing divine beneficence in this life, such as clement weather, good harvests, the avoidance of natural disasters and protection from enemies. Early religions often had a hazy idea of some sort of survival of a soul or spirit, such as the Valhalla of the Vikings or the Hades of the Greeks, and the widespread worship of ancestors throughout the ancient world. This seems to have had some part in early Jewish religious belief too, but the Mosaic Covenant had nothing to do with that. The Covenant was about how Jews behaved in *this* life, and how God would favour their nation as a result. But now they began to think that perhaps the earthly Kingdom of God would in turn come to an end, and then there would be some form of eternal life, enjoyable for the righteous and miserable for sinners. Observation of the Mosaic and Noahic Covenants would secure salvation for Jews and God-fearing Gentiles respectively. Like the Messiah concept, these ideas are nowhere in the Bible set out coherently as worked-through theology, but they provide the intellectual backdrop to much of the prophetic writings. And the attraction of such ideas is obvious: then as now, the promise of eternal paradise made earthly oppression and suffering easier to bear and preserved the idea that God would, in the end, remain true to his Covenants with mankind.

It is important to emphasize that for the Jews, the twin concepts of Messiah and salvation from sin were separate. As we have noted, life after death was not a key theme in the traditional Jewish religious life, so the need to be forgiven for one's sins did not have the urgent necessity prompted by a belief in eternal punishment. The relationship between God and the Jewish nation was all about the here and now. Salvation was about the fortunes of the Jewish nation in history, not the destiny of the individual human soul in eternity. And hence, the Christian theological problem of how God can tolerate human sin without a suitable act of atonement did not arise. It is a peculiarly Christian perspective, probably developed by the Apostle Paul and deriving from his perception of 'original sin': when Adam and Eve sinned in Eden and fell from God's grace, the whole of future humanity fell with them, and all humankind thereafter is born with the stain of inherited sinfulness that requires atonement, without which eternal punishment in the flames of Hell is inescapable. Paul regarded forgiveness for original sin as problematical. An infinite God requires an infinite act of atonement in order to forgive infinite sin. The only way God could achieve this was effectively to make that atonement himself on behalf of his Creation, through the death of his own Son. Paul associated that atonement with the concept of Messiah, and saw both fulfilled in the figure of Jesus Christ and his atoning sacrifice on the cross. But this theological conclusion came at the very end of a long process of developing Jewish thought and remains as alien a conclusion to Jews today as it was to mainstream Judaism up to and including the first century AD.

This is not to say that God's forgiveness for sin was not an issue in Jewish thought. Obviously, as the story of Noah and the Flood demonstrated, God took sin very seriously and it was the sinfulness of the Jewish nation that was blamed by the prophets for the successive punishments that God inflicted, or allowed to be inflicted, on the Jewish nation. But the very concept of sin was vastly different from Pauline 'original' sin, which sees human nature itself as inherently sinful. The Christian obsession with sinful thoughts and inclinations would have been incomprehensible to pre-Christian era Jews. The God of the Old Testament punished wilful disobedience, not unconscious inclination; the Old Testament prophets railed against sinful behaviour, not weak thoughts. And forgiveness from sin was more easily obtained than Christian theology presupposes. For the Jew, God seemed to require nothing more than a genuine repentance: a recognition of wrongdoing and a return to the path of righteousness. Time and again, the prophets would assure the Jewish nation that if it would only turn from its wilful wickedness, then God would forgive and readily bless. For early Jewish thinking at least, there seems to have been no perception at all that such forgiveness would require some extraordinary act of atonement. And as we have seen, sacrifice at the Jerusalem Temple was regarded as symbolic ritual rather than efficacious in atonement.

Many if not most ancient religions practised some form of sacrifice. An animal would be ritually slaughtered and in some ritualistic way, through burning or blood-sprinkling, some or all the animal would be offered to the deity to win his favour. The more valuable the animal, the more valuable the sacrifice, hence the practice in some ancient societies of human sacrifice. The sacrificial offering was both a gift to the deity and a self-denial by the individual making, or paying for, the sacrificial offering. In the former case, the deity was effectively bribed to overlook sin, and in the latter case he was persuaded to accept the self-denial as evidence of genuine contrition for sin. The Jews too practised animal sacrifice, but after the return from Exile in Babylon only at the new Temple in Jerusalem, and only via the rituals of the Temple priesthood. For most Jews, therefore, sacrifice was not central to their religion. The God of the Old Testament was more interested in a contrite heart, expressed through prayer and praise, and seems to have had no difficulty in offering free forgiveness in return. One of the most well-known Bible stories is that of Abraham, the founder of the Jewish race, being prepared to sacrifice his son Isaac to God. But not for atonement of any act of sinfulness. God requires it as a test of Abraham's faith in and commitment to his deity, and at the last moment Isaac is spared and a lamb is substituted on the sacrificial altar.[37] Later Jewish ritual also involved a substitutional 'scapegoat' onto which the nation would symbolically place its sins once a year: a sacrificial ritual that hardly points to an understanding of divine forgiveness as in any way problematical. Far more important to Jews throughout history, and right up to the present day, is the annual ritual of the Passover, which celebrates the Old Testament story of the Exodus of the Jewish people under Moses from Egypt. The Egyptian pharaoh only allows them to depart because God has inflicted a succession of terrible plagues upon his people, culminating in the death of every firstborn child. The Jews are spared from this because they ritually slaughter a lamb that is physically unblemished and sprinkle the blood on the doorways of Jewish homes as a sign and seal that they are to be left untouched. Again, the story is not about the sins of the Jewish people, merely about their physical salvation from Egyptian oppression.

---

37 In Volume I, I show how in the original version of this story the sacrifice of Isaac reflected real, contemporary practice.

But whatever its significance for the Jew, the idea of sacrifice was there from the beginning. What Christianity did was to take the idea of sacrifice and associate it with the idea of Messiah in the unified concept of an atoning Messiah. To emphasize again: this is entirely alien to Judaism, but from those two seeds grew the ideas that eventually found their way into the central tenets of Christianity. And as I shall argue in this and the next volume, the idea of the Passover Lamb is central to that process of evolution. In order to trace this evolution, we need to go back to the original 'suffering servant' image that we noted earlier was developed by Isaiah to symbolize the sufferings of God's people – the Jewish nation. In Isaiah Chapter 53, we find the quintessential expression of the idea in this magnificent, moving and renowned passage, and at the heart of it is also the symbol of the sacrificial lamb:

> Who hath believed our report? And to whom is the arm of the Lord revealed? For he shall grow up before him as a tender plant, and as a root out of a dry ground: he hath no form nor comeliness; and when we shall see him, there is no beauty that we should desire him. He is despised and rejected of men; a man of sorrows and acquainted with grief: and we hid as it were our faces from him; he was despised, and we esteemed him not. Surely he hath borne our griefs and carried our sorrows: yet we did esteem him stricken, smitten of God, and afflicted. But he was wounded for our transgressions, he was bruised for our iniquities: the chastisement of our peace was upon him; and with his stripes we are healed. All we like sheep have gone astray; we have turned every one to his own way; and the Lord hath laid on him the iniquity of us all. He was oppressed, and he was afflicted, yet he opened not his mouth: he is brought as a lamb to the slaughter, and as a sheep before her shearers is dumb, so he openeth not his

mouth. He was taken from prison and from judgment: and who shall declare his generation? for he was cut off out of the land of the living: for the transgression of my people was he stricken. And he made his grave with the wicked, and with the rich in his death; because he had done no violence, neither was any deceit in his mouth. Yet it pleased the Lord to bruise him; he hath put him to grief: when thou shalt make his soul an offering for sin, he shall see his seed, he shall prolong his days, and the pleasure of the Lord shall prosper in his hand. He shall see of the travail of his soul, and shall be satisfied: by his knowledge shall my righteous servant justify many; for he shall bear their iniquities. Therefore will I divide him a portion with the great, and he shall divide the spoil with the strong; because he hath poured out his soul unto death: and he was numbered with the transgressors; and he bore the sin of many, and made intercession for the transgressors.[38]

Of course, this passage from an ancient Jewish prophet is renowned because it is regarded by Christians as a miraculous prophecy of their Messiah, *Jesus* Christ. Here we have the Gospel story of *Jesus* all in a nutshell – his rejection and his message; the pain and sorrow of the crucifixion; the redemption of sins; the silence of *Jesus* before Pilate; the crucifixion between two 'robbers'; the division of spoils at the foot of the cross. We shall examine this again later and see it for what it is – an ancient scriptural text, ransacked by the Gospel writers to give them material for the life of a *Jesus* about whom they knew next to nothing.

But we read this as about the Messiah because we have become used to the Christian conflation of Messiah and atonement in the single person of *Jesus* Christ. The Jews

---

[38] Isaiah 53:4-12.

were expecting two Messianic figures, and the 'suffering servant' of Isaiah does not seem to match the requirements for either. The Jews are described as 'like sheep [that] have gone astray' and the 'suffering servant' is pictured as 'a lamb to the slaughter' – hardly a conquering hero. Christians of course will say that that is the point: the Jews got it wrong in expecting physical salvation. In fact, the Jews seem to have been expecting both, but not all rolled into one single, Messianic figure. The suffering servant is a symbol of the Jewish people and their suffering through history. And it is a human figure Isaiah describes, not a divine being in human form, crucified for the sins of believers. It is not a future deliverer from physical oppression either, if only because – and this is a point Christians glibly overlook – Isaiah is describing a figure from the past: everywhere, he uses the past not the present tense. The symbolism in this passage is twofold. The servant represents the Jewish nation, and in turn the servant is symbolized as a sacrificial lamb. This is a crucial development. Isaiah's image of a lamb caught on with other prophets: it seemed to capture for Jews their feelings about their oppression and sufferings, but also their hope that it was all to be endured for some divine, heavenly purpose that would be revealed and manifested in the Last Days.

Over the next couple of centuries, as these ideas developed and grew, Israel, having been 'liberated' from the Babylonians by the Persian King Cyrus, was now governed as part of the Persian Empire instead. But power in the eastern Mediterranean was by this time starting to shift away from the great eastern powers – Egypt, Syria and Persia – that had dominated events previously, and move towards the classical 'western' civilizations of Greece and then Rome. In 332 BC, the Persian Empire in turn was itself defeated by Alexander the Great, who came from Macedonia in northern Greece, and Israel then became part of *his* European empire. After

Jewish Origins

Alexander's death, his empire was divided among his generals. The General Seleucus founded the Seleucid Dynasty, which at the height of its power included central Anatolia, Mesopotamia, Persia, Afghanistan, Turkmenistan, India and Pakistan, as well as the whole of the Levant, including Israel. Greek culture was spread eastwards by the Alexandrian and then Seleucid empires, and at the same time Jews themselves began to emigrate into the wider empire territories. By the first century AD, there were probably about 4 million Jews, only half of whom lived in Palestine.

There were two important results of this, both of which may surprise some readers. First, many Gentiles encountered Judaism and were impressed by what they saw. Compared with the polytheism prevalent throughout the classical world, the Jewish insistence on just one God was regarded as 'fashionable' and 'modern'. Jews outside Jerusalem would meet in what later became known as synagogues, and some of these Gentile admirers would associate themselves with their local synagogue to hear the Torah expounded. Some converted to full Judaism, including being circumcised as adults, but most were content to remain as what was called Gentile 'God-fearers' and there seems to have been little or no external pressure on them to go any further. The second result was that Jewish culture generally, as well as Judaism itself, was in turn affected by exposure to Hellenistic[39] ideas and philosophies, both in Israel itself and in the Diaspora.[40] Tensions, therefore, began to arise between Jews who favoured integration of their society into the 'modern' classical world, and Orthodox Jews who wanted to hold fast to the old ways.[41]

---

39 i.e. Greek-inspired

40 i.e. the scattered Jewish communities outside Israel

41 Looking at modern Israel, one is tempted to say that not a lot has changed in over 2,000 years.

By the mid-second century BC, relations between Hellenized Jews and Orthodox Jews had deteriorated to such an extent that the Seleucid king, Antiochus IV Epiphanes, decided (not unreasonably from his own point of view) to force the issue once and for all in favour of integration. He imposed decrees banning all the important Jewish religious rites and traditions, as a result of which many Orthodox Jews revolted, under the leadership of a family called the Maccabees. If the Babylonian captivity in the sixth century BC had prompted the Jews to rethink what their Covenant with God was all about, the period of the Maccabees was to focus minds on another major issue: what was the responsibility of the Jews in relation to the Last Days? Two approaches seemed possible, as we began to note above. The 'passivist' approach, as had been the case with the Jewish nation in captivity in Egypt, was to wait patiently on God in faith that He would intervene in His own good time: human responsibility was to live according to the appropriate Covenant, and to persuade others to do the same. The 'activist' approach, modelled on leaders like Moses and Joshua, was to work proactively to bring about the conditions on earth for God's final intervention. Indeed, for activists, this came to be seen as the ultimate purpose of the Jewish nation; if scripture could be mined for information as to the necessary conditions for the establishment of the Kingdom of God, it was then the responsibility of the pious Jew to do whatever was necessary to make those conditions a reality.

There is an important parallel to be drawn here. The Protestant Christian belief in salvation by faith alone is, in my view, in direct descent from Judaism's passivist tradition; both submit themselves humbly to the Will of God and accept that no human action can contribute to salvation: Christ's sacrifice on the cross is both necessary and entirely sufficient. By contrast, the Roman Catholic Christian tradition is that human action can be efficacious in salvation: that faith and 'works' together are necessary. This is in direct descent from the Judaic activist tradition, and indeed, the idea that God helps those who help themselves, as we shall see, goes right to the heart of the beliefs of those that founded the Jesus Movement. Both approaches in historical Judaism involved a constant alertness for the coming Messiah(s), but the activists would not hesitate to take up arms, if necessary, to put him/them on the throne(s). The Maccabee uprising was really the first time since Moses and Joshua that activism took centre stage, and for many Jews thereafter, it never left it.

The uprising was led by Judas Maccabee, his father Mattathias, and his four brothers: John, Eleazar (or Lazarus), Simon and Jonathan. These names are to be found in the stories about Jesus too, which shows how popular they became in succeeding generations but also indicates a more direct tradition of rebellion. And the Maccabee Rebellion, like the Babylonian Captivity, became a major psychic trauma in Jewish history, remembered to this day in the Jewish festival of Hanukkah. The uprising eventually led to the formation of an independent Jewish kingdom again, known as the Hasmonean Dynasty, which lasted about a hundred years from 165 to 63 BC. The success of the uprising suggested to many, both at the time and in later generations, that the activist philosophy was in accordance with God's Will and that, therefore, acts of violent revolt contrary to the laws of man might nevertheless be righteous in God's sight. In the early days of the dynasty, the Hasmonean leaders took the office of High Priest, effectively creating a Jewish theocracy for the first time in Jewish history. But at some point they began also to call themselves 'king', so that the traditional separation of powers disappeared, both in reality and in name. This period is particularly important to this book because the consensus scholarly view is that the

Dead Sea Scrolls are to be dated to this time, and key figures that appear in the Scrolls are held to be figures from Hasmonean history. There are, however, dissenting scholars who, although their precise identifications differ, regard the Scrolls as relating to the first century AD and, therefore, contemporary with *Jesus*. We shall take a closer look at this debate a little later.

The Hasmonean Dynasty eventually began to disintegrate by the mid-first century BC, and at the same time the Roman Empire was becoming active in the eastern Mediterranean. When actual civil war broke out in Israel between Hellenized and Orthodox Jews, the Roman general Pompey seized the opportunity to intervene. In 63 BC, he conquered the country and reorganized Israel into a client state of the Roman Empire, to be known as Judæa. The Hasmoneans clung on as client rulers until eventually, in 37 BC, Herod 'the Great' was appointed 'King of the Jews' by the Romans, finally supplanting the Hasmonean Dynasty. He was to rule Judæa on behalf of Rome with a rod of iron until his death in 4 BC. Thereafter, several of his offspring ruled different parts of Judæa and surrounding countries, appointed at different times by Rome. They all took the name Herod as a title, so texts from the time can get very confusing about which member of the Herodian Dynasty is in question. Judæa under the Herodians was made a satellite of Roman Syria, controlled by a series of Roman Prefects and then Procurators.

This was also the period when Messianic and apocalyptic fervour in Judæa reached its peak. It is a matter of debate what Orthodox Jews wanted exactly – a return to the Hasmonean model, or the separation of powers they had enjoyed previous to that. But all were agreed that they wanted rid of Roman rule. Passivists were content to await the Will of God. But it was increasingly the activists who dominated the political stage, and their level of violence towards Romans, and indeed, towards Hellenistic and collaborationist Jews, escalated wildly. Foremost among the activists seems to have been someone called Judas the Galilean, who we learn about from the Jewish historian Josephus. Judas seems to have begun his activities in the first decade of the first century AD. The immediate cause was the census conducted in AD 6 by the Roman authorities under the governor Quirinius as a basis for Roman taxation in Judæa. Josephus tells us little more about the life of Judas and notably fails to mention his death, but he explicitly blames him and the movement he founded, which Josephus calls the Fourth Philosophy of Judaism, as at the root of all the disturbances of the first half of the century. According to Josephus, followers of Judas seem to have called themselves Zealots because they were zealous for Jewish culture and religion; others seem to have referred to them as Sicarii after the *sicae* or small curved knife they carried concealed in their clothes and with which they carried out a series of political assassinations.

Sectarian religious leaders and revolutionary claimants to the Jewish throne rose up time and again during these decades, only to be ruthlessly suppressed by a succession of Herodian and Roman governors, so that by the middle of the first century AD, Judæa seems to have been in an almost permanent state of civil unrest. Finally, in AD 66, the Jewish nation as a whole rose up against Roman rule in what has become known as the First Jewish War. Once the war began, Jews of whatever sectarian persuasion seem to have come together in united revolt, supported in many cases by sympathetic Diaspora Jews in surrounding territories. The rising was inevitably and ruthlessly put down by the Roman general Vespasian and his son, Titus, both of whom were to become Roman emperors. The war ended with the Siege of Jerusalem in AD 70, when the Romans destroyed much of the Temple in Jerusalem. For the next half a century, the Jews were allowed to continue to live in Judæa in significant numbers. However, another uprising in AD 132, known as the Bar Kokhba revolt, tried the patience of Rome too far. By AD 136, this revolt had also been brutally put down. As a result, almost a thousand Judæan villages were destroyed and most of the Jewish population of central Judæa had been killed, sold into slavery or forced to flee. It was not until the establishment of the modern state of Israel, 2,000 years later, that this was reversed – ironically at the behest of western politicians who, influenced by their childhood Bible reading, believed that the Jews had a God-given right to their ancient lands.

This then is the historical context in which we must seek to fit *Jesus* and the early Christian Church. From the earliest times, the Jewish nation had regarded themselves as special: chosen by their God for an important destiny. Over the centuries, this idea evolved into a conviction that their God, Yahweh, was the only God, and that their destiny was to be His priests in a new world order that He would establish. Some Jews were content to wait passively for God to make His move, but others believed they had a responsibility to work towards the new world order. The latter took their inspiration from the great activist leaders of Jewish history: Moses and Joshua, who led the Jewish people out of Egypt and into possession of their promised land; and the Maccabees, who overthrew the Seleucids and regained independence for a time. By the first century AD, the Jews found themselves subjugated again, living in the police state of Herod and his successors, enforced with all the brutal power of the Roman Empire at its height. Rebellion and revolt were in the air. The last years of Herod's reign were dominated by uprisings, and as the early decades of the first century AD progressed, the situation in Judæa became more and more violent, building towards outright war throughout the region.

According to the biblical account, *Jesus* was born at the time of the census of Quirinius and his crucifixion was ordered by the Procurator, Pontius Pilate, and King Herod Antipas. These provide the traditional dates for *Jesus'* life. The census was, as we have seen, a historical event that can be dated with certainty to AD 6, and if *Jesus* was in his early thirties when he died, as the Gospel accounts imply, then this generally fits well with the periods of Pilate and Herod Antipas. But perhaps the first surprise for anyone acquainted with the traditional story is the turbulent political background to these times. *Jesus* is commonly pictured as an itinerant preacher, surrounded by humble working-class disciples, wandering peacefully around the Galilean countryside, preaching and performing miracles. There is little hint in this picture of the harsh realities of Roman occupation: of the continuous rebellions, uprisings, civil wars and political assassinations that form the real backdrop to these years. Yet there are indications enough in the Bible, if you look for them, that the traditional picture may not tell the whole story. Indeed, that the story itself may owe more to Roman and Gentile rosy spectacles than to reality. Remember that history is written by the winners, not the losers. In the next chapter we shall begin to examine that story.

CHAPTER 3

Christian Origins

THE NEW TESTAMENT (AND OTHER SOURCES)

The New Testament is a collection of twenty-seven texts relating to the purported New Covenant between God and mankind, heralded by the reported life of *Jesus* Christ. It begins with four Gospels – Matthew, Mark, Luke and John – each narrating variously the life, death and resurrection of *Jesus*. These are followed by the Acts of the Apostles, which deals with events in the early church after the Ascension of the resurrected *Jesus* to heaven. Then there is a collection of Epistles – pastoral letters written by early church leaders, and most notably the Apostle Paul, to various early church congregations in the Middle East, Rome and Greece. The final Book, the Revelation of St John, is the only example in the New Testament of a book of prophecy; it concerns the coming of Christ in glory and the final establishment of the Kingdom of God on Earth. Scholars vary significantly on dates for all these texts, but all calculations of absolute dates of composition for the Books of the New Testament depend on the dates one accepts for the life of *Jesus*; if those are wrong (as I shall argue they are), then the dates for everything else are wrong too.

These twenty-seven texts are only a fraction of the texts that we know of that could have been included in the New Testament canon. Some have survived in several manuscripts, some survive only in fragments, and some we only know about because other writers mention them. There were undoubtedly others that have left no trace at all. I list them here (in no particular order and I may have missed some) by the names usually given to them just to demonstrate the sheer scale of these early writings.

Infancy of Jesus Gospels
Infancy Gospel of James
Infancy Gospel of Thomas
Gospel of Pseudo-Matthew
Syriac Infancy Gospel
History of Joseph the Carpenter
Life of John the Baptist

Other non-canonical Gospels
Gospel of the Ebionites
Gospel of the Hebrews
Gospel of the Nazarenes
Gospel of Marcion
Gospel of Mani
Gospel of Apelles
Gospel of Bardesanes
Gospel of Basilides
Gospel of Thomas
Gospel of Peter
Gospel of Nicodemus
Pseudo-Cyril of Jerusalem on the Life and the Passion of Christ
Gospel of Bartholomew
Questions of Bartholomew
Resurrection of Jesus Christ

Apocryphon of James
Book of Thomas the Contender
Dialogue of the Saviour
Gospel of Judas
Gospel of Mary
Gospel of Philip
Greek Gospel of the Egyptians
The Sophia of Jesus Christ

General texts concerning Jesus
Coptic Apocalypse of Paul
Gospel of Truth
Gnostic Apocalypse of Peter
Pistis Sophia
Second Treatise of the Great Seth
Apocryphon of John
Coptic Gospel of the Egyptians
Trimorphic Protennoia

Acts
Acts of Andrew
Acts of Andrew and Bartholomew Among the Parthians
Acts of Barnabas

Acts of John
Acts of the Martyrs
Acts of Paul
Acts of Paul and Thecla
Acts of Peter
Acts of Peter and Andrew
Acts of Peter and Paul
Acts of Peter and the Twelve
Acts of Philip
Acts of Pilate
Acts of Thomas
Acts of Timothy
Acts of Xanthippe, Polyxena, and Rebecca

Epistles
*Epistle of Barnabas
*Epistles of Clement
Epistle of the Corinthians to Paul
Epistle of Ignatius to the Smyrnaeans
Epistle of Ignatius to the Trallians
Epistle of Polycarp to the Philippians
Epistle to Diognetus
Epistle to the Laodiceans
Epistle to Seneca the Younger
Third Epistle of Paul to the Corinthians

Apocalypses
Apocalypse of Paul
Apocalypse of Peter
Apocalypse of Pseudo-Methodius
Apocalypse of Thomas
Apocalypse of Stephen
First Apocalypse of James
Second Apocalypse of James
*The Pastor of Hermas

Stories of Mary
Over fifty texts survive. I list here only the best known three:
The Home Going of Mary
The Falling Asleep of the Mother of God
The Descent of Mary

Miscellaneous
Apostolic Constitutions
Book of Nepos
Canons of the Apostles
Cave of Treasures
Pseudo-Clementines
*Didache
Liturgy of St James
Penitence of Origen
Prayer of Paul
Sentences of Sextus
Physiologus
Book of the Bee

Fragments
The Unknown Berlin Gospel
The Naassene Fragment

The Fayyum Fragment	Gospel of the Four Heavenly
The Secret Gospel of Mark	Realms
The Oxyrhynchus Gospels	Gospel of Matthias
The Egerton Gospel	Gospel of Perfection
The Gospel of Jesus' Wife	Gospel of the Seventy
	Gospel of Thaddaeus
Lost works	Gospel of the Twelve
Gospel of Eve	Memoria Apostolorum

[*Plausibly dated to the first century AD – see below].

So, what are we to make of all this? Who decided what went into the Bible and what did not make the cut? In fact, a consensus only evolved over a period of centuries, and it evolved as Christian theology itself evolved. Christianity was not a religion, invented by *Jesus* and handed down to his followers in clear-cut dogma. Nor was it developed out of his original ideas by his followers after his death. As we shall see, from the very beginning, the Jesus Movement was riven by disagreement and dissension. It very quickly split into a variety of related but competing sects, and all of these produced their own literature. The long list above is the result. The New Testament canon only evolved over a period of centuries as these competing sects vied with one another for dominance. As a result, some texts were tolerated and even revered for many years before being eventually discarded; some on the other hand were vigorously suppressed because they did not accord with evolving orthodoxy. Two centuries were needed to finalize the canon: from the beginning of the second century AD to the mid-fourth century AD. All the Books that finally made the cut were ones that had had no serious objections as either spurious or heretical. (The only exception to this was the Revelation of St John, which was rejected by the Council of Laodicea in AD 363-364 but later incorporated.) The final establishment of the canon reflected not so much recognition that these texts were in some way more authentic, but that they embodied better than any others the growing imposition of orthodoxy in the Church – an orthodoxy that was based on Church tradition and philosophical/theological evolution rather than scripture. The victors in this struggle to establish this orthodoxy not only won their theological battles, but they also rewrote the history of the conflict; later readers then naturally assumed that the victorious views had been embraced by most Christians from the very beginning.

Because the four canonical Gospels come first in the New Testament, the not unreasonable assumption by the lay reader is that they are the earliest texts. This is far from the truth. In fact, no one knows who wrote the Gospels; they were originally written in Greek rather than the Aramaic spoken by Jews in the first century AD, and the names attached to them were a later addition, based on little if any evidence.[1] The arguments between scholars about precise dates, given the evidence we have, will probably never be resolved to everyone's satisfaction. But there is certainly a consensus that they are, in fact, later than the letters of Paul. The very earliest seems to have been Mark, but it could have been written at any time between about AD 70 and the early part of the second century AD. And even if we accept the earliest possible date, we are still *at least* a couple of generations after the events the Gospel purports to describe. Such a dating allows (just) the possibility that Mark knew *Jesus* personally, but if this were the case surely he would have

---

[1] Rather than engage with this issue, which is beyond the scope of this volume, I shall refer to these Books by the names of their traditional authors: this should not be taken as endorsement of the traditional attributions.

said so, and he doesn't. Matthew and Luke seem to be partly based on Mark, but also on another text now lost, which scholars call the Q Document. John is the latest of the four. The internal evidence that allows this relative dating is the way in which the Gospels show the development of the *Jesus* story over time, and particularly the evolution of the theological implications of Christ's death and resurrection. At a time when there was widespread illiteracy, no mass media and no tradition of historical recording, the relatively late authorship of the Gospels alone makes them suspect as historical documents.

Nonetheless, all Christians believe that these four texts (and none of the many others) are, in some sense at least, inspired of God. Yet surely such a belief requires at the very least that there should be a version of these texts that can be trusted as endorsed by God; after all, we are told that God will consign humanity to eternal bliss or damnation based on belief in what these texts say, so the least He could do is make sure that they are clear and unambiguous and free of mistakes. A perfect God cannot (presumably) endorse a less than perfect revelation. Yet of course, neither of these requirements is met in any way by the four Gospels. First, the texts that have come down to us in our Bibles are the result of hundreds of years of editorial harmonization, obfuscation and augmentation. And scholars will still be wrestling with the textual problems hundreds of years on from now, such is the extent of the textual corruption. In what sense, therefore, are we to understand the Gospels to be infallible? Furthermore, the sheer number of contradictions and mistakes in the texts – even after two millennia of conscientious emendation by pious editors – makes the cause of scriptural infallibility a long lost one. In fact, the level of ignorance shown in all the Gospels, both of elementary Palestinian geography and of Jewish customs and laws, makes it a near certainty that these Greek texts must have been written by Greek authors in the second century AD, rather than Jewish disciples of the first century AD.

However, the letters of Paul not only predate the Gospels, but (with the exception of some parts of Revelation) are probably the earliest Christian documents we have and were written closest to the time *Jesus* is supposed to have lived. They are usually dated to AD 50-60, but some could even be as early as the forties, based on Jesus having lived in the first three decades of the century. Not all the Pauline letters in the Bible are accepted by all scholars as authentic, but the letters to the Romans, Corinthians and Galatians emerge as a central core, and we can be reasonably sure that these represent Christianity as it was understood in the mid-first century AD. We shall return to these later, but right now we need to see what these letters have to say about the life of *Jesus*. And it is here that we reach the heart of the matters addressed by this book. Paul was alive when *Jesus* is supposed to have lived. He wrote very soon after when *Jesus* was supposed to have been crucified. He is, therefore, potentially, a more reliable source for the truth about *Jesus* than any other. Yet, *and one cannot emphasize this enough*, he never *met Jesus*; he shows virtually no *knowledge* of the facts of the life of *Jesus* and, incredibly from our point of view, even shows no apparent *interest* in *Jesus*' life. Paul refers to someone he calls variously 'Jesus', 'Christ' and 'Lord'. He knows that this person died and was raised from the dead by God. He seems to know that the death was by crucifixion. And he is aware of a bread-and-wine ritual, instituted by Christ, although this seems to have been revealed to him in a vision rather than knowledge of an actual real-life event.[2] But that is it. All the myriad details in the canonical Gospels (which, I emphasize

---

[2] And in any case it seems to have evolved from the Jewish *Qiddish* ritual that precedes the Jewish Sabbath meal.

again, were written after Paul's letters) is missing from these earliest documents. There is surely something very strange about this. And I am not the only one who thinks so.

Professor Alvar Ellegard[3] has examined in impressive detail all the early, non-canonical Christian texts listed above and has identified four that might reasonably be dated to the first century AD rather than later.[4] He has then painstakingly examined these four, together with Paul's Epistle to the Hebrews and the Book of Revelation, both of which did make it into the New Testament, and finds the same absence of knowledge of, or interest in, the earthly existence of *Jesus*. He concludes:

> ... not only Paul, but *all* Christian writers who can plausibly be dated to the first century AD looked upon Jesus in the same light. They certainly believed that Jesus had once lived ... But ... they saw him as a heavenly figure, sitting on a throne beside God, the Father. On the other hand, the Gospels' picture of Jesus as a Palestinian wonderworker and preacher is ... a creation of the second century AD ... None of this mythical history is supported by *any* first century writings, whether Christian or not.[5]

He also points out that the writers who created the myth were all outside Palestine – they were all Diaspora Jews living in Asia Minor, Syria, Greece and Rome: this is important because, although Christianity obviously has deep Jewish roots, its Jewishness was from the start strongly influenced by its Hellenistic environment.[6]

---

3 See his book, *Jesus: One Hundred Years Before Christ. A Study in Creative Mythology*. Ellegard is a Swedish academic with (like me) a background in literary and linguistic studies.
4 *The Pastor of Hermas, Didache, I Clement,* and the *Letter of Barnabus*.
5 Ellegard, *A Study in Creative Mythology*, pp. 4-5.
6 Ibid., p. 5.

Thus, the straightforward acceptance of *Jesus'* life, as portrayed in the Gospels, is problematical to say the least: the four Gospels themselves represent only a fraction of the texts relating to the life of Jesus that we know to have existed; they were written *at least* half a century after the events they describe; and when we look at other documents written closer to that time, we find extraordinarily little evidence to support their assertions. This, of course, raises the question: if the stories of *Jesus'* life are not *historical*, where did they come from? Were they just imagined by the writers? Were they consciously writing fictions?

To answer these questions, we need to understand how writers of that time regarded historical truth. Today we expect historians to apply strict scientific standards to the narration of history. The historian needs to be able to demonstrate his sources for every statement he makes. But in the ancient and classical worlds, different standards applied. What mattered was not what we regard as literal truth but the deeper truth behind a narrative. It was a mindset that failed to distinguish between history and myth because, in some sense, the myth tells a 'truth' that goes deeper than any history. This was particularly true of ancient Greek historiography, which is the most appropriate context in which to read the Gospels and Acts. If the ancient Greek historian wanted to describe an event, he would invent dialogue, actions, gestures, and even the intervention of gods, to provide a deeper understanding of the event he was attempting to convey. This was commonplace practice in the Hellenistic world at the time of the Gospels, and we must not make the mistake of imposing modern concepts of historical 'truth' on a world where creative invention of this kind was regarded as entirely legitimate. And this was particularly true of spiritual matters: in a very real sense, what did it matter what happened in 'reality'? What was important was the spiritual implications and consequences, and any literary technique was considered legitimate if it helped convey through concrete words the realities of the invisible, spiritual world. It is hard for us now to retrieve the mindset that regarded such creative invention to generate polemical texts as legitimate, but we must try because otherwise we fall into the trap of mistaking fiction for fact.

But in the case of Jews in the period we are interested in, there was much more to it even than this. They had techniques of their own for expressing spiritual truth, which by their standards were also legitimate. We have seen how, scattered throughout the writings of the prophets and the wisdom literature, there are references to a coming time when God would send a prophet followed by a Messiah (or two Messiahs) who would establish a new Covenant with Jews (and in some texts with Gentiles as well) and a new Kingdom of God on Earth. These references do not represent a single coherent picture of these events – they are fragmentary, undeveloped and obscure. But together they convinced many Jews that they were living at the end of the old dispensation. This belief grew as, during the last couple of centuries BC and into the first century AD, the classical world in general increasingly infected Judæa with ideas and customs wholly alien to the traditional Jewish outlook. And with the arrival of the Roman Empire in direct control of Jewish affairs, the belief in an imminent intervention by God became intermittently fervent. In these times, pious Jews would ransack their scriptures for clues as to the timing and nature of this intervention. Scriptural texts were routinely ripped from context and re-interpreted in this way – particularly by Jews of a mystical bent (and there were many of these). One sect in particular took this to extremes: the Dead Sea Scrolls sect. We therefore need to pause at this point and take a closer look at this contentious sect.

From the earliest days following the discovery of the first scrolls in 1949, in caves near Qumran on the west bank of the Dead Sea, there has been controversy about how they were found, how they were then handled and what they mean for Christianity. They were found, preserved in sealed pottery jars, by shepherds whose livestock had wandered into the caves where they had been hidden two millennia before. Those shepherds were poor men, with little understanding of what they had found and no interest in anything other than getting the best price for them on the thriving antiquities market in Palestine and Egypt. Gradually, news of the finds leaked out to the west, and most of the scrolls were gathered together (one way or another) in Jerusalem and an international team of scholars were brought together to study them. That team maintained very tight control indeed. No one was allowed access except themselves and their hand-picked research students. For anyone not familiar with the cut-and-thrust world of international academia, it may seem strange that access was not opened to everyone. But scholarly publications and theses containing new and original material are the currency of success in the academic world, and from this point of view it is perhaps not surprising that these scholars should have held on jealously to what they had. However, by the very nature of things, scholars of biblical manuscripts tend themselves to be believing Christians and, with a few exceptions, this was true of the international team, many of whom were ordained Catholic priests. As a result, suspicions arose over time that the team were hiding something: that there was a religious time bomb ticking in the Scrolls.

The team vigorously denied this. Very soon after studying the scrolls they reached a consensus opinion that the scrolls represent the library of a sectarian community which was based at Qumran and were hidden in the caves at the time of the first Jewish war against the Romans in the Sixties AD. The sect in question they believed to have been the Essenes. Unlike the other established Jewish sects in the first century AD, the Pharisees and the Sadducees, the Essenes do not seem to appear in the Bible, but they are well attested in Josephus and other writers of the time. The team maintained, from the evidence of the scrolls themselves, that the sect's history began at the time of the Maccabees, in or around the second century BC, and that the characters and events described in the scrolls belong to that period. And that remains the consensus, official scholarly view to this day. The scrolls are regarded as a mine of information about Judaism in the centuries before Christ, and as we have seen, about Messianic belief in particular; but their only relevance to Christianity is to provide the context out of which Christianity and other Messianic sects arose.

Over time, partly because of the protests of conspiracy theorists, and partly because the international team were their own worst enemies and failed to publish vast swathes of the texts for decades, one way and another the original restricted access to the scrolls has been gradually loosened, and, as of today, all the texts are freely available. As a result, as other scholars have been able to work on them, a variety of dissenting views have been developed about the scrolls. Some have argued that the scrolls come from a library in Jerusalem and therefore represent a wider spectrum of Jewish religious belief than just one sect. Others have questioned the Essene association, or the Qumran connection, or both. Others have challenged the consensus dating and regard the events and characters depicted in some of the scrolls as relating to Judaism as it existed in the first century AD rather than the second century BC. And some have gone further and identified the scrolls with the early Christian church. It is therefore important to the concerns of the present book that we endeavour at this point to reach a view about these issues.

The Essene connection, adhered to by most scholars, is based partly on the geographical coincidence of Qumran and the caves, and a reference by the contemporary Roman writer, Pliny the Younger, to an Essene community in that area. But it is also based on detailed descriptions in some of the scrolls of a religious community that in many respects sounds like the Essenes as described by Josephus and Philo – the two Jewish historians of the period. The Christian connection is also based partly on the Essene connection, because the same descriptions of the religious community also sound like the early Christian church as described in Acts and the Epistles of Paul. But it is also based on the language used – terms used to describe the community like the 'poor', and their beliefs as the 'way' sound genuinely like Christianity. Unfortunately, attempts to resolve these issues through carbon dating and handwriting styles have failed to produce unanimity.

One reason it is so tempting to make these connections is that there are some vivid characters that emerge from some of the scrolls, and if they can be identified with their counterparts in history, interpretation of the scrolls would be more secure on the one hand, and light would be shed on that period of history on the other. The Scrolls sect – whoever they were – claim they were founded (a 'root of planting') in an 'age of wrath' some 390 years after the destruction of Jerusalem by the Babylonian Empire. This event, as we have seen, took place in 587 BC, which gives a date of 197 BC for the founding of the sect. This brings us roughly into the Maccabean period – hence the consensus view that the scrolls relate to this period. But time periods and dates in texts of this sort cannot be trusted and are often based on mystical numbers rather than history. Apparently, the sect 'groped their way' for about twenty years before a 'Teacher of Righteousness' came along to guide them. His teachings led to a split in the community; the leader of the schismatics is known in the scrolls as, among other names, 'the Liar'. The split forced the Teacher to take his followers into Exile in the 'land of Damascus', where they entered into a 'new Covenant'.

The Teacher died in Exile, but the community waited for the coming twin messiahs – King and Priest – to establish the Kingdom of God on Earth. Another character, the Wicked Priest, appears in some of the scrolls; he was a corrupt figure who defiled the Temple in some way, persecuted the Teacher and his followers and appears to have had some sort of physical confrontation with the Teacher, but scholars seem divided on whether this is another name for the Liar, or a different character altogether. There is no real consensus among those scholars that accept the Maccabean identification as to exactly who each of these characters were; since their descriptions are so loose, they can be fitted to a number of individuals. This is particularly true of the Teacher himself, and this failure to positively identify him is one of the reasons why there remain dissenting voices who look for a more secure identification in the first century AD. These have variously identified the Teacher with *Jesus*, John the Baptist and James, the brother of *Jesus* (of whom more later).

My own view is that the jury is still out on whether the scrolls relate to the second century BC or the first century AD. None of the arguments look conclusive, and although the weight of scholarly opinion is behind the earlier dating, there is always a bias in scholarship for the establishment view – that is, until an iconoclast comes along and shows it to be wrong. Proponents of the later date include very many non-scholars who are attracted by the conspiracy theory that the Scrolls were withheld from open scrutiny for many years by a cadre of Christian scholars who were frightened by the implications of the scrolls for traditional Christian belief. Given that the scrolls have been freely available to everyone for the last few decades, however, and no one seems yet to have discovered an indisputable smoking gun for Christianity lurking somewhere in them, I think this can be discounted. But the fact remains that no one has proven a case to the satisfaction of all, and the debates continue. However, all this is, in my opinion, while not irrelevant to the subject of this book, nevertheless something of a red herring – and an unfortunate red herring because it has for so long and for so many people, distracted from the real issues.

Let us assume for the moment that the minority view is right and that the scrolls are largely first-century AD texts. In my view, it is the supposed identification between them, the Essenes and Christianity that is shaky. We shall examine the Essenes later when we look at the writings of the Jewish historian Josephus, who described them in considerable detail. Much of what he says is borne out by another ancient Jewish historian, Philo, who also describes them at great length. Both writers differ in certain particulars, suggesting perhaps that there were indeed differences within the sect itself; Philo lived in Egypt and Josephus was Judæan, so perhaps there were regional differences. But the one thing that stands out above all others in both their descriptions is that the Essenes were *peaceful*. This is why both historians write of them at such length and with such approbation; unlike other Jewish Messianic sects, the Essenes were acceptable to the Roman Empire, and both historians were writing for Hellenistic readers of the Empire. Josephus in particular makes a specific point of emphasizing just how universal was the respect with which the Essenes were held. They were regarded as apolitical, unworldly monks, devoted to scriptural study and worship. In sharp contrast to this, the sect described in the Scrolls is Messianic, extremist and violent. I fail to see how the two can be equated.

A leading proponent of the Essene/scrolls identification is Robert Eisenman.[7] He seeks to get round this issue by talking about an 'Opposition Alliance', by this means deliberately blurring the differences between the sects and thereby allowing him to interpret the scrolls as 'Jewish Christian'. But Eisenman and his followers go one step further still. Having identified the Scroll sect with the Essenes, they then identify the Essenes with early Christianity, and conclude from this that the early Christians were Messianic and probably violent. This last may well be true – we shall look more closely at this issue later – but in my view, the case for identification between the Essenes and Christianity is as tenuous as the case for identifying the scrolls sect with the Essenes and certainly has not been accepted by most scholars. There are indeed very many coincidences of language and social structure between the Scrolls, what we know of the Essenes and the early Church, as depicted in the New Testament. But remember, Christianity began as a Jewish sect, and we are discussing here different versions of Judaism, not different religions. One would be surprised *not* to find commonality of language, outlook and structure. Eisenman's entire approach is based on seeking out these commonalities.

An alternative view to Eisenman's has been promulgated by Hyam Maccoby.[8] He has argued that *Jesus* was in fact a Pharisee. The Gospels largely present the Pharisees as opponents of *Jesus* – synonymous with hypocrisy and cant. As with the Essenes, we shall presently look at this group in more detail, but Maccoby demonstrates that the anti-Pharisee tone of the Gospels has more to do with anti-Semitism than

---

[7] See Select Bibliography.

[8] See Select Bibliography.

reality. For example, Chapter 23 of Matthew is a long tirade by *Jesus* against the Pharisees; its repeated refrain is 'Woe unto you, Scribes and Pharisees'. Yet we know the passage could not be a report of words spoken by *Jesus* in the thirties because *Jesus* there also mentions 'Zacharias son of Barachias, whom ye slew between the temple and the altar'[9] – a character of the same name and parentage appears in Josephus and his death, as described, was in AD 67, long after the supposed death of *Jesus*. The Gospels were written for a Roman audience after the Jewish War, by which time the Jews were in bad odour. The Pharisees were the dominant force in Judaism, so to attack the Pharisees was to attack the Jews. If we must identify a group out of which the Jesus Movement emerged, my money is on Pharisees rather than Essenes. But if we want to discover what was unique about Christianity it is not the commonalities that we are after but the differences. Saying that *Jesus* was a Pharisee is certainly surprising, given their usual press, but it does not actually take us far.

However, irrespective of the above issues there is nevertheless one aspect of the Scrolls sect that has a real bearing on the subject of this book, and that is the allegorical way they approached the scriptures. So much of Jewish scripture purported to be history; it described events that had happened in the distant past. It seemed to the Scrolls sect that either this material was no longer any use for guiding current action, or that there must be more universal truths hidden encoded within it. This is a problem faced by Christians today: they feel they should study the Old as well as the New Testament, but so much of the former describes ancient history that, it seems irrelevant to guide day-to-day Christian life. Inevitably, therefore, they tend to use an allegorical approach. Protestant preachers are past

---

9 Matthew 23:35.

masters at this. They will take an obscure Old Testament text with apparently no relevance whatsoever and then find a remarkable and surprising allegorical meaning hidden within.[10]

The writers of the Dead Sea Scrolls did something similar but much more extreme. They developed an interpretive process called *Pesher*[11] designed to uncover and decode the truths they believed God had deliberately hidden within scripture. The writers of *Pesharim* believed that the prophets themselves only had a partial interpretation revealed to them of the prophecies they made. Scripture was thus written on two levels: the surface for ordinary readers with limited knowledge, and the concealed one for specialists with higher knowledge and the religious dedication necessary to uncover it. The Scrolls sect used this *Pesher* technique to find hidden meanings in scriptural passages that could then be used to justify their own specific beliefs and practices. The meanings they found were spiritual and symbolic and bore no relation at all to the physical realities overtly referred to. To modern eyes they seem breathtaking in their willingness to suspend all sense of historical reality and to see hidden messages from God in the most unlikely passages. The technique was used by the sect to interpret scripture relating to the Last Days, and to identify their own role as prophesied in scripture. Today's *Bible Code*[12] and other similar flights of fancy pale to insignificance beside this interpretive enterprise.

The discovery of the hitherto unknown *Pesher* technique

---

[10] The classic parody of this is Alan Bennett's hilarious sketch in *Beyond the Fringe* in which, portraying an Anglican priest, he implies some allegorical meaning from the seemingly banal 'Esau my brother is a hairy man, and I am a smooth man' (Genesis 27:11).

[11] The word comes from a root meaning 'interpretation', in the sense of 'solution'. *Pesharim* (the plural) give a scriptural interpretation, previously partly known but now fully defined.

[12] See Select Bibliography. There have been two sequels, equally banal.

following the discovery of the scrolls themselves has served to throw into sharp relief the importance of such scriptural techniques to Jewish commentators and to demonstrate just how far they could go in their search for hidden meaning. Before scholars had this evidence, they had no real idea of the extent to which the texts they were used to treating as history were, in fact, imaginative fictions.[13] Outside of the Scrolls sect, other Jewish sects, like the Pharisees and Sadducees, habitually did something similar, which they called *Midrash*.[14] Because the Pharisees regarded religious truth as something to be gradually understood through discussion and open debate between different learned rabbis, *Midrash* tends to be less dogmatic and prescriptive than *Pesher*. But in its essentials, *Midrash* too was founded on the belief that the Word of God has different layers of meaning and the deeper the layer, the more esoteric and spiritual the meaning. The devout student would search for those meanings and there was lively debate over differing interpretations. It now seems evident that the Jesus Movement was no different in this regard. Like all the other sects of Judaism, they would approach scripture with an *a priori* idea of what they wanted to find there.

I cannot emphasize enough the importance of this. The idea that allegory is an important biblical technique is not new. After all, we are used to the parables of *Jesus*, which seem just allegorical stories with a moral or spiritual message. And it is hard to understand or justify the inclusion in the Bible of a Book like Song of Solomon (which is an at times graphic celebration of sexual love) except as an extended allegory of divine love. But the discovery of the Dead Sea Scrolls, and the extreme lengths to which the *Pesher* technique could be

---

[13] Some examples will be explored presently.

[14] The word comes from a root word meaning 'to search', 'to seek', 'to examine', and 'to investigate'.

pushed, gave a huge impetus to scholars to recognize that the use of allegorical techniques was not just widespread among New Testament writers – it was endemic. At first, the scholarly effort focused on prophetic texts where, unless one starts with a belief in supernatural prophecy, it seems natural to search for more rational explanations. But it did not take long for scholars to discover they were on a slippery slope towards recognition that *all* the Gospel stories, and even the stories about Paul and the other Apostles in Acts, also had their origins in the Old Testament and other stories about other people and events and times entirely. Given the latitude that the writers of *Pesharim* gave themselves, almost any Old Testament text could be pillaged to find proof for, or evidence of, almost anything else. The Gospel parables themselves were not folk stories meant to explain difficult spiritual concepts to simple people – quite the reverse. They were texts designed to have different layers of meaning for the spiritually adept to discover. And with this dawning realization came the completely new understanding that the writers of New Testament texts were using the *Pesher* technique to flesh out the detail of what would otherwise have been mere myth and hearsay. It provided both the glue and the substance with which they pieced together the fundamental narratives of their faith. In effect:

Today's Christian reader learns what Jesus did by reading the Gospels; his ancient counterpart learned what Jesus did by reading Joshua and 1 Kings. [15]

---

15 This is from the Introduction to Robert M. Price's *The Christ Myth Theory and Its Problems* – see Select Bibliography. Price is an American theologian and writer who, in a succession of books and through his website, has argued extensively and in scholarly detail that Jesus was never a historical figure. His book goes through the Gospels, line by line, showing how everything we think we know about the life of Jesus was lifted from the Old Testament and other sources. For anyone seeking detailed validation of the mythicist stance, it is an indispensable source book.

So, to answer the question we asked a few pages back – did they just make up the Gospel stories of *Jesus*? – the answer is both yes and no. Yes, they created fictions to fill in the detail of a biography of which they had no knowledge. But no, they did not just pluck those fictions from thin air: they diligently searched the scriptures using *Midrash* and *Pesher* to find the hidden meanings that would fit with their preconceived paradigm about *Jesus*.

A couple of examples will serve to illustrate the *midrashic* method. First, we shall examine the biblical accounts of the death of Judas Iscariot, who famously betrayed *Jesus* for thirty pieces of silver. Matthew's Gospel says that Judas returned the money to the priests, who used it to buy a potter's field; Judas then committed suicide by hanging himself. The Acts of the Apostles flatly contradicts this. It says that it was Judas who used the money to buy a field, and he then fell head-first, and 'burst asunder in the midst, and all his bowels gushed out'.[16] Outside of the Bible, there survives a non-canonical Gospel of Judas[17] which gives a third account, different again. It says that Judas had a vision of the disciples stoning and persecuting him. Another account, preserved by the early Christian leader Papias, said that Judas' body swelled up and he was crushed by a chariot, so that his bowels gushed out. I suppose we could invent some narrative that harmonizes all these accounts: Judas buys the field, gives it to the priests, gets sick, has a delirious dream, gets involved in a chariot crash and in despair hangs himself. But just how many multiplied entities must we incorporate before we realize that these are all just fictions? Even just restricting ourselves to the two canonical accounts in Matthew and Acts, it seems inescapably obvious that they cannot both be correct; either Judas bought the field,

---

16 Acts 1:18.

17 Listed above, pp.65–67.

or the priests did. The differing accounts of Judas' death have been a stumbling block over the years for many Christians trying to maintain belief in the inerrancy of scripture – and no wonder. But where do these stories come from?

The Matthew account[18] concludes:

> Then was fulfilled that which was spoken by Jeremy [i.e., Jeremiah] the prophet, saying, and they took the thirty pieces of silver, the price of him that was valued, whom they of the children of Israel did value; And gave them for the potter's field, as the Lord appointed me.

Clearly this is a *Midrash* on an Old Testament text, interpreting it as a prophecy concerning Judas hundreds of years later. Or is it? There is a problem that has puzzled scholars and believers alike for years: there is nothing corresponding to this prophecy in the Book of Jeremiah. The closest passages in Jeremiah are in several chapters where there are unconnected references to potters, jars, the purchase of a field, and silver. But the contexts are entirely different. Chapter 18 compares Israel to a clay vessel on a potter's wheel, moulded and/or destroyed by the hand of God (the potter).[19] Chapter 19 describes how God will destroy the unfaithful like shattering a 'potter's earthen bottle'.[20] And in Chapter 32, Jeremiah relates how God told him to purchase a field from his cousin for 'seventeen shekels of silver' in faith that God would restore the Jews to their lands after the Babylonian captivity.[21] (God certainly looks after his own!) But none of

---

18 27:3-10.
19 18:1-6.
20 19:1-10
21 32:9

these references can be honestly regarded as prophesying the death of Judas.

However, very significantly, as we shall see later in this book, there *is* a relevant passage in *another* Old Testament prophet, Zechariah. This passage *does* mention 'the potter' and 'thirty pieces of silver'. Zechariah says to his Jewish hearers:

If ye think good, give me my price: and if not, forbear.[22]

He is given 'thirty pieces of silver' as the price for his prophesying, and then God tells him to 'cast them to the potter in the house of the Lord'. But again, only a *Midrashist* (or a fundamentalist Christian perhaps) determined to find hidden meanings would see this as referring to events in the first century AD. None of these references relate in any obvious way to the Judas story, but Christian tradition would maintain that these obscure Old Testament references are in some way a prophecy of what actually happens to Judas in Matthew (if one ignores the entirely different account in Acts). Whether or not under this explanation Judas knew he was fulfilling scripture is a moot point, though it is difficult to believe he would have planned such a gruesome suicide for himself.[23] It seems to me a more likely and rational explanation that the account in Matthew is a fictional story, combining imaginatively different elements from the passages in Jeremiah and Zechariah. The Gospel writers, needing a culprit for *Jesus'* betrayal, invented a character that bears a name, Judas, that symbolises all Jews (because, after all, they tell their Gentile

---

[22] 11:12-13.

[23] Or perhaps not – after all, this is precisely what *Jesus* himself is supposed to have done: delivering himself up, with Judas' aid, to the authorities to become a sacrifice for mankind.

audience, it was the Jews who killed Jesus!). They then need him to suffer God's punishment, so they filch a range of handy Old Testament references to potters and silver and weave an unlikely but vivid story. And in their minds they were not making things up – they were uncovering hidden, esoteric truths in the most sacred texts.

Another example, more straightforward this time, also (again, importantly, as we shall see) comes from Zechariah. As we have seen, this book has much to say, albeit obscurely, about the coming of the twin messiahs, and in Chapter 9 Zechariah has a vision of a King-Messiah entering Jerusalem:

> Rejoice greatly, O daughter of Zion; shout O daughter of Jerusalem: behold, thy King cometh unto thee; he is just, and having salvation; lowly, and riding upon an ass, and upon a colt the foal of an ass.[24]

Matthew, in Chapter 21, relating the entry of *Jesus* into Jerusalem, tells how:

> ... when they drew nigh unto Jerusalem ... then sent Jesus two disciples. Saying unto them, Go into the village over against you, and straightway ye shall find an ass tied, and a colt with her: loose them, and bring them unto me ... All this was done, that it might be fulfilled which was spoken by the prophet, saying, Tell ye the daughter of Sion, Behold, thy King cometh unto thee, meek, and sitting upon an ass, and a colt the foal of an ass.[25]

This was clearly a well-established part of the story by the time the Gospels came to be written; the other three Gospels

---

[24] 9:9-10.

[25] 21:1-5

also relate much the same story, although only John also includes the *midrashic* reference:

> ... *as it is written*, Fear not, daughter of Sion: behold, thy King cometh, sitting on an ass's colt'.[26] (Author's emphasis)

In this case of *Midrash*, the source is clear, but the potential explanations more varied. It may be, as in the case of Judas' death, that *Jesus* was fulfilling the prophecy, either unknowingly or deliberately, as part of some sort of 'Passover Plot' to establish him as the Messiah.[27] But surely the simplest explanation is that Matthew (or whoever wrote the story) is filling in imaginative details to his narrative and at the same time establishing *Jesus*' Messianic credentials – by filleting the Old Testament for verses that can be interpreted under the very loose methods of *Midrash* – to apply to his fiction.

The obvious question that arises, therefore, is how much of the Gospel stories of *Jesus* are fiction of this sort, and how much 'true' by modern standards? We have seen how neither Paul nor other first century writers had any knowledge of or, interest in, the life of *Jesus*. We have seen how, coming along later, the Gospel writers filled this need by ransacking the Old Testament for people and events that could be rewritten, using the *Midrash* technique, as applying to *Jesus*. What certainly seems clear from all this is that we cannot trust anything the Gospels say about *Jesus*. Unfortunately, because as we shall see, there is no trustworthy corroborating evidence outside the Bible, it is not possible then to take the uncompromising

---

26 12:14-15.

27 As argued in Schonfield's book of that name – see Select Bibliography. Schonfield evolved a theory of Jesus deliberately setting out to fulfil by enactment the Old Testament Messianic prophecies – a good example of a scholar vainly attempting to explain the inexplicable, before the Dead Sea Scrolls came along to reveal the extent of *Pesher* and *Midrash*.

stance that without such external evidence we accept nothing as authentic. But it *is* possible to take each Gospel statement in turn and see whether we can identify where it came from. And over the last hundred years or so, this is what scholars have done. There is now what amounts to a scholarly industry, spotting the original sources for just about every event in the Gospels. The result of this entire endeavour is that there is virtually nothing left that someone, somewhere has not found a source for. Of course, scholars dispute with each other endlessly about this or that source. But when so much of the Gospel narratives can be explained in this way, surely we are entitled to say, whatever the fine detail, it does look as if the Gospels are fiction. What then can we conclude about the traditional life of *Jesus* as it has come down to us today?

THE LIFE OF JESUS

The prophecy of Isaiah Chapter 53, quoted in full earlier, which contains within it all the key elements of the Gospel story, indicates that the Gospel writers did not have to look too far for their material. Christians will claim that this, and other passages like it, are miraculous prophecies. But, given what we now understand about the process of *Midrash*, we are surely entitled to take the view that this text was simply ransacked by the Gospel writers to give them the key material for the life of a *Jesus* about whom they knew next to nothing. The examples of Judas' fate and *Jesus* on the ass are further grist to the mill. But my book would be twice as long if I went through all the other sources that can be adduced for virtually every line of the Gospel narratives; others, (notably Price: see bibliography) have already done this. However, I do want here to provide sufficient by way of example to provide all but the most sceptical reader with reasonable evidence to confirm the view that, ironically, nothing in the Gospels can be taken as Gospel Truth. There are surely two key articles of Christian faith which, if they can be shown to be drawn from other sources, are a strong indication that all the rest is probably equally fictional. These are the miraculous birth of *Jesus* as the son of God, and his sacrificial crucifixion. If these two acid tests can be shown to originate in other narratives and texts, I would argue that we can safely conclude the same about the rest.

The birth narrative with which we are probably familiar from Sunday School and Christmas Nativity plays is only found in Matthew and Luke; Mark (the earliest Gospel) and John omit mention of it altogether. Mark probably ignores the birth because no one at that point had thought to even ask about the circumstances of *Jesus*' birth. John, of all the Gospel writers, is the least concerned with *any* of the details of *Jesus*' human existence; instead, it is concerned with a range of philosophical ideas, imported into Christian theology from Greek philosophy. Modern writers seeking to show the fallibility of scripture often do so by reference to the passages in Matthew and Luke. The two accounts totally conflict, despite all attempts over the centuries to harmonize them. Matthew places the birth in the last years of Herod the Great, who we know died in 4 BC. Luke places the same event a decade later at the time of the taxation census decreed by Caesar Augustus 'made when Cyrenius was governor of Syria'.[28] Either Matthew is wrong, or Luke is wrong; it is hard to see how the two are capable of reconciliation. But that is just the start of the problems. If the census took place under Herod, it could not have been 'decreed by Augustus' because Herod was responsible for taxation in Judæa – a

---

28 Luke 2:2. 'Cyrenius' is more properly known as 'Quirinius'.

client state of Rome at that time, not under direct Roman administration. We know, in fact, from Josephus that the census in AD 6 was a local affair, organized in order to determine local taxes. According to the narrative, Joseph and Mary were resident in Nazareth because one Old Testament text – (see below) arguably placed the Messiah there. So that is where they would have been census registered. Why then are they depicted as travelling to Bethlehem? Because this is the City of David and another Old Testament prophecy also places the Messiah *there*. In addition, we know from other Roman sources that, as with censuses today, only the head of household needed to make a Roman census return. It really would not have been necessary then as now for a heavily pregnant Mary to make a journey to Bethlehem. Once again, we find ourselves asking whether people were really going to these lengths to fulfil scripture, or whether the Gospel writers, having no historical sources, were inventing them doing so.

And the invention was relatively easy. For the basic outline, Matthew seems to have raided Josephus' account of the nativity of Moses, who is described there in Messianic terms:

> He shall deliver the Hebrew nation . . . [and] . . . His memory shall be famous while the world lasts.[29]

Remember that Moses was one of the great Jewish heroes that provided a model for the coming Messiah. He defied the Egyptian pharaoh and led the Israelites out of Egypt. Just as Pharaoh in the Old Testament, warned by a prophet, decreed the slaughter of all male Jewish infants, so Herod, warned by the wise men, does the same. Moses' parents, like Joseph and Mary, are reassured in a dream of the importance of their forthcoming son. Details of *Jesus*' birth are then filled in by a

---

29 *Antiquities* 2:216.

variety of borrowings from Old Testament texts. For example, the Star of Bethlehem was not a real star – as its astronomically impossible geostationary position would surely imply. It comes from the Old Testament Book of Numbers:

> ... there shall come a star out of Jacob, and a sceptre shall rise out of Israel.[30]

This was a very well-known Messianic prophecy, mentioned in Josephus and applied at the time to any likely Messianic candidate in the first century, including even the Roman conqueror of Jerusalem, Vespasian. All the hours of honest endeavour over the years by well-meaning scholars and enthusiasts to identify the Star of Bethlehem with this comet, or that supernova, could have been saved if those scientists and scholars had just understood what was really going on here. Similarly, the idea of the virgin birth comes from Isaiah:

> Behold, a virgin shall conceive, and bear a son.[31]

In fact, many scholars argue that the word 'virgin' here is in any case a mistranslation of a Hebrew word that more precisely means 'young woman', so the whole edifice of Mary worship built up by the Catholic church over the centuries is probably based itself on a fallacy. The Nazareth origin comes from Judges:

> ... the child shall be a Nazirite unto God from the womb.[32]

This again is in all probability a misconception too. Nazirites

---

[30] Numbers 24:17.
[31] Numbers 7:14.
[32] 13:7. There are other, interesting possibilities as we shall see later.

had nothing to do with a place called Nazareth, which in any case it is doubtful even existed in biblical times. We shall look at the derivation of 'nazir' later in this book, but Nazirites were pious Jews who had made certain purity vows. The Greek writer of the Gospel probably did not understand this Jewish concept and assumed the term referred to a place. As mentioned above, the Bethlehem connection comes from Micah:

> But thou, Bethlehem Ephratah . . . out of thee shall he come forth unto me that is to be ruler of Israel [33]

The flight of the holy family into Egypt comes from Hosea:

> I called my son . . . out of Egypt[34]

One can imagine the Gospel writer's challenge: to invent a story wherein the holy family can be said all at once to hail from Nazareth, Bethlehem and Egypt; he did the job so well we still have our children re-enact the story every Christmas without pausing to notice how completely unlikely the whole narrative is.

Luke, on the other hand, gives us the story of the double birth of Jesus and John the Baptist, who was born to Mary's cousin Elizabeth and her husband Zechariah. We shall see later that the Book of Zechariah provides the solution to all these problems, hence perhaps the name's occurrence in this narrative. And as we shall also see, the real Jesus Movement was founded by two such individuals. But the essentials of this version of the story were taken from, not Moses in this case, but the birth of the Old Testament prophet Samuel. Mary's hymn of praise to God in Luke seems a little strange:

---

[33] 5:2

[34] 11:1

And Mary said, 'My soul doth magnify the Lord, and my spirit hath rejoiced in God my Saviour. For he hath regarded the low estate of his handmaiden: for, behold, from henceforth all generations shall call me blessed. For he that is mighty hath done to me great things; and holy is his name. And his mercy is on them that fear him from generation to generation. He hath shewed strength with his arm; he hath scattered the proud in the imagination of their hearts. He hath put down the mighty from their seats and exalted them of low degree. He hath filled the hungry with good things; and the rich he hath sent empty away. He hath holpen his servant Israel, in remembrance of his mercy; As he spake to our fathers, to Abraham, and to his seed forever.[35]

The references to God bringing down the mighty and filling the hungry seem rather beside the point. But of course, these words have been put in her mouth by Luke, who has taken and reworked them from the Old Testament story of Samuel. In that story, a man called Elkanah had two wives; one of the wives, Hannah, was barren, but by the gift of God bore a son, Samuel. Hannah's hymn of praise uncannily parallels that of Mary:

And Hannah prayed, and said, My heart rejoiceth in the Lord, mine horn is exalted in the Lord: mine mouth is enlarged over mine enemies; because I rejoice in thy salvation. There is none holy as the Lord: for there is none beside thee: neither is there any rock like our God. Talk no more so exceedingly proudly; let not arrogancy come out of your mouth: for the Lord is a God of knowledge, and by him actions are weighed. The bows of the mighty men are broken, and they that stumbled are girded with strength. They that were full have hired out themselves for bread; and they that

---

35 1:46-55.

were hungry ceased: so that the barren hath born seven; and she that hath many children is waxed feeble. The Lord killeth, and maketh alive: he bringeth down to the grave, and bringeth up. The Lord maketh poor, and maketh rich: he bringeth low, and lifteth up. He raiseth up the poor out of the dust, and lifteth up the beggar from the dunghill, to set them among princes, and to make them inherit the throne of glory: for the pillars of the earth are the Lords, and he hath set the world upon them. He will keep the feet of his saints, and the wicked shall be silent in darkness; for by strength shall no man prevail. The adversaries of the Lord shall be broken to pieces; out of heaven shall he thunder upon them: the Lord shall judge the ends of the earth; and he shall give strength unto his king, and exalt the horn of his anointed.[36]

Luke's references to *Jesus*' growth in 'wisdom and stature, and in favour with God and man'[37] also directly quotes Samuel:

And the child Samuel grew on, and in favour both with the Lord, and also with men.[38]

Luke's account of the Annunciation to Mary is similarly lifted from the story of Isaac, son of Abraham:

. . . thy wife shall bear thee a son indeed, and thou shalt call his name . . .[39]

I could cite much more but hopefully the point is made. The nativity narratives are stories, stitched together from various

---

36 1 Samuel 2:1-10.

37 2:52.

38 2:26.

39 Genesis 17:19.

unrelated sources, to provide an account of the birth and childhood of a man the writers had no information about, but whom they needed to portray as fulfilling scriptural prophecies about the coming of a Messiah. There is nothing new in all this. Many Bibles will point out precisely these cross-references – and many more – as proof of the inspiration of the Bible and its prophecies. Many believe that all this happened to fulfil those prophecies – either in ignorance, or in deliberate acts of fulfilment. Surely, as Occam's Razor would suggest, the simplest answer is most likely the right one: that these are just stories, no more and no less.

The narratives of the crucifixion of *Jesus* bear exactly the same characteristics; there are two main sources – Psalm 22 and the Wisdom of Solomon, which is canonical in Catholic Bibles but missing from Protestant ones. I reproduce below the relevant passages from Psalm 22, together with the Gospel parallels:

> My God, my God, why hast thou forsaken me? Why art thou so far from helping me, and from the words of my roaring?
>
> [Psalm 22:1]

> My God, my God, why hast thou forsaken me?
>
> [Mark 15:34]

> All they that see me laugh me to scorn: they shoot out the lip, they shake the head
>
> [Psalm 22:7]

> And they that passed by railed on him, wagging their heads.
>
> [Mark 15:29]

He trusted on the Lord that he would deliver him . . . seeing he delighted in him

[Psalm 22:8]

He trusted in God: let him deliver him now

[Matthew 27:43]

For dogs have compassed me: the assembly of the wicked have inclosed me: they pierced my hands and my feet

[Psalm 22:16]

. . . and they crucified him

[Mark 15:25]

They part my garments among them, and cast lots upon my vesture

[Psalm 22:18]

And when they had crucified him, they parted his garments, casting lots upon them, what every man should take

[Mark 15:24]

The Wisdom of Solomon was written in the last couple of centuries before the Christian era, but prefigures the whole crucifixion story:

Therefore let us lie in wait for the righteous; because . . . he upbraideth us with our offending the law . . . he professeth to have the knowledge of God; and calleth himself the child of the Lord. . . he pronounceth the end of the just to be blessed, and maketh his boast that God is his father. Let us see if his words be true: and let us prove what shall happen in the end of him, and deliver him from the hand of his enemies. Let us examine him with despitefulness and torture, that we may know his meekness, and prove his patience. Let us condemn him with a shameful death: for, by his own saying he shall be respected.[40]

Other details are, as usual, taken from a variety of unconnected, random Old Testament passages. For example:

> And it shall come to pass in that day, saith the Lord God, that I will cause the sun to go down at noon, and I will darken the earth in the clear day
>
> [Amos 8:9]

> Now from the sixth hour there was darkness over all the land unto the ninth hour
>
> [Matthew 27:45]

> He keepeth all his bones: not one of them is broken
>
> [Psalms 34:20]

> They brake not his legs . . . that the scripture should be fulfilled
>
> [John 19:33-6]

> They gave me also gall for my meat: and in my thirst they gave me vinegar to drink
>
> [Psalm 69:21]

---

40 Wisdom of Solomon 2:12-20.

> And straightway one of them ran, and took a sponge, and filled it with vinegar . . . and gave him to drink
>
> [Matthew 27:48]

Why else would one give a dying man vinegar? And the resurrection on the third day?:

> . . . in the third day he will raise us up, and we shall live in his sight.
>
> (Hosea 6:2)

Once again, we must ask what is the most likely rational explanation for these parallels – were all these characters consciously or unconsciously playing out predestined roles, or are we faced here again with fiction based on *midrashic* plunderings?

I suggest that these accounts of *Jesus*' birth and death provide the acid test of my assertion that the Gospel stories are fiction. But many modern Christians, having had some knowledge of these problems, would want to argue that these borrowings really do not matter. For them, it is not the details of *Jesus*' life that matter, but the freshness and originality of *Jesus*' teachings. For example, the 'sublime' Sermon on the Mount, which many Christians believe provides an unparallelled guide to the conduct of a righteous life? Surely these were entirely new ideas at the time, and bear testimony, if not to his divinity, then at least to *Jesus*' status as a unique religious thinker? Not so, I am afraid. The 'sermon' is to be found in Matthew, Chapters 5 to 7. There is a parallel 'sermon' in Luke, Chapter 6,[41] which is only a third the size; this is delivered in a different setting but begins as does the Matthew account with what are called the 'Beatitudes'

---

41 6:20-49.

('Blessed be . . . etc.). The longer Matthew account is the first of five discourses recorded in that Gospel, as the Torah is also divided into five Books. Once again, therefore, we have a deliberate borrowing from Moses, who was supposed to have written the Torah and similarly received God's word on a mountain. But the sermon itself draws less on the Old Testament and more on other classical sources.

We call it now a 'sermon' but this discourse is in fact an example of a classical genre known as *epitome* – a collection of teachings. The point of the *epitome* was to provide short, instructional materials for disciples, to train them in ethical traditions. The closest parallels in genre to the Sermon on the Mount can be found in philosophical texts by Greek philosophers like Epictetus, and Epicurus and closer to home in other works by Jewish thinkers such as Ben Sira, the Wisdom of Solomon, and Philo, the Alexandrian Jewish philosopher. The Sermon itself is populated with stock figures from Hellenistic philosophy; for example, the 'prudent man' and the 'foolish man'.[42] More specifically, the proverb on vision[43] is a commonplace of classical Greek science, and the sayings on anxiety[44] reflect a broad concern with that topic in a range of Greek literature. But what, the modern Christian will say, about the famous injunction to love, not just neighbour and brother, but enemy as well, and to turn the other cheek: surely these, at the heart of the Christian message, were revolutionary ideas for their time? They certainly contradict God's bloodthirsty injunctions in the Old Testament to take 'an eye for an eye' (are deities allowed to change their mind)? The last of these is, of course, an entirely

---

42 Matthew 7:24-27.
43 Matthew 6:22-23.
44 Matthew 6:25-34.

impractical rule for life as many have commented, and it may indeed have been new to Jewish ears: It is hard to say, but it was nothing new in classical philosophy. Plato set out the same philosophy half a millennium earlier, putting these words into the mouth of his hero, Socrates:[45]

> It is never right to do wrong and never right to take revenge; nor is it right to give evil, or in the case of one who has suffered some injury, to attempt to get even[46].

The idea became almost a commonplace of classical philosophy.

More generally, many scholars have noted the similarities between the teachings of *Jesus*, in the Sermon on the Mount, and those of the Cynics. One of the reasons some scholars seek to identify Christianity with the Dead Sea Scrolls sect (or Essenes if you want to make that connection too) is that both seem to call themselves followers of 'The Way'. But the Greek school of philosophy called the Cynics, founded in the 5th century BC, also described themselves as 'The Way' and scholars have pointed out that the *Jesus* of the Gospels sounds like nothing so much as a traditional Cynic philosopher. These were a common sight throughout the first-century Roman Empire, wandering from town to town, preaching their ascetic, moral philosophy. Other scholars have noted that *Jesus* also looks at times like a Stoic philosopher. Stoicism emerged as a Greek philosophy a couple of centuries after Cynicism and some of its central concepts seem to have deeply influenced the writings of Paul. Like Paul, Stoicism

---

45 It might just be noted in passing this example of creative fictionalizing to express a greater truth in a classical author. Socrates never spoke these words – but they are consistent with Plato's understanding of Socrates' philosophy.

46 *Crito*, 49b-e.

asserted an inner freedom combined with a sense of the innate depravity of mankind.

But it is not just the Sermon on the Mount that owes much to pagan influences. Earlier we saw how the Gospel story of *Jesus* entering Jerusalem on the back of an ass was lifted from a prophecy in Zechariah. It is worth pausing to consider for a moment what a strange prophecy this is. Why an ass? What significance did Zechariah place upon it? There was another chief god of the ancient world who became a man and rode to his death upon a donkey – Dionysus. He is often depicted in this way on pottery from the classical period. Indeed, the whole story of *Jesus* on an ass, entering Jerusalem in triumph, welcomed by cheering crowds who strew his path with palm leaves owes everything to the celebration of the ancient Eleusinian mysteries in Athens. Pilgrims walking the Sacred Way were accompanied by a sacred donkey and were greeted by crowds of Dionysus worshippers waving palm branches. The significance of the ass or donkey to the ancient mystery religions, rooted in traditional beliefs about its lusty nature, was as a symbol of the lower self, dominated by lust and animal passions – the story of Pinocchio turned into an ass from overindulgence in pleasures has its roots in the same tradition. By riding a donkey, Dionysus symbolically showed his triumph over his animal self. The parallels between Dionysus and *Jesus* are more than coincidence; they illustrate just how much Judaism became infected by the Greek world in the last few centuries BC, and again, how stories about *Jesus* were borrowed not just from the Old Testament, but from the classical world generally – either directly, or through previous influences on prophets like Zechariah.

Dionysus was revered because he was born twice; there are differing classical accounts of how this came about, but his death and rebirth were at the heart of the mystery cult that bore his name. He was, however, only one such ancient deity revered in the classical world for this reason. There were many others, with similar myths attaching to them, who became the subject of mystery cults. Indeed, so widespread was the phenomenon that sophisticated commentators in the ancient world recognized the common theme and regarded all these dying and reviving gods as syncretic avatars of each other. Thus, Marduk in Babylon, Osiris in Egypt, Mithras in Persia, and Attis or Adonis elsewhere in the Middle East all melt into each other at times and clearly all represent a similar concept. In Canaan, the 'promised land' that the Jews made their own, the chief God was originally called El, and in the Old Testament this name is sometimes adopted as an alternative to Yahweh for the Jewish chief God. But his son, who was called Baal or Hadad, took over as chief God from his father El and stories of Baal/Hadad also refer to him dying and being reborn. When the Jews moved into the land of Canaan, they naturally used the name Baal to refer to any number of what they regarded as minor or false local gods. But tales of Baal's death and resurrection, along with all the other deities mentioned above, clearly influenced the Gospel writers. The similarity to the story of *Jesus*' death and resurrection hardly needs emphasis.

Many scholars at the turn of the twentieth century became very enamoured of all this, and elaborate anthropological theories were constructed around the similarities by writers like Frazer and Weston.[47] In more recent times, some scholars have emphasized the differences between all these myths: such is the pendulum of fashion in scholarship. But there can be no doubt that the similarities do exist, whatever

---

47 T.S. Eliot's *The Waste Land* drew heavily on the fashionable writings of J. Weston and J. G. Frazer.

anthropological conclusions one might want to draw from them. And the mystery cult myths do seem to have their roots far back in prehistory, to the very earliest beliefs of mankind. The most important event in the lives of early agrarian peoples was the coming of Spring, celebrated by the numerous pagan festivals that eventually transmuted into our own festival of Easter. Spring was the time of renewal and rebirth that gave new life to the land, and faith that it would arrive was vital to see mankind through the long winter months. Early religious rituals were designed to ensure that it happened. Almost universal among primitive societies were rituals surrounding a god who dies in winter and is reborn in spring. Over time, these simple rituals became elaborated and differentiated in different societies until they emerge in classical times as the great mystery cults.

The worship of this group of deities, through the mystery cults, was carried out alongside the state-sanctioned worship of the Olympian gods and their Roman successors, but they met deeper needs of the human psyche. They are known as mystery cults because their beliefs and rituals were closely guarded secrets, revealed to initiates gradually, level by level – rather like the layers of meaning discerned in *Pesher* and *Midrash*. The outer levels of the mystery were easily accessible, but the inner mysteries were known only to initiates and concerned themselves with theological and philosophical interpretation of the outer rituals and festivals. Scholars over the last couple of hundred years have uncovered more and more of these mysteries, and they have found quite startling parallels with Christianity. For example, it has always been a puzzle why so many churches throughout Europe have much-venerated sculptures of a 'black' Madonna holding an infant Jesus; it now seems clear that these were originally representations of the Egyptian goddess Isis holding Horus, the offspring of her liaison with the god Osiris. Indeed, the emergence of

Christian Origins

veneration of the Virgin Mary in the early church, which has no foundation in the New Testament scriptures, can now be confidently ascribed to the absorption into the Christian belief system of the ancient myths of Isis (Mary) and Horus (Jesus). The parallel development of the story of Mary Magdalene, who in the Gospels is a sketchy figure, reflects the need to provide another Mary/Isis who is not *Jesus'* mother but his consort. In fact, the latest Gospel, John, has no less than *three* Marys at the foot of *Jesus'* cross: the Virgin, the Magdalene, and (confusingly) the Virgin's sister![48] What are the chances of two sisters having the same first name? Clearly, here we are dealing with evolving myth rather than history. I am not suggesting that the Jesus Movement was a mystery cult itself; it was a different sort of beast. But I am suggesting that the Hellenistic writers of the New Testament drew from the mystery cults, as they drew from other pagan sources, in stitching together their wonderful (in the literal sense) narratives.

Thus, contrary to much popular belief today, there is nothing about the teachings of Jesus, or indeed of Judaism in the first century, that cannot be parallelled in the writings of the pagan philosophers and/or in the teachings of the mystery cults. These parallels have given rise to the most unlikely theories over the years – from the Jesus Movement being based on magic mushrooms, to Jesus being an Egyptian adept in the monotheistic religion of Akhenaton – and in one form or another have been sufficient to unsettle the Christian beliefs of many. Not surprisingly, therefore, the Church has its answer to all this. Some theologians argue that these coincidences are the result of vague, mythical memories of God's original revelation of his purpose and plan for humanity's salvation to Adam and Eve and/or His continuing revelation through Creation, which is open to all, including

---

[48] John 19:25.

pagan philosophers, to interpret. Indeed, it is also argued that without such a general revelation, it is hard to see how a just God could condemn to eternal damnation all the generations of humanity that lived in the millennia before Christ, or before the later activities of missionaries. Others argue the exact opposite – that these myths are the snares of the devil, deliberately fostered by Satan through the infernal mystery cults, not merely to lead their adherents astray, but also to confuse and undermine the faith of latter-day believers. As ever, let us apply Occam's Razor to these fantasies. The simplest answer must surely be that Christianity adopted these pre-existent myths into its own mythology from the start. And then, as Christianity spread into the world, its own theology further evolved and was deliberately adapted to these myths, to remove obstacles to belief in the new religion. If later Church rituals like Easter and Christmas were deliberately coincided with existing pagan festivals, it is not hard to believe that similar adoption and transmutation took place at the very birth of Christianity. The writers of the Gospels drew on these myths directly and through the medium of the Jewish prophets, and the early Church continued the process, utilizing the existing myths, understood and interpreted by the inner mysteries, to flesh out the detail of Christian theology.

I recognise that all this flies in the face of common understanding of Judaism and Christianity. We are used to the idea that the Jews and their religion were in some way isolated from the rest of the world and its beliefs and that Christianity itself was a startling new revelation, as much to the Jews as to the Gentiles. But in fact, there is no room for doubt that this is not just over-simplistic – it is plain wrong. Judaism itself for several centuries before the Christian era was increasingly influenced by Hellenistic culture and beliefs; Christianity itself began as a Jewish sect, and then over time became a Gentile religion, founded as much on ancient pagan ideas as on its Jewish inheritance. But as with the Dead Sea Scrolls, while all this is interesting and not without relevance, it does not get us far in identifying who exactly *Jesus* was. Some modern writers and scholars conclude that *Jesus* never existed – that Paul invented Christianity as a new mystery religion, a Jewish version of all the other dying and resurrecting gods. But as I have indicated, the contention of this book is that there *was* a Jesus; it is just that he was not who the Church preaches him to be.

The precise process by which all these pagan influences came to bear on the original Jesus Movement to create the essence of the Christian religion is complex, probably unrecoverable except in general terms, and certainly well beyond the scope of this book to map out; but it does seem that Paul was a key figure in pulling it all together. His fundamental perception was that all believers, Jew and Gentile alike, were now freed by faith from the Mosaic and Noahic Laws and it is this perception that ultimately led to his split with the originators of the Jesus Movement. Out of Paul's original perception flowed two separate strands of belief. On the one hand, the Catholic Church ironically developed a whole raft of new behavioural requirements as Christian belief became institutionalized. But for a period of a few centuries, coexisting with the Catholic Church was a range of beliefs we now call Gnosticism,[49] founded equally on Paul's ideas about freedom from law, but resistant to any attempt to shackle that freedom. Gnosticism was eventually killed off by the Church, which stigmatised Gnostic belief as heresy, which is to say, at variance with its own evolving dogma.

Until very recently, we knew of Gnostic belief only as it

---

[49] 'Gnosis' is Greek for 'knowledge'.

was filtered through the writings of the established Church. Our understanding of its beliefs was so severely hampered by this, it was not even clear to many scholars exactly how it related to Christianity, and it was possible to argue, as some did, that it had its roots in pagan religious ideas that predated and were independent of Christianity. But all this changed in 1945 when a considerable library of Gnostic literature was discovered in a cave near Nag Hammadi in Egypt. The manuscripts included dozens of 'Gospels' attributed to a variety of characters familiar to us from the New Testament,[50] and it left little room for doubt that Gnosticism was an offshoot of early Christianity. Gnostics saw themselves as Christians; they took to heart the freedom preached by Paul and took it to extremes. In essence, they believed that every individual has God (as the Holy Spirit) inside them, and that the task of the believer was to follow the guidance of that internal voice. As a result, of course, we cannot speak of Gnosticism as a 'religion'; there were as many different sets of beliefs as there were Gnostics. But certain beliefs seem to have been largely common to them all, and different groups of Gnostics followed the guidance/ teachings of different influential Gnostic leaders. In the early days, some of those leaders managed to maintain positions in the established Church. Leaders such as Clement, for example, who is remembered still as a Catholic Saint and yet was in many respects a Gnostic. Others such as Simon Magus (of whom, much more later in this Volume and in Volume III) established, in effect, their own new mystery cults in which the deeper, hidden truths of the cult were reserved for initiates only. These leaders were vilified by the established Church as heretics, and in many cases suffered the consequences, until

---

50 All included in the list of non-canonical texts on pp. 65–67.

Gnosticism itself became so diffuse it could no longer be called a movement.

As Gnosticism developed, it felt itself free to absorb whatever seemed appropriate from pagan philosophy, so that the result was perplexingly multi-layered. At its roots lay the original Jesus Movement beliefs, founded on Old Testament ideas which themselves were infected with Hellenistic concepts. Over this lay a set of ideas developed by Paul, drawing on the mystery cults and the relatively sophisticated ideas of the great Greek and Roman philosophers. And then the Gnostics added more layers, deriving from their own visions and influenced by an even wider set of religious ideas drawn from Asia and the East. No wonder scholars had difficulty interpreting Gnosticism until the Nag Hammadi discovery, and teasing out the detail of Gnostic belief will keep them occupied now for many years to come. But in amongst all this, one core belief that seems to have been shared by all Gnostics was that this world is subject to a sort of semi-God or Demiurge,[51] who is not the ultimate Creator of all things, but who exercises local power. This belief presumably arose in order to deal with the disparity between the God of Love of Christianity, and the jealous, vengeful Yahweh of the Old Testament. In the Gnostic concept, the Creator of the Universe is a perfectly good, omnipotent being but Yahweh rules this world on his behalf and this explains the existence of sin and evil. When Jesus is called the Son of God, it is the ultimate Creator who is his Father, not Yahweh. Various names were given to this Demiurge, one being *Samael* or *Samyel*, a name lifted from Jewish tradition in which he features as an angelic being. His name in Aramaic means 'Blind God' – blind because he is limited in his power and influence; he is not the omnipotent Creator

---

[51] A term coined by Plato.

God. We shall return to Samyel in Volume III where he will be found central to understanding the Book of Revelation.

DISCREPANCIES, INCONSISTENCIES AND CONTRADICTIONS

Gnosticism was eventually suppressed by the growing orthodoxy of the Christian Church, and in similar fashion, a whole range of other versions of Christianity fell by the wayside, along with their own sectarian texts so that, as the various writings that make up the New Testament were gathered together and absorbed into an evolving Christian theology, the number of variants gradually reduced. Particularly under the influence of the Roman Empire, which adopted Christianity as the state religion, the evolving orthodoxy was reinforced by dogmatic religious intolerance, which itself became an integral part of the belief system. By the fourth century, two dominant dogmas emerged triumphant: the Roman Catholic Church in the West and the Orthodox Catholic Church in the East. No one challenged these monolithic sets of dogma because the Bible stayed in Greek and Latin and only the priests could read it. They conveyed to their congregations a version of Christianity that was fully sanctioned by the Church, based on a canon accepted by the Church, and with all inconsistencies ironed out of existence by centuries of theological hair-splitting.

For over a millennium this remained the case as the two Catholic Churches became increasingly integrated with secular power structures and provided a world view that both underpinned those structures and provided the potential solace of a better world to come. All this only changed with the invention of printing in the sixteenth century and the subsequent wider availability of the Bible, in Latin at first, and then in the modern languages of Europe. It gradually became evident to many devout men that the world system of the Catholic Churches was, while based on the Bible, divergent from it in key areas and had developed doctrines which had little or no basis in scripture. From the Catholic viewpoint, this was entirely reasonable; Catholic doctrine taught that God's revelation to mankind did not end with the Bible, but was a progressive process mediated through God's Holy Catholic Church. Doctrines such as the status of the Virgin Mary, or the existence of an intermediate state between Heaven and Hell called Purgatory, while hard if not impossible to justify by recourse to the Bible alone, were nonetheless true because Church tradition, guided by God, asserted them to be true. But along with more widespread access to the Bible arose the concomitant belief by many that the Bible itself was the inerrant, infallible Word of God, and as such, Holy Writ was the sole source of God's particular revelation to man: God revealed His truth through inerrant scripture, interpreted by each believer, guided by the Holy Spirit.[52] The Catholic Church was at best an unnecessary intercessor between believers and their God, and at worst, a Satan-inspired institution responsible for dangerous and ultimately evil lies about the true way to salvation.

We now call this new development in Christianity, and indeed in western civilization, the Reformation – and it changed everything. Reformers like Luther and Calvin now openly challenged the Church of Rome over unbiblical doctrines, some of which, like the practice of 'indulgences'[53] arguably no longer exist (at least in a naked form), but some

---

[52] One of the muddles in the Bible is that God seems to manifest himself in different ways; the Catholic Church harmonized this into the doctrine of the Holy Trinity – God the Father, the Son and the Holy Spirit.

[53] The promise of a reduced period in Purgatory in return for money.

of which, like the existence of Purgatory and the veneration of the Virgin Mary, persist at the heart of Catholic dogma to this day. Luther even challenged the Roman Catholic canon itself, doubting, for example, that the Book of James should be included in the New Testament.[54] Now that the Bible and other sources began to be available in modern languages, all the old debates about what was to be included in the canon; how scripture should be read and by whom; and how the inconsistencies should be explained away, rose again. At first, the focus was on what distinguished the new Protestant belief system from the old Catholic. But as time went by, within the Protestant faith itself it became apparent that, inerrant though it might be, scripture itself is full of *prima facie* inconsistencies and contradictions. Some of these could be argued away in one way or another, but wherever an individual interpreter of the Bible, guided by the Holy Spirit, felt there was a sticking point – an interpretation felt to be so crucial it could not be quietly ignored – a new Christian sect would arise, so that, ironically, in the post-Reformation world Christianity returned to the ferment of conflicting sects with which it had begun.

But one thing still united all these sects and, indeed, the Catholic Church as well – a fundamental belief that, in one way or another, the scriptures were inspired of God and properly understood would provide a guide to conduct in this world and salvation in the world to come. At the heart of most if not all versions of Christianity, there was and is acceptance of a harmonized, 'debugged' story, familiar to many of us in the West from Scripture lessons at school, Sunday School stories and Nativity re-enactments. It goes something like the following:

---

54 He felt it preached salvation by 'works' rather than 'faith' – interesting, given who James will turn out to be later in this book!

The Virgin Mary, betrothed to Joseph, is visited by an angel and told she is miraculously pregnant with the Messiah, descended from King David. A census requires her to travel to Joseph's hometown of Bethlehem, where she gives birth, attended by a star, shepherds and wise men. The child, *Jesus*, is taken home via a detour into Egypt. *Jesus* grows up full of wisdom and, on reaching adulthood, is publicly recognized as the Messiah by John the Baptist, and as God's Son at his baptism. He then embarks on a three-year ministry, wandering the Galilean countryside with His twelve disciples, teaching the new religion of Christianity and working various miracles as evidence of His powers. Eventually, He enters Jerusalem in triumph where, after cleansing the Temple of defiling activities, He is betrayed by Judas Iscariot, arrested, tried by the religious and secular authorities and, at the insistence of the Jewish populace, is crucified. He dies, descends to Hell, and rises on the third day as evidence that He has conquered death and sin. He is seen by various people before ascending to sit at God's right hand. He will return one day and then everyone who has ever lived will be resurrected and judged before being ultimately consigned for eternity to Heaven or Hell. Precise requirements for 'salvation' from this fate vary between Christian denominations and sects, but all agree that belief/faith in *Jesus* as the Christ is an important, and for some the sole, factor.

As soon as one looks a little closer at this harmonized account, however, discrepancies become apparent. The genealogies of *Jesus*[55] provided in the different Gospels do not coincide; the nativity stories themselves conflict with each

---

[55] Based in any case on descent from Joseph, who is not *Jesus*' real father – Mary is impregnated in some way by the Holy Spirit.

other; the lists of disciples differ from Gospel to Gospel and the accounts of the trial of Jesus conflict with each other, as do the stories of who saw *Jesus* and in what order after his resurrection. Two thousand years of harmonization means that these problems are all habitually skated over. We have seen some of these already and we shall uncover more later.

A similar process of harmonization and debugging characterizes the accepted story of the early Church:

> After *Jesus*' ascension to heaven, the downhearted disciples return to Jerusalem, attend the Temple regularly, vote to replace Judas Iscariot with someone called Matthias, and wonder what to do next. At the festival of Pentecost, the Holy Spirit descends on them, and from that point they embark on their missionary activity, preaching faith in *Jesus* as the only salvation from sin. Initially, they preach this only to the Jews but their leader, Peter, soon comes to understand that the Gospel is for Gentiles as well. Various tales of miracle working and conversion follow as the early Church fulfils its missionary destiny. The first martyr for this cause is Stephen, who is stoned to death for his faith. Instrumental in this stoning is one Saul, who then goes on to persecute the early Church on behalf of the High Priest. However, in the original 'Road to Damascus Conversion', Saul then experiences visions of *Jesus*, repents of his former persecution of the Church, and changing his name to Paul (or Paulus – Latin for small), becomes the main 'Apostle' (i.e. messenger) to the Gentiles. The Church is naturally wary of him at first, but soon accepts him enthusiastically. As Paul founds Gentile churches in the lands north of Judæa, it becomes apparent that a decision needs to be made concerning whether Gentiles need to accept the Mosaic Covenant on conversion, but this is amicably settled at a Council of Jerusalem, where it is

determined that Gentiles need not embrace the full Jewish Covenant. Thereafter, Paul, in a series of epic missionary journeys, takes the Gospel out to Gentiles in Syria, and then westwards towards Greece, finally arriving in Rome.

Even a casual glance at this narrative of the early Church reveals some unexplained dislocations in the story. The dispiritedness of the disciples following the death of *Jesus* seems very strange because, according to the *Jesus* story, he has instructed them, both before and after his death, in his true mission of salvation. Indeed, throughout the Gospels the disciples are portrayed as obtuse if not downright stupid; no matter how many times *Jesus* explains to them what he is really about they just never seem to understand. Another example is the revelation to Peter that Gentiles are to be included in the Jesus Movement – one would have thought that *Jesus* would have made this crucial fact abundantly clear through his teachings, and if not, why not? It seems very strange just how little the disciples seem to have understood about the purpose of *Jesus*' life and death and their own roles. It is all just psychologically implausible. The main source for the story of Christianity immediately after the death of *Jesus* is the Book of the Acts of the Apostles. We shall examine this in some detail later, but here it would be as well to point up some of the difficulties it presents and with which we shall deal. The difficulties arise because Paul gives an account of his life in his letter to the Galatian Church, and this seems at variance with Acts on two points – and these happen to be the most important points of all: the events surrounding the conversion of Paul to the Christian faith, and the subsequent Council of Jerusalem.

The discrepancies around Paul's conversion largely concern what happened after he had his visions on the road to Damascus. In Paul's own account, he says that he immediately went off to Arabia, then returned to Damascus and did not go to Jerusalem for three years. The Acts account is quite different: it has Paul being instructed by *Jesus* in a vision to go to Damascus and be instructed in the faith by someone called Ananias before 'after many days' going to Jerusalem to visit the Apostles and disciples there. The implication of Paul's own account seems to be that he ploughed his own furrow from the beginning, steering clear of the Jerusalem Church, while Acts on the other hand wants to portray Paul as reconciled to the Jerusalem Church and accepting their leadership from the start. Making sense of this discrepancy will prove to be relatively straightforward, once we have established who exactly Paul was trying to avoid and what the real issues were that guided his actions. At this point, however, it is worth pointing out again that such discrepancies do nothing to support belief in scriptural inerrancy.

The second set of discrepancies concern the Council of Jerusalem. You will not find an event named in this way anywhere in the New Testament; it is what theologians have come to call a particular event, described by Paul in Galatians and by the writer of Acts, which seems to have marked a major watershed in the history of the Church. It is clear from both accounts that there were issues between Paul and the Jerusalem Church; these are declared more overtly in Paul's own account and glossed over as much as possible in the Acts account, but they hover in the background of these early years of the Christian faith and seem to have required formal resolution. Both accounts are agreed that at some point Paul travelled to Jerusalem and met with the Apostles there, under the leadership of someone called James, and reached an understanding that was then promulgated throughout the churches. The issue concerned whether Gentile converts needed to be circumcised and in other respects be bound like Jews by the requirements of the Mosaic Covenant.

The problem is that it is far from clear exactly when this key event took place, who the key players were, or indeed, the precise details of either the problem itself, or the solution that was agreed. Nobody has ever managed to offer a solution to these issues that satisfactorily resolves the discrepancies. I believe that all these matters can be settled by close attention to the texts concerned. Crucially, we need to trust Paul's own account as earliest and most authentic, and then be prepared to reinterpret the Acts account in its light. That reinterpretation will be made possible by applying Occam's Razor to two examples in the Acts text of 'multiplication of entities'.

The first of these concerns a character called Agabus, who appears twice and makes prophecies both times: Occam's Razor would suggest that these were one event, and I shall show that this is indeed the case. The second involves emissaries from James and the Apostles. In Acts,[56] 'certain men . . . came down from Judæa' to criticize Paul, and this leads directly to the Council of Jerusalem. In Galatians,[57] Paul says that 'certain came from James' to criticize him, but this event is *described after* the description of the Council of Jerusalem and has therefore always been regarded as *taking place after* the Council. Again, Occam's Razor would suggest that these were the same event, and I shall demonstrate how this can be – in simple terms, just because one event is *related* after another does not mean that it necessarily *took place* after the other. Close attention to the text shows that Paul's narration involves him *remembering* earlier events. Once this is clarified, all falls neatly into place, but the implications for the traditional narrative are far reaching and help clarify both the relationship between Paul and the early Church in Jerusalem, and that between John the Baptist and the disciple John.

---

[56] 15:1.

[57] 3:12.

The Reformers of the sixteenth century worried about all these things, but their unshakeable faith in the inerrancy of Holy Writ meant that all their efforts went into harmonization and justification, rather than letting scepticism enter their heads. Until the eighteenth century, no one in Europe seriously doubted – in print at least, because to do so would be to invite imprisonment, torture and death – the essential truth of Christianity. But then it occurred to some scholars for the first time that perhaps all the inconsistencies were pointing to a more fundamental truth: the hitherto unthinkable idea that perhaps it was not human understanding that was at fault, but the idea of inerrancy itself. This heresy could only have arisen in the eighteenth century, the so-called Age of Reason – when philosophers and intellectuals generally became emboldened by the belief that there was nothing that was not accessible to the human faculty of reason. In the natural world, alchemy gave way to rational science. And in the humanities, the great literature of the classical Greek and Roman worlds was rediscovered after a millennium of neglect and a whole new world of philosophical and historical enquiry was opened up. The same atmosphere of rational thinking that motivated Isaac Newton to discover the fundamental laws of nature led others to undertake a fundamental reappraisal of the stories of *Jesus* and the early Church; rationalist scholars, trained to look at classical historical texts with a critical eye, began to study biblical texts in the same way.

And they discovered that, just as Christianity itself had begun with a plethora of conflicting ideas and interpretations, so had the Bible. They recognized that it comprises a wide range of texts written at highly diverse times and places by a diverse range of people, each with their own agendas, biases and blind spots. These scholars saw that the accepted version of events was a harmonization of a range of accounts that did not always coincide, and they began a process of deconstruction of the scriptures that continues to this day. They approached the scriptures not as inerrant revelations from God; they saw their job as scholars, not to seek to explain away inconsistencies and contradictions in order to reinforce belief in inerrancy in the face of obvious problems, but to examine the scriptures critically as historical texts, written by men who not only had their own axes to grind, but a different attitude to what constitutes historical 'Truth' to that of our own age. Texts that happened to have been included in the biblical canon were no longer seen as in some way superior to those that had not; all texts started out as equal in validity and were to be trusted or not based on their internal evidence of veracity – not some assumption of supernatural guidance or imprimatur.

The first rationalist scholar to raise his concerns to a wider audience and receive mass attention across the western world was a German theologian called David Strauss. He was educated in a tradition of textual criticism as applied to the Classics and saw no reason in principle why the same techniques should not be applied to sacred texts. He set about examining the Bible as if it were any other set of ancient writings. In particular, he examined the miraculous events of *Jesus*' life in the Gospels and concluded that they were all myths. He published his conclusions in German in the 1830s,[58] and in 1846 his ideas became easily available in the English-speaking world through the translation of the fourth German edition into English by George Eliot.[59] In fact, although as a rationalist Strauss could not accept divine intervention in the natural order, he nevertheless argued that although the miracles were 'myths' they need not necessarily be 'untrue'. He argued that what the Gospels presented as miracles in history were in reality a product of the early

---

58 *Das Leben Jesu Kritisch Bearbeitet* (Tübingen, 1835–1836).
59 *The Life of Jesus, Critically Examined* (London, 1846).

Church's use of Jewish ideas about what the Messiah would be like, in order to express the conviction that Jesus was indeed the Messiah. But such philosophical hair-splitting was not the impact of his book. For many readers, the implications seemed clear. If the miracles never happened then the greatest miracle of all – the Resurrection – was also just a myth, and in that case the whole edifice of Christianity came tumbling down. Strauss's book ushered in a new epoch in the textual and historical treatment of the rise of Christianity.

With the belief in scriptural infallibility seriously challenged, it became evident that all the contradictions and inconsistencies in the Bible that over a millennium had led to sectarian splitting on the one hand, and heroic efforts of theological harmonization on the other, were just the inevitable outcome of fallible human writing. The New Testament was the work of many hands, writing at different times with differing understandings and interpretations of what may or may not have happened, and those varied writings were then cobbled together by editors who themselves had strong axes to grind and felt free to suppress or alter what did not fit with their own biases. In particular, the various writers of the texts that make up the New Testament were all writing in Greek for a Hellenistic/Roman audience. For them, the Romans had to be presented as the good guys so, by definition, the bad guys had to be the Jews. It was *the Jews* that killed *Jesus*, and it was *the Jews* that persecuted Paul and the early Church, ignoring the fact of the matter which was that *Jesus* himself was (of course) a Jew and the early Church was a Jewish institution.

Because Christianity came to teach that *Jesus* had abolished the Mosaic Law, the Jewish religion, like the Jews themselves, is a target for New Testament hostility and abuse. As soon as this was apparent, it became clear that Christianity was originally not a new religion, founded by *Jesus* out of a Jewish background; it was a branch of Judaism itself, and the early

Christians were devout Jews. The reason why the disciples seem so confused about exactly what Jesus had been about was because he had never taught those things in the first place. *Jesus* had never claimed to be the Son of God, part of the Holy Trinity; he had been a devout Jew who would never have sanctioned the abandonment of the Mosaic Covenant, and his crucifixion had nothing whatsoever to do with salvation. All these doctrines arose after his death and were then written back into the story of his life at some later date.

All these perceptions came together in the work of F.C. Baur and the school of scriptural interpretation that he founded at the University of Tübingen in the generation after Strauss. He recognised that the Church had begun as a Jewish sect and that after *Jesus'* death there was a split. The Council of Jerusalem had not been as harmonious as the standard version taught; the 'harmony' was a result of deliberate harmonization after the event to disguise the fact that Paul's Gentile churches were disowned by the Jewish Church in Jerusalem. The latter continued to regard themselves as Jews, observing the Mosaic Laws and attending the Temple, under the leadership of Peter. The former, led by Paul, abandoned the Mosaic Laws and embraced freedom from all such necessities; the doctrine of salvation by faith alone in the death and resurrection of Jesus as atonement for the sins of all that believe was evolved by Paul and was anathema to the Jewish Church. Indeed, Baur made the opposition of Peter and the Jewish Church in Jerusalem, with Paul and his Gentile converts outside Judæa the key to interpreting all early Christianity.

Since Baur, we have had over 150 years of further scholarship, and every possible view about these matters seems to have been explored.[60] At one extreme, as noted already, there

---

60 Two scholars since Baur have been particularly influential – Bultmann and Brandon; see Select Bibliography for works by these and others.

are many now who would deny the existence of *Jesus* at all. For them, the whole Jesus Movement is founded on nothing more than a myth, concocted by Paul and turned by him into a religion that would be acceptable to Rome. Many such theologians doubt whether there is any material of historical value at all in the New Testament. This extreme scepticism is, however, two-edged. On the one hand, it leads inexorably to a complete rejection of Christianity: a religion based on historical events that turn out to be mythical must therefore be false. But ironically, it is also used to re-establish the credibility of Christianity in the face of historical and textual criticism: since the quest for a historical *Jesus* is impossible, the believer is thrown back, as he had always been, on 'faith'. Baur's arguments are rejected by such Christians with the counterview that the existence of a Jewish Christian Church in Jerusalem is not evidence of what *Jesus* originally taught, but of a 'Judaizing' tendency in the decades after his birth. Their contention is that Jesus did originally teach the Christian Gospel of salvation through His atoning death, but that some of his followers reverted over time to a sectarian version of the Jewish faith. Under this interpretation, Paul was just reasserting what Jesus had originally taught. Does this sound psychologically likely?

This is what continues to sustain the Church into the twenty-first century – a belief that the search for a historical Jesus is irrelevant to what really matters: spiritual conviction and the life of faith. For those for whom this just is not enough, the rest of this book starts to look at the texts themselves on which all this is based, to see whether with a fresh set of eyes we can discern where, in all this muddle of conjecture and assertion, the truth might be found. But before that, a word about dates. The key events surrounding the foundation of the Christian religion took place from right at the end of the BC period and extend to the beginning of the second century AD. And at the heart of this period are the years when *Jesus* is supposed to have lived, followed by the period in which the Apostles, and particularly Paul, were establishing the early Church. In broad terms, this all took place in the first half of the first century AD, but exactly when in this 50-year time frame is a moot question.

Establishing a chronology for the founding events of the Christian religion is notoriously difficult. I shall be proposing a revised chronology in this book that will enable us finally to identify the key players and events. But as a preliminary it would be as well to briefly review the standard chronology as accepted by the churches and by Christian scholars and theologians. It will be immediately apparent that this accepted chronology is based on little hard evidence. And there is a tendency for arguments about chronology to become circular: searching for external confirmation of a biblical event can lead to confident scholarly assertions of dates which on closer examination turn out themselves to be based on nothing firmer than the biblical event one started with. Furthermore, that dating turns out to be based on the overall standard chronology, which itself is based on a handful at most of 'assured' correspondences. All very shaky indeed.

The standard harmonized and 'debugged' narrative of *Jesus'* life, recapitulated in the previous section, has *Jesus* born in AD 1 (i.e. Anno Domini 1, or 'the first year of Our Lord) and starting his ministry in AD 30 at the age of 30 years old. Here is how this can be calculated. The first clue is provided by the dates of construction of the new Temple by Herod the Great. In the Gospel of John, which was probably the latest of the four Gospels to be written, *Jesus* goes to the Temple in Jerusalem around the start of his ministry[61] and is told:

---

[61] John 2:13.

MISTAKEN MESSIAHS

Forty and six years was this temple in building, and wilt thou rear it up in three days?[62]

This either means that the Temple was *completed* after forty-six years, or the visit took place forty-six years after building started, but it was still *unfinished*. Josephus[63] states that the Temple's reconstruction was started by Herod the Great in the eighteenth year of his reign. Herod was made King of Judæa in 39/40 BC, so eighteen years on from that date gives us a start date for the Temple of around 22 BC. Forty-six years on from 22 BC takes us to AD 24. If it were finished after forty-six years and *Jesus* visited it at the start of his ministry, on this reckoning, his ministry could not have begun until some date after this. This interpretation does not confirm AD 30, but it does not preclude it. On the other hand, if it was still in progress after forty-six years, the AD 24 date indicates the date of *Jesus*' visit and therefore a date of a little before then for the start of his ministry.

Another clue is the date of John the Baptist's death. In the *Antiquities of the Jews*, Josephus states[64] that a defeat of Herod Antipas (one of Herod the Great's successors) in battle was widely considered by the Jews of the time as misfortune brought about by Herod's unjust execution of John the Baptist. We can date the battle (from Josephus) with some confidence to AD 36, so presumably John was imprisoned and executed some (little?) time before that date. But, according to Matthew and Mark, *Jesus* began his ministry by being baptized by John the Baptist who was then some time afterwards imprisoned. If John were imprisoned and killed in the mid-thirties, *Jesus* must have begun his ministry before that date – again, not a precise

---

62 John 2:20.
63 *Antiquities of the Jews*, 15.380.
64 18.142.

dating, but entirely consistent with AD 30 and it establishes the latest date at which *Jesus* could have started out.

So, *Jesus* could have begun his ministry no earlier than AD 24 and no later than AD 36 – a gap of over a decade; how does the standard account narrow things down to AD 30? It is Luke that provides the answer, based on calculations of the date when John the Baptist commenced his ministry, preceding that of *Jesus*:

> Now in the fifteenth year of the reign of Tiberius Caesar, Pontius Pilate being governor of Judæa, and Herod being tetrarch of Galilee, and his brother Philip tetrarch of Ituraea and of the region of Trachonitis, and Lysanias the tetrarch of Abilene, Annas and Caiaphas being the high priests, the word of God came unto John the son of Zacharias in the wilderness[65].

Tiberius was co-regent with his predecessor Augustus from AD 11 before Augustus died in AD 14, but the latter date is the most obvious interpretation of Luke's reference. So, the 'fifteenth year' of Tiberius' reign referred to by Luke gives AD 29 for the beginning of John the Baptist's ministry. We are told that John was the predecessor of *Jesus*, so this means that, by this reckoning, Jesus could not have begun his own ministry until about AD 30. And Luke states quite clearly that Jesus began his ministry when he was thirty years old; if he was born in AD 1 (of course!), that gives AD 30 for the start of his ministry. QED you might think?

Unfortunately, not. This may be where the standard story comes from, but it is totally in conflict with what the Gospels tell us about the *birth* of *Jesus*. At first glance that seems to be very securely founded, because the Gospel accounts of

---

[65] Luke 3:1-2.

his life give some very precise indications of the date of his birth, but closer inspection reveals that the birth narratives are both inconsistent with each other (as we saw earlier) *and* with the dates we have just arrived at for *Jesus'* ministry. Mark and John's accounts say nothing at all about *Jesus'* birth but Matthew's account, which comes first in the Bible, states quite clearly that *Jesus* was born in 'Bethlehem of Judæa in the days of Herod the King'.[66] Then a little later we learn that this was right at the end of Herod's reign: the Holy Family flee from Bethlehem into Egypt after the birth, then Herod dies and the Holy Family return to Judæa, which is now governed by Herod's successor, Archelaus. The mention of Archelaus[67] confirms that the Herod in question here is Herod the Great, and not one of his sons who also took 'Herod' as a title. Herod the Great died in 4 BC, and Archelaus ruled from then until AD 6. So, if Jesus was born at the end of the reign of Herod the Great, we must date his birth to, say, 3–4 BC. Ironically, this date is a few years before the beginning of the 'Christian Era' itself, but since the BC/AD designation uses the year-numbering system introduced by a sixth-century monk – who was probably influenced by the argument deriving from *Jesus'* ministry, above, but had no more idea of when *Jesus* was actually born than anyone else – this is not the paradox it may seem. And more important still, it drives a coach and horses through the standard chronology we have just established.

More problems arise with the narrative in the Gospel of Luke. We have no idea who Luke was. The attribution of this Gospel to him was made by the early Church: Luke is described in the New Testament as a 'fellow worker' with Paul, and as a 'beloved physician'. The Gospel of Luke

---

66 Matthew 2:1.
67 Matthew 2:22.

begins with the conception by Elizabeth of John the Baptist in the 'days of Herod, the king of Judæa'; *Jesus* is then conceived six months later. But then the problems begin. Luke explains that 'in those days' – when 'Cyrenius' [properly, Quirinius] was Governor of Syria – there was a census. This is the cause of Mary travelling to Bethlehem, where *Jesus* is born. This census did indeed occur in the governorship of Quirinius because we know of it from the Jewish historian Josephus. But we also know that it took place in AD 6, which is in direct conflict with the 3–4 BC dating for the conception and birth of *Jesus* given in Matthew. How could *Jesus* have been conceived under Herod, who died in 4 BC, and then be born in AD 6? And if AD 6 is correct, how does that square with Matthew's assertion that Jesus was born in around 4 BC? And how does any of this square with the standard chronology?

Another approach to the problem entirely is to estimate the date that the Apostle Paul was converted after *Jesus*' death, and this requires a chronology for Paul. The standard chronology has the date of conversion of Paul as immediately after the standard view of *Jesus*' death in the thirties AD. The chronology for Paul then has him travelling on his missionary journeys in the forties and fifties before arriving in Rome in the sixties. For all events in Paul's life, the standard chronology relies on a series of calculations that work backwards from the Book of Acts' account of his trial before Junius Gallio in Greece.[68] Gallio's presence in Greece has been dated from external sources to around AD 51–52 on a reasonably secure basis. However, I shall show later that this lynchpin of the traditional chronology is false, not because the dates are wrong for Gallio, but because the introduction

---

68 Acts 18:12-17.

of Gallio in the Acts account is fiction not fact. Whoever wrote Acts was also the writer of Luke.[69] And on matters of history, Luke the writer just cannot be trusted. All the references in the Gospel of Luke to historical governors and Herods and the census are lifted straight from Josephus. Luke, more than any of the other New Testament writers, was very fond of salting his two narratives (his Gospel and his Acts) with references to historically verifiable characters and events. For committed Christians, this is evidence of the truth of the Bible. But they cannot be relied upon to date anything; their function is to provide a spurious air of authenticity to the writings of someone who really had no more idea of events and dates than we have. He inserted Gallio into his story of Paul, just as he inserted the census into his story of *Jesus*; in both cases to convince the reader he was writing history not fiction. We shall see that in the story of Paul, as with that of *Jesus,* the resulting conflicts and implausibilities give the game away.

But there is something of importance to be noticed in all this. Put aside the standard chronology for the moment and accept it for what it is: a harmonized fiction invented by a monk a millennium and a half ago. First, we have a span of up to a decade between differing calculations for the ministry of *Jesus*: from AD 24 to AD 36. And second, it will be recalled that we have a similar span of a decade between dates for *Jesus*' birth as well: from 4 BC to AD 6. We thus have a chronological puzzle with evidence for both the birth of *Jesus* and the start of his ministry, both scenarios a decade apart. Perhaps this provides a clue to what is going on. It looks as if we are dealing here with two distinct traditions about *Jesus* that place his life and activities a decade apart.

---

[69] Both Books are dedicated to 'Theophilus' and Acts refers to a 'former treatise' – presumably Luke's Gospel.

We shall see that this shift of a decade in time occurs too often to be coincidence. It is an example of the multiplication of entities that Occam's Razor warns us to be on the lookout for. As we shall see, the shift seems to have been to move events *forward* in time by a decade – a perception we might have arrived at already on the basis that, if we strike out Luke's evidence, we are left with what appears to be an early association between the birth of *Jesus* and the last days of Herod the Great, as suggested by the Matthew account. I have begun to show here how shaky is the standard chronology, and how there seems to have been a parallel, early tradition that placed all these events a decade earlier. It is now time (at last) for us to turn from background to substantive argument, from hints and possibilities, to a step-by-step dismantling of the whole fallacy that is the life of *Jesus*.

CHAPTER 4

The Jesus Fallacy

With all the preceding background in mind, we are now ready to embark on the dismantlement of the *Jesus* fallacy. I chose the words 'fallacy' and 'dismantle' with care. Christianity is built on falsehoods from the start, but I do not believe that its founders were deliberately lying. The deliberate, cynical invention of new religions for personal gain – financial, psychological and sexual – is perhaps a phenomenon of more recent centuries. The original Jesus Movement arose naturally from the Messianic expectations that we have traced through the history of the Jewish people. It evolved into the religion we know as Christianity over a period of decades and then centuries, based first on the sincerely held visionary insights of Paul, and then on the misunderstandings and misconceptions of Greek-speaking Gentiles living far from Palestine with no acquaintance with the Jewish roots of the movement. So, I am not pointing any fingers of blame; no one lied, but falsehood resulted, nonetheless. And given the complexity of these origins, the only way to approach that fallacy is to dismantle it, text by text, step by step. It is all too easy to erect theories about Christianity, based on extracts and quotations from those texts. As we have seen, a multi-layered, multi-authored book like the Bible is inevitably full of inconsistencies and errors. Ripping passages from it out of context with little or no regard for original authorial intent began with *Pesher* and *Midrash*, but it has continued down the millennia and lies behind the formation of every variety and sect of Christianity, from the mainstream to the bizarre. And modern revisionist commentators are often guilty of the same: they seize on some aspect of the texts, point out the inconsistencies and erect their theories on their blinkered selections.

In this book we shall endeavour to avoid these errors by the simple expedient of working our way through the relevant texts in their entirety, to understand who wrote them and why and to take full account of context and style. Remember the quotation from Arnold: 'Not deep the poet sees but wide.' In the end, it is about seeing the wood rather than the individual trees. I make no apology for the fact that, as with real woods, the going will get a little tough at times; we have 2,000 years of undergrowth to clear away before we can see clearly. But I promise here, at the outset, that the effort will be worthwhile. We shall be able to sweep away the fallacy of a human called *Jesus* who died a grisly death in an eternal gesture of supernatural atonement for human sin, and in the process free ourselves from the pernicious concept of sin itself. Sin exists only if there is a God to define it; if *Jesus* was not the son of that God and did not die for our sins, we are free to recognize that it is the evolving human sense of morality that should determine our actions – not the arbitrary *fiats* of a remote deity. We shall replace the fallacies with a psychologically satisfying and historically recognizable account of human beings who lived two millennia ago, trying to throw off the shackles of oppression and in the end make sense, like us, of the absurdities of life.

We need to address a core issue: if all the stories of the Gospels were borrowed fictions, what are we left with? The concept of a character called *Jesus* must have come from somewhere. It is not enough to state that he probably did not exist. Who then invented him and why? Or, if he was not invented, who on earth was he and why did people feel the need to invent these stories about him? We shall start in the obvious place if we want history not myth, with the writings of the Jewish historian Josephus, who lived in the first century AD and was a detailed chronicler of contemporary events. As we shall see, there is a single reference to *Jesus* in the texts of his writings as they have come down to us, but I shall argue that this is partly, if not entirely, a later Christian insertion in the text. There is also a single reference to a 'James, brother of Jesus', and we shall see similarly that this James is the brother of another Jesus entirely and nothing at all to do with Christianity. What is of far more interest in Josephus is the way in which the texts seem to be confused at best, and deliberately misleading at worst, about the chronology of events in the first half of the first century AD. We shall trace the shifting forward of events by about a decade, which we have begun to suspect on other grounds. This will then make possible what otherwise would be difficult to see – that the Jesus Movement and the resistance movement founded by Judas the Galilean are, in fact, identical.

We shall then move on to look at the Old Testament prophet Zechariah, whose visions of another Jesus are the real source for the *Jesus* of Christian faith. We shall see that these visions prophesied in fact *two* Messiahs – King and Priest; the Jesus Movement regarded these roles as fulfilled by Zechariah's Jesus, who was long dead before the Christian era but resurrected by God to be judge of mankind at the end of time, and by Judas the Galilean who sought to bring about the final apocalypse on the Mount of Olives around AD 19.

Having established exactly who the real Jesus was and what the original Jesus Movement was all about, we shall move on in Chapter 5, The Pauline Fallacy, to examine how that parochial Jewish Messianic movement became over time the worldwide, Gentile religion of Christianity. Our focus in that chapter will be the Apostle Paul. As already explained, one cannot begin to get to grips with Christian origins without reaching an understanding of this charismatic figure: who he was, when he lived, and his relationship with the original Jesus Movement. As we also saw earlier, we can embark on this quest with some considerable confidence, not because we have an independent historical account to work with, as was the case with Josephus, but because all scholars seem agreed that some at least of Paul's Epistles are both genuine and early. They are personal letters, not considered history, but if approached with an understanding of whom Paul was writing to and why, a fresh interpretation of them will emerge, and that interpretation will explain the puzzles that have dogged an understanding of Paul for centuries in a way that makes psychological sense. We shall then be able to turn finally to the Acts of the Apostles. We shall see that although most of Acts is a fictionalized account rivalled in imaginative storytelling only by the Gospels themselves, we shall nevertheless be able to make some sense of it because we can re-interpret it in the light of Paul's letters. This process will uncover a new chronology that removes all the key players from the scene much earlier than hitherto realized, and thus explain how, years later, the fictions that we call the Gospels and Acts could have come to be written. Read in this light, it will turn out that Acts really does help us trace how the distinctly Jewish Jesus Movement became the Christianity that we now know.

JOSEPHUS: 'THE *WARS*'

The best place to start in the search for the historical Jesus is with the writings of the first-century Jewish historian,

Josephus. If *Jesus* were as prominent a figure as the Gospels maintain, attracting huge crowds with his preaching and his miracles, to say nothing of his raising of the dead and his own resurrection, supposedly witnessed by many, surely he would get a mention in the writings of the key historian of the period. Josephus was a Jew, born into a wealthy, aristocratic Jerusalem family with priestly connections in AD 37 – that is, around the time *Jesus* is supposed to have been crucified. In his early twenties, he travelled to Rome as part of an official deputation to negotiate with Nero for the release of several Jewish priests. By this time, the ongoing tension between the Jews and the Roman Empire that forms the background to the *Jesus* narrative was erupting towards outright rebellion. Upon his return to Jerusalem, Josephus became a commander of the Galilean forces, and when war with Rome finally broke out in AD 66 he was a prominent military leader in that area. If Jesus had been active in Galilee in the thirties, as usually supposed, it is hard to imagine that Josephus, in the very next generation, and spending some years in Galilee, would not be conversant with the story. As we shall see, he almost certainly was not.

After the fall and subsequent massacre of a Jewish garrison in Galilee in AD 67, many of the Jewish survivors committed suicide, but Josephus was trapped in a cave with forty of his companions. The Romans offered them surrender terms, but they refused. Josephus by his own account then suggested a method of collective suicide: they drew lots and killed each other, one by one. The sole survivor was Josephus, who surrendered to the Roman forces and became a prisoner. He then claimed to have experienced a divine revelation that Vespasian, who with his son Titus led the invading army, would become emperor, thus fulfilling the Jewish *Star* prophecy mentioned above.[1] He also formed the conviction that Vespasian's defeat of the Jewish people was ordained of God for their punishment, and he proceeded to change sides. When Vespasian did become emperor in AD 69 he released Josephus, who then acted as a negotiator with the defenders during the Siege of Jerusalem in AD 70, in which his parents and first wife died. When the war ended in AD 71, Josephus went to Rome, becoming a Roman citizen, a member of the ruling Flavian household, and taking the name Flavius Josephus. He spent the rest of his life in Rome.

Josephus has always had his supporters and his detractors. For some, his accommodation with the fact of Roman supremacy was no more than recognition and acceptance of the inevitable. Some would even go so far as to claim him a Christian. For others, he was a traitor – a duplicitous turncoat who betrayed his own people, and probably 'fixed' the suicide pact lottery that only he survived. However, what concerns us here is not the dubious morality of the man, but the reliability of Josephus the historian. During his later years in Rome he wrote several works, two of which provide the fullest historical account of first century Judæa that has come down to us. The first was an account of the Jewish War itself, written initially in his native Aramaic, and then an extended version in Greek. It starts in the period between the Old and New Testaments with the story of the Maccabee Revolt, continues through the Jewish War in which he took part, and concludes with the siege and massacre at Masada that effectively ended the war. In line with his own defection and new loyalties, he blames the Jewish War on what he calls 'unrepresentative and over-zealous fanatics'[2] among the

---

1 Numbers 24:17.

2 Remember – according to Josephus, followers of Judas were called Zealots.

Jews, who led the masses away from their traditional leaders. He then followed the *Wars of the Jews* with his monumental *Antiquities of the Jews*. In this, he outlines Jewish history beginning with the Genesis creation stories and following the Old Testament narrative through the period of the Maccabees, up to the outbreak of the first Jewish war in AD 66. So, while there is no overlap between the two works concerning the first Jewish War itself, the period of the first half of the first century, when *Jesus* is supposed to have lived and the early Christian Church began, is covered in both works – with some interesting similarities and differences as we shall now examine.

Before doing so, a brief word about manuscripts and translations. A few manuscripts of Josephus have come down to us in the original Greek, and although these contain many variations as one might expect, they do not affect the arguments in this book. The first English translation of Josephus appeared in 1602, but the 1732 translation by William Whiston quickly became the standard text in the English-speaking world. It achieved enormous popularity and was often the book – after the Bible – that Christians in succeeding centuries most frequently owned. It is far from perfect as a translation, but given its ready availability still today, in cheap reprint and for free online download, it is the version I have used. References to Josephus in this book are to book and verse, ignoring the Whiston chapter numberings. There also exist late, 'Old Slavonic' translations of the Greek Josephus, which contain several Christian references that most reputable scholars reject as later interpolations. I shall ignore these for two reasons. First, any arguments based on the 'Old Slavonic Josephus' will be controversial and, as elsewhere in this book, I am trying to avoid controversy and rely simply on texts universally accepted as authentic. And second because, as I shall argue below, such overtly Christian references, if genuine at all, are solely evidence that towards the end of the first century the Jesus Movement was gaining momentum, and Josephus would have picked up on stories circulating about *Jesus*.[3]

The *Wars of the Jews* (in seven books) was commissioned by the Emperor Vespasian himself sometime in the late seventies and it was finished and 'published' in AD 78. It was created, therefore, when the events to which it relates were very recent, and one must assume, therefore, that sensitivities on all sides were still very sore. Indeed, certain facts may well have been dangerous for people still alive. Modern governments place time restrictions on information release for these very reasons, and we can assume that Josephus would have been careful not to upset any apple carts; his own position in the ruling Roman dynasty, achieved by desertion of his own people, must have still been precarious. On the other hand, however, Josephus seems to set out from the beginning to be a good historian, even judged by modern standards. He has his biases to be sure. The Romans are portrayed as the good guys and the Jewish insurgents are blamed for bringing down the wrath of the Empire on their heads; and Josephus is far from reticent to inject these by way of judgements about people and events into his accounts. But these biases are not difficult to spot; he wears his heart very much on his sleeve.

---

[3] However, it is worth recording here that a reference in the Slavonic Josephus to John the Baptist suggests that there was tradition of John's ministry starting much earlier than the AD 29 date that is derived from Luke. In this version, John is brought before Archelaus, who was Herod the Great's main successor, ruling between AD 4 and AD 7. This suggests that John's ministry must have begun about that time and coincident with the AD 6 census revolt of Judas the Galilean. As we shall see below, I reach this conclusion from other evidence, and would prefer to build my argument on that. But perhaps if that is accepted by the reader, it might warrant a re-examination of the potential authenticity of at least parts of the Slavonic Josephus.

And to set against these defects as a historian, he records events in enormous detail. It really seems to matter to him to get the record straight, and the result is an almost encyclopaedic presentation of people and events. Certainly, reading Josephus, the four Gospels and the Acts of the Apostles alongside one another, one becomes aware of the yawning gulf between them. Josephus for all his flaws is trying to be a good historian, and relatively speaking he succeeds; the writers of the Gospels and Acts were writing creative propaganda, with a spurious aura of authenticity cast by *midrashic* and contemporary allusion (including, as I shall argue, to Josephus himself) – that is why they make such great stories, enacted in mystery and nativity plays and illustrated in church windows, down through the centuries. I am not suggesting we should trust Josephus uncritically. We should never just take him at his word, particularly if his account seems to conflict in some way with other information. And we should be on the lookout for changes that have crept into his account, by accident or design, over the centuries since he wrote. But he is the best source we have and that is where we must start.

Wars of the Jews begins with the period following the death of Alexander the Great, whose empire extended to cover the Middle East, including Palestine and Egypt. After his death in 323 BC, his eastern empire was ruled by his generals and their descendants. In Egypt, these were known as the Ptolemaic dynasty, of whom the most famous was to be Cleopatra; in Syria they were known as the Seleucids. Judæa lay between these two powerful regimes. At first, it fell under Ptolemaic control, and then, as we enter the period covered by Book 1, it came under the Seleucids. But in either case, Judæa was gradually altered by this exposure over the three centuries before the Christian era to the European culture of the Greek world – a process known as 'Hellenization'. Some

Jews, mainly those of the urban upper class, came to relinquish the old Jewish ways based on the Mosaic Covenant and Old Testament laws, and to adopt a Greek lifestyle. They abandoned circumcision, the physical mark of the Mosaic Covenant between God and the Jews, and lived as citizens of a more modern, Greek civilization, enjoying the economic and political benefits that accrued from it. But the mass of the people, though undoubtedly affected to some degree, resisted these influences and were increasingly outraged by the desecration of their proud religious heritage by many of their leaders.

When Antiochus IV Epiphanes became ruler of the Seleucid Empire, he determined to accelerate the Hellenization process in Judæa, and this is the point at which Book 1 of *Wars of the Jews* actually begins. It relates how Antiochus converted the Jewish office of High Priest from a divinely ordained performer of temple rituals into, effectively, a Seleucid political appointment – a local governor within an overarching Greek state. He then followed this through with edicts outlawing the Torah, banning the key Jewish rituals, including circumcision, and setting up altars to Greek gods. These acts were regarded by Orthodox Jews at the time as outrageous blasphemies, and when Antiochus went so far as to place a statue of Zeus on the Jerusalem Temple altar itself, this was the last straw.[4] Open revolt resulted, led at first by a rural Jewish priest, Mattathias the Hasmonean, and then by one of his sons, Judas Maccabee: (the name Maccabee means 'hammer'), who eventually expelled the Seleucids from Judæa. Following this successful revolt, all the pagan

---

4 Pollution of the Temple in this way became a major issue again in Roman times, when, on a number of occasions, Roman governors sought to bring Roman symbols into Jerusalem and even into the Temple itself. As we shall see, these 'pollutions' are almost certainly the roots of the stories about Jesus cleansing the temple.

altars were pulled down, and traditional Judaism was re-established: circumcision was re-introduced; the Jerusalem Temple was cleansed and rededicated to the Jewish God; and another of Matthias' sons, Jonathan, became High Priest.

Judas Maccabee founded what became known as the Hasmonean Dynasty, initially still as a province of the Seleucid Empire, but after the death of Antiochus as an independent state. This dynasty lasted a further half century until 63 BC, when the Roman general Pompey captured Jerusalem and brought Judæa into the Roman Empire. The Hasmonean Dynasty itself was finally ended in 37 BC when Herod the Great became King of the Jews. Herod was an Idumean from the area south of the Dead Sea, historically known as Edom. He became governor of Galilee under the Hasmoneans, and following a subsequent power struggle became King of Judæa in around 36 BC, founding his own Herodian Dynasty, in which religious and secular power were separated – but with Herod firmly in control through the selection and appointment of High Priests, who under his administration came and went with alarming regularity. Like many of his Idumean countrymen, he ostensibly practised Judaism, but he was never considered a genuine Jew by the conservative Jews of Judæa. He banished his existing wife and child and married a Hasmonean heiress, Mariamne, in an attempt to legitimize the Herodian claim to the throne and gain conservative Jewish favour. But whatever success this might have had was undermined from the start by his brutality in maintaining power; under his dictatorship, Judæa became a police state, with an active secret police force, the suppression of public assembly and frequent imprisonment without trial.

As with dictatorships in the modern era, Herod was keen on grandiloquent public works. These included fortresses such as Masada,[5] and new cities such as Caesarea, which replaced Jerusalem as the centre of political power. But Herod's most famous and ambitious project was the rebuilding and expansion of the Jewish Temple in Jerusalem. The original Temple, the one we read of in the Old Testament, was destroyed when the Babylonian Empire sacked Jerusalem some five centuries before the Christian era. The second Temple was built by the Jews that returned from Exile but was always a rather modest affair. Herod's revamped Temple, the one that *Jesus* cleansed in the Gospel accounts, was designed to amaze and impress. It was destroyed in AD 70 as a result of the Jewish War with Rome; today only the four retaining walls remain standing, including the Western ('Wailing') Wall.

Herod achieved his lasting ascendancy because, from the first, he cultivated the support of Rome. In doing so, he continued the process of Hellenization, introducing Roman culture and customs, including, for example, a theatre and amphitheatre where entertainments were staged that will be familiar to anyone who has seen the films *Ben Hur* and *Gladiator*, but were entirely foreign to traditional Judaism and met with animosity and resistance. As Herod's reign wore on, it inevitably provoked sedition and revolt, notably an uprising led by a certain Judas, 'the son of Sepphoris'. The immediate cause of this specific uprising was the introduction by Herod of a Roman Eagle effigy into the holy Jewish Temple, echoing the previous action by Antiochus IV Epiphanes. But very soon after this, in around 4 BC, Herod died,[6] and there, Book 1 of the *Jewish Wars* ends.

Book 2 is 654 verses long and covers the seventy or so

---

[5] The site of the Jews' last stand in the Jewish War with Rome.

[6] According to Josephus, from something very nasty, including 'a putrefaction of his privy member, that produced worms'.

years between Herod's death and the outbreak of the Jewish War.[7] It is, therefore, the crucial Book covering the first half of the first century. After Herod's death, the emperor, Augustus Caesar decided to break up Herod's power base by dividing his old kingdom between his three sons: Archelaus, Antipas and Philip. Archelaus was made Ethnarch over about half the country – Judæa itself, plus Idumea to the south and Samaria to the north – with a promise that if he behaved himself like his father, he would eventually get the other territories. The other half, Augustus divided between two Tetrarchies;[8] Philip got the lands east of the Jordan River, and Antipas got Galilee to the west. Because all these Herods can get confusing, here is an *aide memoire*:

Herod the Great	37 – 4 BC
Archelaus, Ethnarch of Judæa	4 BC – AD 7
Herod Antipas, Tetrarch	4 BC – AD 39
Philip, Tetrarch	4 BC – AD 34
Agrippa I, Tetrarch & King	AD 37 – AD 44
Herod of Chalcis	AD 44 – AD 49
Agrippa II	AD 49 – AD 93[9]

Coincident with the power struggles of the three Tetrarchs of Herod's old kingdom, Josephus describes a continuation of the rebellions that had begun in the latter part of Herod the Great's reign. He reports in particular that in Sepphoris, a

---

7 Books 3 to 7 cover the war itself.

8 The etymology of the word 'tetrarch' suggests four rulers, not three. There are two possible explanations. One is that the area was already regarded as being divided into quarters and that Archelaus' half comprised two such quarters. The alternative is that there was a fourth tetrarch not mentioned by Josephus – Lysanius, Tetrarch of Abilene.

9 Note that there were seven in all – this will be important in Volume III when we consider the identity of a certain seven kings in the Book of Revelation.

large Hellenistic city in Galilee,[10] a certain 'Judas' broke into the royal armouries and raised a rebellion. There has always been debate about whether this was the same as 'Judas, the son of Sepphoris', referred to above, who led the revolt over the Eagle effigy at the end of Herod the Great's reign. And indeed, some scholars believe that one or both of these is also the same as the third Judas – known as 'the Galilean'. Right now, we lack the evidence to determine either way although Occam's Razor might suggest we are dealing with one individual here.

According to Josephus, Archelaus the Ethnarch very quickly proved to be a disastrous ruler, and around AD 6–7, Augustus Caesar removed him from office and placed his territories, including Judæa, under direct Roman rule, exercised by a Procurator called Coponius. Augustus left the two Tetrarchies of Philip and Antipas in place. Having related these events, Josephus introduces the third 'Judas':

> Under his [Coponius] administration it was that a certain Galilean, whose name was Judas, prevailed with his countrymen to revolt; and said they were cowards if they would endure to pay a tax to the Romans, and would, after God, submit to mortal men as their Lords. This man was a teacher of a particular sect of his own and was not at all like the rest of those their leaders.[11]

This Judas, whether or not identical with the previous two, turns out to be most interesting in the pursuit of the truth about *Jesus*. The name Judas has many resonances. It derives of course from the tribe of Judah from which modern Jews are said to be descended, and therefore can symbolize the

---

10 Very close in fact to modern-day Nazareth.
11 *Wars of the Jews* 2:117.

Jewish people as a whole. The betrayal of *Jesus* by another Judas (Iscariot) has been a major element in the demonization and persecution of the whole Jewish race by Christians for the last two 2,000. Yet in Jewish history, Judas Maccabee is remembered annually at Hanukkah as the greatest of Jewish heroes, and it can be no coincidence that all these three subsequent rebel leaders are also called Judas – after Judas Maccabee. One imagines that every little Jewish boy with that name would grow up in the hope that he would fulfil a similar destiny. And furthermore, any conservative Jewish family that could trace its lineage back to the royal house of David would likely call their first son Judas, in the hope that he would be the one to fulfil the nation's Messianic hopes. If the angel Gabriel had not told Mary to call her son *Jesus*, she would surely have called him Judas – and as we shall see, perhaps in a way she did.

But Judas the Galilean was not just another rebel, one among many. Josephus says that he was 'not at all like the rest of those their leaders' because he was 'a teacher of a particular sect of his own'.[12] This raises the obvious question of the nature of this sect and of the teachings that underlay it. There *must* have been more to it than just resistance to Roman rule in general, and Roman taxation in particular; neither of these would mark out Judas' teachings as different in any way from, for example, the preceding two Judases, or indeed any of the other activist rebels that Josephus describes. And as Josephus continues his narrative, it looks as if he is going to tell us the answer. Immediately following the quotation above, he writes:

For there are three philosophical sects among the Jews. The followers of the first of whom are the Pharisees; of the second

---

12 *Wars of the Jews* 2:117.

the Sadducees; and the third sect, who pretends to a severer discipline, and called Essenes.[13]

Then he launches immediately into a detailed description, over forty-three verses, of the Essene sect. At the end of this description, almost as if he has caught himself getting carried away, he switches to the other two sects – the Pharisees and Sadducees – and covers them both in just four verses. Yet we know that, numerically speaking, the Pharisees were far and away the biggest and arguably the most popular group in first-century Judæa. Indeed, the Pharisee movement saw itself as embracing the people as a whole, as well as the 6,000 or so Pharisee leaders, known variously as Sages, Scribes and Rabbis. It has been argued by Hyam Maccoby[14] in particular, and seems to me very probable, that the Pharisees were less of a sect and more the normative version of Judaism of the Jewish people at this time.

The Sadducees were politically powerful but numerically smaller – numbering about 4,000 – and the Essenes, though much admired and respected, probably also numbered only about 4,000 in Palestine. Yet none of these three sects seem to be the sect of Judas the Galilean. Josephus at this point says no more about him, or his movement, and after describing the Pharisees and Sadducees simply resumes his historical narrative with information about the two Tetrarchs – Philip and Antipas. There is no further mention of Judas the Galilean in *Wars of the Jews* at all;[15] this is very strange and has puzzled commentators on Josephus for centuries. (We know that some passages at least have gone missing from the texts that have

---

13 *Wars of the Jews* 2:118.

14 Notably in his *Judaism in the First Century*, see Select Bibliography.

15 There is more information in the *Antiquities of the Jews*, as we shall see, but for the moment we shall stay with the present text.

come down to us, because Josephus makes cross-reference to them. Clearly, either the passage of time or something more deliberate means that we cannot trust that we have the whole story before us.)

The temptation is to look for the roots of the Jesus Movement in one of these four sects. We have touched on the Essenes and the Pharisees earlier; it is time we looked a little closer. The main source we have for the Essenes is in fact Josephus, who had first-hand knowledge of them and wrote about them in *Wars of the Jews*, *Antiquities of the Jews*, and in his autobiography, *The Life of Flavius Josephus*. But they are also described by the contemporary Alexandrian writer Philo, and they are mentioned by the Roman historian Pliny. The meaning of the name Essene remains a matter of debate, but if there is any consensus at all among scholars, it seems to mean something like 'Observers of the Torah', or 'Holy/Pious Ones'. This seems appropriate since they were a group that separated themselves to varying degrees from normal life to pursue the pious life, rather as in a Christian monastery. According to Josephus, they could be found in large numbers in every Judæan town, and it is Philo who confirms that there were more than 4,000 in the Middle East as a whole.[16] Pliny refers to a community of Essenes living by the Dead Sea, and many scholars have identified this with the settlement at Qumran, near which the Dead Sea Scrolls were found.[17]

On this basis many have identified the Essenes with the community described in some of the Scrolls – an identification which as we have seen is far from proven or universally accepted. Scholars who do accept that identification believe that they were probably a breakaway sect from the Sadducees

---

16 *Every Good Man is Free*, XII:75.
17 *Natural History* 5:73.

as the latter became corrupted by political power from the Ptolemaic period onwards.[18] These scholars argue that the 'Temple Scroll', one of the key Dead Sea Scrolls found at Qumran, describes their idealized Temple and its associated rituals, which they seem to have established at Qumran as an unpolluted alternative Temple that would serve the Lord until he established his new Kingdom and Temple in the Last Days. In this interpretation, they adopted the name Sons of Zadok, this deriving from the same linguistic root as the word 'Sadducee'. Zadok was the first Priest in Solomon's first Temple and the priest caste in Jerusalem liked to trace itself back to this Zadokite tradition.

Be all that as it may, all sources for the Essenes *per se* confirm that they led a communal, in many ways 'communist', life and, indeed, that some at least were celibate, although Josephus speaks of others that married for the procreation of children. Most importantly, however, they are portrayed in all sources as pacifist, and seem to have been widely trusted and admired, in the Hellenized, classical world as well as the Jewish, for their apolitical peacefulness. They believed in the immortality of the soul and, like many religious groups at the time, practised some form of baptism or water purification ritual, for which they constructed rainwater storage cisterns. The description in the New Testament Acts of the Apostles of the early Christian Church has many similarities with all these aspects of Essene practice, and on this basis the Essenes have also been linked by some scholars with early Christianity. But the Essene/Qumran/Dead Sea Scrolls/Early Christianity nexus is so fraught with contradiction and disagreement that in this book I have determined to steer as clear from it as possible. In

---

[18] Notably Geza Vermes, who in his edition of the Dead Sea Scrolls (see Select Bibliography) concludes: '. . . the identification of Essenism and the Qumran sect remains in my view the likeliest of all proposed solutions.' (p.48).

my view, it is possible to determine the truth about Jesus and the beginnings of Christianity without resort to these controversial areas. However, one conclusion can be drawn and, although I made it earlier, it needs emphasis because in the search for parallels it often gets lost. Whoever or whatever was the movement – Josephus' Fourth Philosophy – founded by Judas the Galilean, it was *not* the Essenes for one simple reason; they were pacifists and Judas clearly was not. It may be that Judas' movement had any number of aspects in common with the Essenes – indeed, it would be surprising if there was not a degree of overlap between all these sects, as there is between the various Christian sects today. But a simplistic identification can be ruled out.

This is also true of the Pharisees. Jumping ahead a little, Josephus tells us in the *Antiquities of the Jews* that Judas the Galilean's movement was effectively a Pharisee offshoot, but it clearly had a distinct identity of its own.[19] Modern scholars now believe that the picture of the Pharisees presented in the Gospels is historically inaccurate, driven as it is by anti-Jewish bias. Pharisees believed in preservation of the traditional Jewish political system in which power was divided between King, High Priest and Prophets. The priesthood had always been a relatively minor office under this system, but since the time of the Ptolemies it had gained the ascendancy, and the Pharisees fought to limit its powers. They favoured the retention of monarchy in principle, but in the first century when Herodian monarchs were little more than Roman mouthpieces, they tended to be anti-establishment to varying degrees. Their power base and influence were with the common people – the traditional believers in Judaism, and resisters of Hellenization.

---

19 'These men [i.e. followers of Judas] agree in all things with the Pharisaic notions; but they have an inviolable attachment to liberty; and say their God is to be their only Ruler and Lord' (*Antiquities*, 18:23.)

The Pharisees were effectively the lawyers of Judæa. They believed, like the Essenes, in an immortal soul and, therefore, in matters of morality and right behaviour. They recognized, however, that the laws set out in the Old Testament needed interpretation and arbitration, and they provided these services to the Jewish community. Over time, they created an oral tradition of moral and legal judgements that could stand alongside the written Torah – in effect, a fully worked through, detailed legal system. In creating this oral legal tradition, the Pharisees did not just pluck their judgements from thin air; they based them on *midrashic* interpretations of scripture. *Midrash* was essentially their invention and their working method. Differing *midrashic* interpretations led to differing sects or 'schools' of Phariseeism, founded by particularly revered Rabbis. Because they recognized that society only works with give and take, and that many social and moral issues have shades of grey rather than black and white, they were popular with the community and formed the largest 'party' by far in the Judæan state. Indeed, after the war with Rome, their pragmatic form of Judaism was the only one the Roman state was prepared to tolerate, and rabbinical Judaism, which is the basis of the Jewish faith to this day, traces its roots back to the great Pharisee Rabbis.

Their opponents, therefore, were the religious extremists: people who saw only black and white, no shades of grey; who believed pragmatism and flexibility had no place in a society run according to God's immutable laws; and who believed that there were no moral dilemmas, just sin and righteousness. The Sadducees were such extremists. They were the beneficiaries of the shift in power towards the priesthood and believed in a theocratic system under an omnipotent High Priest. Drawing its members from the aristocratic, priestly classes, this sect did not believe in immortal souls and therefore had no interest in moral or legal niceties, upon which eternal salvation might depend. They recognized only the written Torah and regarded the oral traditions of the Pharisees as unnecessary. What mattered to them was priestly ritual, ordained by a God who cared little if at all for human morality, but did require strict obedience to his Will – the true definition of righteousness. The Temple and its satellites and trappings were their province, and the means by which they pursued power and material gain. Given that the High Priest was appointed by the secular power, they were deeply engaged in political matters and committed to conservatism and working within the existing Roman power structures.

As we have seen, Eisenman has suggested that the best way to think about all these sects and their various offshoots is in terms of their attitude to Roman power. He talks of an 'opposition alliance' of militant, xenophobic Jews who are behind the increasing violence and sedition in Judæa from the end of Herod the Great's reign up to the outbreak of war in the sixties AD.[20] Given the uncertainty, confusion and discrepancies in the surviving textual sources, this is probably a realistic, pragmatic approach to a broad understanding of these events. But as this book will show, there is another broad categorization that is vital to unlocking the truth. Within the opposition alliance, there was a split between two camps. On the one hand, there were those that Eisenman focuses on – the militants who believed in a coming Messianic age, but also believed that it was their responsibility to usher in that age by taking action themselves. Judas the Galilean – whether or not he is to be identified with the previous two

---

20 See *James, The Brother of Jesus* (see Select Bibliography), p.36: '... Jewish or Palestinian Christians (whatever may be meant by such designations), James' Jerusalem Church or Jerusalem Community, succeeded by Ebionites, Essenes, Zealots, and the group responsible for the documents found at Qumran – all can be thought of as the various constituents of the Opposition Alliance.'

Judases – seems to have been of this sort, and insofar as the Zealots and Sicarii[21] can be seen to descend from his movement, then the identification seems secure. But there was another camp – those that believed that human action was unnecessary at best, and perhaps counterproductive at worst: that only God's intervention in human affairs could end Roman power and restore Jewish self-determination. Their rhetoric would have sounded like that of the militants, but they believed their task was to prepare people for the coming Messiah(s), and to watch and pray for signs of the coming millennial intervention. This dichotomy between militant action and patient faith emerges at the very heart of Christianity as it transcends the events of first-century Judæa. The argument about whether personal salvation from God comes from faith alone, or from work, or a combination of both, reflects this argument about how to bring about Jewish national salvation.[22]

So, to return to Josephus' *Wars of the Jews*: in describing the decade after Herod the Great's death, Josephus introduces us to the three main Jewish sects, plus a fourth, founded at around that time, by Judas the Galilean. The only one of the four described in any detail is the Essene sect. Josephus then returns to his chronological narrative, where we have reached verse 167. In this and the next verse, he describes very briefly some key and precisely datable events in the Middle East at the time, most notably the death of Augustus Caesar and the subsequent accession of Tiberius Caesar. This took place in AD 14. Then, in verse 169, Josephus refers to 'Pilate' who was 'sent as Procurator into Judæa by Tiberius'. This is, of course, the famous Pontius

---

21 The Jewish guerrilla fighters of the first century.

22 The tension between the two beliefs can be seen even in the New Testament, where St Paul is clearly on the side of 'faith' and St James emphasizes 'work'.

Pilate, who is pictured in the Gospels as washing his hands of the crucifixion of *Jesus*. Based on Josephus' account here, we can conclude at this stage that Pilate must have arrived on the Judæan scene sometime soon after AD 14. Over the next eight verses, Josephus relates two stories about Pilate's administration, both of which suggest that either he was extremely callous and insensitive to Jewish religious feeling, or perhaps more likely, he arrived with a brief from Tiberius' new administration to accelerate the Hellenization of the Jews in order to facilitate their absorption into the Roman polity.

The first of these two stories concerns Pilate's introduction of Roman military standards with images of Caesar into the holy city of Jerusalem. As we have seen, this had been a crucial issue for the Maccabees, and then under Herod the Great; either Pilate was extraordinarily ignorant of history or he was deliberately seeking confrontation. Either way, this action predictably provoked uproar and then an outright confrontation between the Roman military and 'vast numbers' of Jews, who together resisted authority with passive resistance – offering their bare necks for beheading rather than move and allow the desecration to continue. Pilate on this occasion backed down and removed the effigies. The second story involves Pilate's construction of an aqueduct to bring fresh water into Jerusalem. He used temple funds, known as Corban, to do this. The Jews opposed this for reasons that are not entirely clear since Corban was often used for this kind of public works. However this may be, the Jews used the same passive resistance tactics, but this time Pilate did not back down and his forces set about the demonstrators with wooden staves, killing many in the process. The aqueduct was built and survives to this day.

Then, immediately after describing these two actions by

Pilate,[23] Josephus relates events surrounding the death of Tiberius and the accession of the Emperor Caius.[24] This took place in AD 37. So, between AD 14 or thereabouts and AD 37 we have a twenty-three-year period in which Josephus tells us virtually nothing except that Pilate arrived in Judæa at some time during that period and upset the Jews on at least two occasions. But we are provided with no information about when exactly in that twenty-three-year period these events took place. It will be recalled at this point that in our earlier discussion about traditional dates for the life of *Jesus*, this period from AD 14 to AD 37 is precisely the time when, by traditional Christian calculation, *Jesus* was growing up, fulfilling his destiny, and was crucified and raised from the grave. Yet there is not even the slightest hint of these momentous events in Josephus' account. I have made the point already, but it bears repeating: if *Jesus* really did wander the countryside for three years, performing amazing miracles, healing the sick and raising the dead, if He really were the victim of a crucifixion from which He miraculously returned, surely, we could have expected some mention at least by Josephus. But there is nothing. Josephus is obviously not ignorant of events at that time since he relates the two Jewish disturbances. And we can be sure that if there had been any favourable mention of *Jesus*, it would have come down to us; the manuscripts of Josephus were preserved by Christian communities, not Jewish ones. So, either *Jesus* did not exist, at least, in the form described in the Gospels, or perhaps, it has been argued, Josephus knew all about him but neglected to mention him because so soon after the war, it would have been in some way provocative and dangerous to do so. This explanation does seem unlikely. Whoever *Jesus*

---

23 *Wars of the Jews* 2:178–180.

24 More popularly known by his nickname, Caligula ('little boots').

turns out to have been, all accounts are agreed that from the Roman perspective he was a troublemaker. And one thing we know for certain is that the Roman Empire did not tolerate troublemakers. This was as true in the seventies AD when Josephus was writing his account as it was when Jesus and Pilate had their confrontation. So, I fail to see where any possible sensitivity or embarrassment might lie. The descriptions of Pilate's behaviour must have been equally tendentious to a Roman audience, given that they surely imply some measure of guilt to the Roman administration for the outbreak of war that followed. On the other hand, one might speculate that Josephus did indeed mention *Jesus* at this point, but the revolutionary nature of his activities made some later Christian scribe uncomfortable and he excised the reference. Whatever the truth – and all these viewpoints have been propounded at different times – this does all seems very strange; but the story does not end there.

JOSEPHUS: 'THE *ANTIQUITIES*'

The time has now come to turn to *Antiquities of the Jews*, written twenty years later than *Wars of the Jews* and finished in AD 93 when, arguably, another generation had succeeded and the political sensitivities, if any, would have receded. Is there extra information about this twenty-three-year period available from the later work? The first seventeen Books of *Antiquities of the Jews* retell the biblical history of the Jews from God's creation of the world right up to the events surrounding the death of Herod the Great; it therefore covers the Old Testament and inter-testamental periods. Book 18 then deals with the thirty-two years between the downfall of the Ethnarch Archelaus in around AD 6 and the death of Caius/Caligula in AD 41. It therefore roughly parallels the crucial period covered in Book 2 of *Wars of the Jews*. Book 18 begins with the census of Quirinius, which we are told was coincident with the arrival of Coponius as Procurator of Judæa – around AD 4–5. Then Josephus immediately introduces the important figure of Judas the Galilean, and this time, unlike in *Wars of the Jews*, provides a little more information.

First, it now appears that Judas has an accomplice of some sort: a man called simply Sadduc, which is presumably a corruption or variant of the Zadok designation discussed above. We are told he was a Pharisee, which is a surprise given that it was the Sadducees that took their name from Zadok, the first priest in the original temple. It seems likely that he represented some form of alternative, anti-establishment and anti-Sadducee priesthood within Judas' movement. If true, this will provide an important clue as to his identity: we know of only one man who offered an alternative rite to that of the Temple – John the Baptist.[25] We shall return to this identification later. Second, Josephus makes clear that the census was conducted as a basis for determining Roman taxation, and the revolt of Judas and Sadduc was occasioned by precisely this event:

> ... both said that this taxation was no better than an introduction to slavery, and exhorted the nation to assert their liberty: ... *they also said that God would not otherwise be assisting to them*, than upon their joining with one another in such counsels as might be successful, and for their own advantage; and this especially, if they would set about great exploits, and not grow weary in executing the same; ...[26] [Author's emphasis]

---

[25] And I cannot resist at this point referring back to the footnote p. 139 regarding the Slavonic Josephus that provides evidence that John the Baptist began his ministry at this time – AD 6-7.

[26] *Antiquities of the Jews* 18:4-5.

This passage is key to our understanding of events. Most if not all commentators seem to gloss over its detail because the sentiment it describes seems so obvious to us in this day and age, but for Jews who were used to relying on their God to intercede on their behalf, it issued an activist challenge. Read carefully, it makes explicit what was unique about Judas the Galilean's teaching. He did not just exhort his countrymen to rebellion. He said that *this was the only way to bring about God's intervention in human affairs*. God 'would not otherwise be assisting to them' unless the Jews took action themselves. To use the vocabulary we have discussed earlier, passivism and faith alone were not enough. God would only come to the salvation of Judæa once activist Jews took matters into their own hands. A committed revolt would, in effect, force God's hand and usher in the End of Days. Others had and would preach rebellion; but Judas offered more. His Fourth Philosophy was new because he urged his followers to search the scriptures for clues as to events that would precede the apocalypse, and to work to bring those events about; God had promised that he would only then intervene directly in human affairs and restore the Jewish nation once more. That was the heart of his Philosophy.

Josephus then goes on to assert that:

> All sorts of misfortunes also sprang from these men, and the nation was infected with this doctrine to an incredible degree; one violent war came upon us after another, and we lost our friends, who used to alleviate our pains; there were also very great robberies and murders of our principal men. This was done in pretence indeed for the public welfare, but in reality for the hopes of gain to themselves; *whence arose seditions, and from them murders of men, which sometimes fell on those their own people (by the madness of these men towards one another, while their desire was that none of the adverse*

party might be left), and sometimes on their enemies; a famine also coming upon us, reduced us to the last degree of despair, as did also the taking and demolishing of cities; nay, the sedition at last increased so high, that the very temple of God was burnt down by their enemy's fire. Such were the consequences of this, that the customs of our fathers were altered and such a change was made, as added a mighty weight toward bringing all to destruction, which these men occasioned by thus conspiring together; for Judas and Sadduc, who excited a fourth philosophic sect among us, and had a great many followers therein, filled our civil government with tumults at present, and laid the foundation of our future miseries, by this system of philosophy, which we were before unacquainted withal; concerning which I shall discourse a little, and this the rather, because the infection which spread thence among the younger sort, who were zealous for it, brought the public to destruction.[27] [Author's emphasis]

This is another crucial passage that tells us a great deal. In effect, Josephus here blames the activist Fourth Philosophy of Judas and Sadduc for all that befell the Jews as the first century unfolded; the increasing sedition and revolt, and the introduction of political assassination by Zealots, all leading up to outright war with Rome, the destruction of the Temple, and, ultimately, the undoing of the Jewish State.[28] It also confirms (in the passage in italics) that there were two camps within the opposition alliance, one of which – presumably that which believed in trusting in faith rather than direct action – was physically attacked, even to the extent of murder, by those seeking to bring about the End of Days

---

27 *Antiquities of the Jews* 18:6-10.

28 He also blames famine. This was a major problem in the forties AD and provides the context to much of the Book of Acts, as we shall see.

ushering in the Kingdom of God through violence. Finally, Josephus says that this new 'system of philosophy' was one 'which we were before unacquainted withal'. If rebellion alone was the message of Judas' Fourth Philosophy, it seems hard to understand what was so new about it. Rebellion against secular authority can hardly be characterized as a 'system' of philosophy, and it is hardly a new idea for the Jewish people – hadn't this been the philosophy of the previous Judases, stretching back to the Maccabees? Clearly from the Maccabees onwards, the Jews had been well 'acquainted' with violent rebellion. What was new and exciting about Judas was that he promised God's 'assistance', were the Jews only to set the ball rolling.

Josephus (above) promises to 'discourse a little' more on the Fourth Philosophy, and as in *Wars of the Jews*, he finds it necessary to preface that discourse with a description of the other three Philosophies. This he does in verses 12–22, and unlike in *Wars of the Jews*, he gives each of the first three sects roughly equal weight. Then in verse 23, he turns at last, and as promised, to the Fourth Philosophy. But again, what he has to say is a disappointment:

> But of the fourth sect of Jewish philosophy, Judas the Galilean was the author. These men agree in all other things with the Pharisaic notions; but they have an inviolable attachment to liberty; and say that God is to be their only Ruler and Lord. They also do not value dying any kind of death, *nor indeed do they heed the deaths of their relations and friends,* nor can any such fear make them call any man Lord; and since this immovable resolution of theirs is well known to a great many, I shall speak no more on that matter . . .[29] [Author's emphasis]

---

29 18:23-25.

And that is it. Just a restatement of what we have already been told. Note the hint again of a split in their ranks with the reference to 'deaths of their relations and friends'. But otherwise, Josephus just seems to veer off from the subject every time he approaches it. Unless, of course, someone has tampered with the text and Josephus said more than we now have; perhaps he did say more but parallels with the Jesus Movement were too much temptation for some Christian scribe not to tamper with. We will probably never know, and it is no part of the argument of this book to rest upon conspiracy theories: we can uncover the truth without resorting to that.

In the next verse, Josephus confirms the date we have reached in his chronology of events. He says that the census and associated taxation (together with Judas' revolt) took place 'in the thirty-seventh year of Caesar's victory over Antony at Actium'.[30] This is, of course, the famous Battle of Actium at which Octavius Caesar defeated Mark Antony and his lover, Cleopatra. We know from Roman historians that this took place in 31 BC, so 37 years on from that brings us to AD 6 – the date of the census and the start of Judas the Galilean's[31] career. Over the next half dozen verses, Josephus briefly describes a few events, bringing the story up to the death of Octavius Caesar and the accession of Tiberius as emperor in AD 14. We saw in *Wars of the Jews* that Pilate arrived as Procurator sometime after the accession of Tiberius. But *Antiquities of the Jews* here makes clear that Pilate was not the first such, for we learn that Tiberius originally sent someone called Gratus to be the new Procurator of Judæa.[32] The implication from the context is that this was at the start

---

30 18:26.

31 And according to the Slavonic Josephus, John the Baptist's career.

32 18:33

of Tiberius' reign, so we can assume Gratus arrived sometime around AD 15; it would seem likely that the appointment of Gratus by Tiberius was part of a series of appointments made by the latter at the outset of his reign to put his own people in positions of power.

Gratus had similar concerns. One of his first acts on arriving in Judæa was to sack the High Priest. For three decades prior to Judæa becoming a Roman province, and for most of the reign of Herod the Great, the High Priesthood had been dominated by the family of a man called Boethus, starting with Simon, son of Boethus, whose daughter was one of Herod's wives, and whose family were elevated in status as a result. When Quirinius became the first Governor of Roman Judæa, he decided to break the power of the Boethus family and in AD 6 appointed a man called Ananus to the High Priesthood. Ananus held the post for almost a decade, making himself rich in the process. Perhaps Ananus had grown too powerful for Gratus' liking, but whatever the reason, Gratus sacked him and replaced him with Ishmael, son of Phabi – a scion of another old and influential priestly family. However, Ananus' influence seems to have been too powerful to resist, and Ishmael lasted only a year before being replaced again by Eleazar, one of Ananus' sons. Josephus records that Gratus thereafter proceeded to appoint and sack a sequence of High Priests on a regular, annual basis. Throughout all the changes, however, Ananus continued to dominate the High Priesthood for at least the next two decades; he seems to have retained the honorific title of High Priest, whoever was performing the executive role at the time, and to have dominated the Jerusalem High Court (the Sanhedrin), despite having been officially removed from office. Furthermore, five of his sons in all, over time, became High Priest in their turn, and his son-in-law Caiaphas was the High Priest who in the Gospels was responsible for *Jesus'* death.

This was an extremely powerful, dangerous dynasty who directly influenced and, as often as not, controlled events in Judæa throughout the period that interests us. There is a very telling illustration of the power of Ananus and his kin. *Jesus* is credited with a parable concerning a rich man (Dives) and a poor man (Lazarus); in this, the rich man dies and goes to Hell and wants to warn his still-living four brothers and father of his fate. There can be little doubt that this is a clear reference to the family of Ananus and their consignment to Hell is confirmation of the way they were seen by the Jesus Movement. But the other powerful Sadducee families continued to vie for the High Priesthood over the next half a century. The Phabi family made a comeback now and then, and one or two other families make an appearance in the list, but the family that appears most often to challenge Ananus is that of Boethus, who lost power with the death of Herod but never stopped their attempts to regain it. Another family to hold office, Cantheras, seems to have also been a branch of the Boethus clan. There can be no doubt that these two Sadducee families, like many in that sect, were collaborators with Roman authority, and their dominance over the High Priesthood, extending through several decades, provides the key background detail to later events we shall discuss below.

So, returning to Josephus' narrative, Gratus first sacked Ananus in AD 15 and replaced him with Ishmael, son of Phabi. However, Ishmael lasted only 'a little time', and was then replaced by Eleazar, one of Ananus' sons, probably in the following year, in AD 16, because annual appointments now became the norm. Simon ben Camithus was then appointed in AD 17, and he was replaced by Caiaphas (Ananus' son-in-law) in AD 18.

These events and the shifting fortunes of the Boethus and Ananus clans are illustrated in the following chart:

High Priests at the Time of *Jesus* and Paul
(*Coded as follows:*)
Bold   Families of Boethus/Cantheras
Italic: Family of Ananus

BC
23–4	**Simon, son of Boethus**
4	Matthias, son of Theophilus
4	**Joazar, son of Boethus**
4–3	**Eleazar, son of Boethus**
3–?	Jesus, son of Sie

AD
?–6	**Joazar, son of Boethus**
6–15	*Ananus, son of Seth*
15–16	Ishmael, son of Phabi
16–17	*Eleazar, son of Ananus*
17–18	Simon, son of Camithus
18–36	*Caiaphas, son-in-law of Ananus*
36–37	*Jonathan, son of Ananus*
37–41	*Theophilus, son of Ananus*
41–43	**Simon Cantheras, son of Boethus**
43	*Matthias, son of Ananus*
43–44	**Elioneus, son of Simon Cantheras**
44	*Jonathan, son of Ananus*
44–46	Josephus, son of Camydus
46–52	Ananias, son of Nebedeus
52–56	*Jonathan, son of Ananus*
56–62	Ishmael, son of Fabus
62–63	**Joseph [called Cabi], son of Simon [Cantheras]**
63	*Ananus, son of Ananus*
63	Jesus, son of Damneus
63–64	Jesus, son of Gamaliel

At this point in AD 18, all seems clear. But then Josephus' narrative seems to get chronologically confused:

> When Gratus had done those things, he went back to Rome, *after he had tarried in Judæa eleven years*, when Pontius Pilate came as his successor.[33] [Author's emphasis]

So now we know that Pilate was Procurator after Gratus. Apart from the clause that I have put in italics, everything about this passage and the chronology that precedes it seems to be telling us that Gratus was in Judæa for about four years, from AD 15 to AD 19. Remember, he sacked Ananus in AD 15, Eleazar in AD 16, and then Simon ben Camithus in AD 18. But the italicized passage adds eight years to this calculation, bringing the chronology in one jump to AD 26. Where did the extra eight or so years come from? What was going on between AD 18 and AD 26? Here is the puzzle in chart form:

Roman Procurators/Governors (AD)

6–9	Coponius
9–12	Ambivulus
12–15	Rufus
15–26	Gratus (or 15–18)
26–37	Pilate (or 18–37)
44–46	Fadus
46–48	Tiberius Alexander
48–52	Cumanus
52–60	Felix

Something seems very wrong here, yet the later date of AD 26 for Pilate's arrival has been accepted over the centuries since as the date Pilate arrived in Judæa – in time to have

---

33 18:35.

Jesus crucified in the early thirties. And the anomaly gets worse. The very next three verses describe the founding of the city of Tiberias, named after the emperor:

> And now Herod the Tetrarch, who was in great favour with Tiberius, built a city of the same name with him, and called it Tiberias.[34]

We know from Roman records that Tiberias was established in AD 20 – not in AD 26, as would be implied by Josephus' eleven-year chronology, but exactly as would be implied by his narrative without that eleven-year interpolation. Verses 39-53 that follow jump back in time to AD 4 to bring the reader up to speed with parallel events in Parthia. They conclude with the Roman general Germanicus being sent to the region 'to settle the affairs of the east' and his subsequent death, which in fact took place in AD 19 – again consistent with the shorter chronology for Gratus' term of office.[35] (We know from Tacitus, that just before his death, Germanicus visited Egypt, ostensibly because there was famine there that year; he solved the problem by opening the grain stores. We shall revert to this later.[36])

None of this would be at all problematical, were it not for my italicized phrase: *after he had tarried in Judæa eleven years*. In my view, it is inescapable that the phrase was never in Josephus' original account. Gratus was replaced by Pilate in around AD 19, not AD 26. Some Christian scribe has inserted the italicized reference to 'eleven years' there in the version that has come down to us for one simple reason

---

34 18:36.
35 18:53.
36 Tacitus: *Annals* Book 2 [59].

– to shift events relating to *Jesus* forward in time, to fit a chronological framework for the life and death of Jesus that by then had become established. It will be remembered that there seem to have been two traditions for *Jesus'* life – one a decade earlier than the other. Something similar is happening here. If Pilate did not arrive in Judæa until AD 26, then *Jesus* could not have been crucified until then. But if he arrived in AD 19, it could have happened earlier. And in that case, Pilate's outrages – the imperial effigy and the aqueduct – would have been either bold, deliberate moves, consequent upon the suppression of the movement led by *Jesus*; or perhaps even the events that *preceded* and *occasioned* the death of *Jesus*. As we shall see later, there is evidence that something momentous did happen in or around AD 19. But for now, let us return to the story as Josephus tells it.

He now relates the same tales as in *Wars of the Jews* regarding the actions of Pilate on arriving as Procurator of Judæa. First, the introduction of the effigies of Caesar into Jerusalem; Josephus here confirms that this was a deliberate act of provocation 'in order to abolish the Jewish laws'. Second, the use of Corban to build a new aqueduct to bring water into Jerusalem. And then we find the following important passage, entirely missing from *Wars of the Jews*:

> There was about this time Jesus, a wise man, *if it be lawful to call him a man, for he was a doer of wonderful works* – a teacher of such men as receive the truth with pleasure. He drew over to him both many of the Jews and many of the Gentiles. *He was [the] Christ; and when Pilate, at the suggestion of the principle men amongst us had condemned him to the cross, those that loved him at the first did not forsake him, for he appeared to them alive again the third day, as the divine*

prophets had foretold these and ten thousand other wonderful things concerning him; and the tribe of Christians, so named from him, are not extinct at this day.[37] [Author's emphasis]

Here we have it – the *only* direct reference in the first century, outside of the Bible, to *Jesus'* life.[38] This apparently decisive reference to Jesus, confirming his life, death and resurrection, has been known over the centuries as the *Testimonium Flavium* – the testimony of Flavius Josephus [to the truth of Jesus]. But it has never been universally accepted as authentic, and today most scholars would question it in part if not in its entirety. The two phrases in italics seem to most scholars to be highly suspect, not being in Josephus' style, and suggesting as they do that Josephus must have been a Christian convert – a most unlikely scenario, given all that we know of him. Controversy still rages around this passage and this book would be twice as long if we fully engaged in it.

However, the first thing to say is that if this is the best that Christianity can do by way of independent confirmation of the New Testament, it is not very impressive – even if we accept it as one hundred per cent authentic. As I have said before, if Jesus really did do the things we are told about in the Gospels, and Josephus really did have first-hand knowledge of them, why on earth would he not have written about them in *Wars of the Jews* twenty years earlier? And why is this such a brief account of events which, if true, must have dwarfed into insignificance all the other stories that Josephus relates at much greater length? I think there are only two rational conclusions that can be drawn from this passage. Either the whole thing is a later Christian interpolation into

---

37 *Antiquities of the Jews* 18:63-4.

38 There is another single reference to 'Jesus' in Josephus and we shall deal with this shortly.

Josephus' text, perhaps by the same scribe who added the extra years to Gratus' administration. Or, alternatively, by the nineties AD, when Josephus came to write this account, the *Jesus* story was already becoming well-known in Rome, where Christianity was flourishing, and Josephus, with no first-hand knowledge but not wanting to omit something that seemed to have happened, put in a short reference. In my view, in that scenario, the original reference was probably the non-italicized clauses above, which would thus read:

> There was about this time Jesus, a wise man – a teacher of such men as receive the truth with pleasure. He drew over to him both many of the Jews and many of the Gentiles and the tribe of Christians, so named from him, are not extinct at this day.

In this scenario, the italicized clauses would have been added by someone much later, clearly a believing Christian, who would have felt the need to modify the word 'man' with 'if it be lawful to call him a man' and while he was at it, to insert what look like excerpts from some early Christian credo. In plain terms, even if Josephus wrote these words, or something like them, all that it is evidence of is that by the nineties AD a Jew in Rome would have heard the stories that eventually became the Gospels.

There is also another chronological problem here. This passage about Jesus is immediately followed by an extended excursion into two tales of events in Rome.[39] The first involves the seduction of a chaste, married woman called Paulina in the temple of Isis by a young man named Mundus, posing as the God Anubis. It seems most strange that this should immediately follow the reference to *Jesus* – almost as

---

39 18:65-82.

if Josephus were mocking the story of *Jesus'* virgin birth, in which Mary is impregnated by the Jewish God. The second story involves a fraud perpetrated by a Jew on a rich Roman aristocratic convert to Judaism, in which money intended for the Jerusalem Temple is diverted for personal gain. As a result, Tiberius 'ordered all the Jews to be banished out of Rome'. In fact, we know from the Roman historian Tacitus that these events did indeed take place in Rome, and they happened in AD 19. And we have argued that Pilate arrived in Judæa in AD 19; so, the *Testimonium Flavium* is firmly sandwiched in Josephus' account between two events that we know both took place in AD 19. And the actions by Pilate to antagonize the Jews, described in both *Wars of the Jews* and *Antiquities of the Jews* also seem to have taken place at around that time.

Following the description of the AD 19 expulsion of Jews from Rome, Josephus' narrative jumps again – a full seventeen years to events that we can date from other sources to AD 36. This gap is roughly the same as the gap already noticed in *Wars of the Jews*, precisely covering the period when Jesus was supposed to have lived and died. To repeat once more – something very strange is going on here. Can we conclude perhaps that *Jesus,* assuming that he was a historic figure, was crucified in AD 19, a decade before the traditional dating, and at the same time as Pilate was outraging the Jews in the other ways recounted by Josephus? Or, if *Jesus* turns out not to have been a historical figure, perhaps some other figure died at this time and his story became associated with that of *Jesus*? We have seen how all the other elements of the Gospel story derive from such borrowings – why not this one?

It is my contention that by shifting events backwards by a decade we have removed the barriers to an identification that otherwise now seems irresistible: that the new, revolutionary movements founded by Judas the Galilean, and *Jesus* the Galilean are one and the same. Judas was not *Jesus*, but the Gospel writers used elements of Judas' life to create elements in their portraits of *Jesus*. It seems most strange that Josephus says so much about Judas the Galilean in both his books, ascribing all the catastrophic events of first-century Judæa to him and his movement, and yet nowhere in the texts of Josephus that have come down to us does he tell us when or how Judas died. Perhaps a clue to what is going on here is provided by Pilate's introduction of Roman effigies into Jerusalem.[40] Although Josephus does not say that he went as far as introducing them into the Temple itself, the event does seem to echo the two previous occasions noted above, where Antiochus and then Herod did just that. In both cases, someone called Judas (Maccabee and then Sepphoris) is involved in the subsequent uprisings. In my view, Judas the Galilean (who in any case may have been the same person as Judas Sepphoris, as some commentators believe), led the uprising in this case also. And interestingly of course, a key event in the life of *Jesus*, described in all four of the Gospels, is *His* cleansing of the Temple.

For many scholars, the Gospel story of *Jesus* cleansing the Temple seems problematical. The Gospel writers take the view that *Jesus* was angry with the activities of money changers and sellers of sacrificial livestock in the Temple – they seem to have regarded these activities as in some way desecrating the holiness of the Temple. Yet a moment's thought suffices to indicate that this is an anachronism, or perhaps a Greek misunderstanding of Jewish practice. All religious institutions throughout history have needed money to function; in our own day, no one objects to the passing of a collection plate in Christian services, and some British

---

40 *Antiquities of the Jews* 18:55.

cathedrals now charge for entrance. Certainly, temples and priesthoods in antiquity supported themselves with just the sort of activity that *Jesus* seems to be objecting to. Without money changers, how were Diaspora Jews, visiting the Temple from foreign lands, to exchange their native coinage for the purchase of sacrifices? And how could there be any sacrifices without livestock breeders to provide them for money? These activities were not taking place in the Holy of Holies where God was believed to dwell, but in the outer precincts and courtyards that existed for precisely these legitimate and necessary activities. It is hard not to draw the conclusion that this story is a garbled recollection of a different kind of Temple cleansing entirely – that of Roman effigies of one sort or another that definitely *were* sacrilegious. Of course, for the Gospel authors, writing in Greek for a Greco-Roman audience, *Jesus*' objection to the effigies would have seemed hard to understand at best, and an insult to the Roman state at worst. Indeed, from the point of view of an orthodox Roman, it would be the cleansing of the effigies that would itself have been the sacrilegious act. In fact, the writer of the Gospel of John describes *two* such Temple cleansings by *Jesus* – one at the start and a second at the end of his ministry. In one view (encouraged by Occam's Razor), John was just getting confused about what had in reality been a single event; but another view would be that the story of *Jesus* in all these cleansing narratives is being filled out with detail from the activities of one or more revolutionaries called Judas. **In my view we can go one step further and say that, on balance of probabilities, Judas the Galilean's resistance to just such sacrilege led to his arrest and execution in 19 AD, and it is this event which lies behind the Gospel story of Jesus' Temple cleansing, his subsequent arrest, and his execution.** You may wish to read that last sentence again. It cannot be proved; but as we proceed with our analysis, I will show how this and related identifications unlocks so much else that is otherwise puzzling, that the probability becomes overwhelming.

Many people have concluded on the sort of evidence I have outlined above, external to the Bible and therefore more reliably objective, that there was no historical person living in the early decades of the first century AD who lived the life set out in the Gospels. But there is one further reference in Josephus which for most has represented a huge obstacle to this mythical view of Jesus. To find it, we need to skip forward a few decades and a couple of Books in Josephus to Book 20, just a few pages before the end of *Antiquities of the Jews*. At this stage in Josephus' narrative, Nero was Roman emperor and Judæa was still overseen by a Roman Procurator, Felix, but there was also a local king, Agrippa II, on the throne of Judæa and Galilee. The rebellions and revolts that had rumbled on from the beginning of the century were now reaching their height and the outbreak of full war was only a few years away. Anarchy seems to have reigned:

> Now, as for the affairs of the Jews, they grew worse and worse continually; for the country was again filled with robbers and imposters, who deluded the multitude.[41]

The Procurator, Felix, was hard pushed to maintain control and this was not helped by a power struggle between himself and the High Priest, Jonathan, who seems to have disapproved of Felix's strong hand with the rebels. Eventually, Felix paid a bribe for Jonathan to be murdered by the Sicarii, who subsequently seem to have gone completely out of control and to have carried out assassinations of other priests,

---

41 20:160.

even in the Temple precincts. This was a major incident in the lead up to the war: an act of such utter sacrilege that Josephus wonders whether this was not the reason, in effect the final straw, that persuaded God to allow the Romans to sack Jerusalem and destroy the Temple, which was now so defiled by such monstrous acts that it could no longer be His 'home' on earth.

One 'imposter' who 'deluded the multitude' at this time was known as the 'Egyptian':

> These works, that were done by the robbers, filled the city with all sorts of impiety. And now these imposters and deceivers persuaded the multitude to follow them into the wilderness and pretended that they would exhibit manifest wonders and signs, that should be performed by the providence of God... Moreover, there came out of Egypt about this time to Jerusalem, one that said he was a prophet, and advised the multitude of the common people to go along with him to the Mount of Olives... He said farther, that he would show them from hence, how, at his command, the walls of Jerusalem would fall down...[42]

Signs, wonders and the Mount of Olives. We are in familiar New Testament territory here; surely it was *Jesus* who performed such signs and wonders? For the moment at least, Felix put this particular uprising down with brutal force, but the situation was deteriorating:

> And again the robbers stirred up the people to make war with the Romans, and said they ought not to obey them at all; and when any persons would not comply with them, they set fire to their villages, and plundered them.[43]

---

[42] 20:167-170.

[43] 20:172.

Josephus calls them 'robbers', just as he had termed Judas the Galilean, but one must remember when he was writing and who he was writing for. There is no doubt that all these 'robbers' would today be called freedom fighters, and the way they are described here, rejecting Roman authority, leaves no doubt that these are the followers of Judas the Galilean. The Egyptian, being one such, connects not only with Judas, but also with *Jesus* and other Messianic figures. It will be recalled that Hosea had prophesied that the Messiah would come out of Egypt – hence the need in the Gospels to have the holy family flee from Bethlehem to Egypt. And of course, the Mount of Olives is where *Jesus* went to initiate his own bid to instigate the new millennium and raise a new Temple.

In AD 56, following the murder of Jonathan at the behest of Felix, the new High Priest appointed by King Agrippa was called Ismael ben Phabi. But this seems to have made matters even worse as, under his direction, some sort of civil war broke out even *within* the ranks of the priesthood:

> And now arose a sedition between the high priests and the principal men of the multitude of Jerusalem; each of whom got them a company of the boldest sort of men, and of those that loved innovations, about them, and became leaders to them; and when they struggled together, they did it by casting reproachful words against one another, and by throwing stones also. And there was nobody to reprove them; but these disorders were done after a licentious manner in the city, as if it had no government over it. And such was the impudence and boldness that had seized on the high priests, that they had the hardness to send their servants into the threshing floors, to take away the tithes that were due to the priests, insomuch that it so fell out that the poorer sort of the priests

died for want. To this degree did the violence of the seditious prevail over all right and justice.[44]

At this point, in AD 60, matters had got so far out of control that the Emperor Nero himself intervened. He recalled Felix to Rome and sent a man called Festus out to Judæa as Procurator, with a clear brief to sort the Jews out once and for all:

> Upon Festus' coming into Judæa, it happened that Judæa was afflicted by the robbers, while all the villages were set on fire, and plundered by them. And then it was that the Sicarii, as they were called, who were robbers, grew numerous.[45]

Remember, we are now only a few short years from the outbreak of the war that was ultimately to result in the destruction of the Jewish State for 2,000 years. It is too easy to gloss over an account like this: Judæa was by now in a state of virtual anarchy; law and order had largely broken down; and the authorities were very worried indeed. Whether Festus would have succeeded in calming all this down, we will never know. In AD 62, he died suddenly and was replaced as Procurator by a man called Albinus, sent out from Rome for the purpose. Remember also, that at this time Judæa was governed locally by a king who was himself playing political games. King Agrippa now sacked the then current High Priest, Joseph ben Simon, (Ismael ben Phabi's successor) and replaced him with one of the sons of Ananus that we referred to earlier, putting back into power a strong priestly family that could be counted on to be loyal to secular authority. Just to be confusing, this son was also called Ananus.

---

44 20:179-181.
45 *Antiquities of the Jews* 20:185-6.

So, to recap, the situation in AD 62 was as follows: against a background of civil disturbance and internecine warfare among the priestly class, when the new Procurator – Albinus – is still *en route* from Rome to Judæa, the most avaricious and powerful priestly family of the period regain control of the High Priesthood. Seizing his opportunity before Albinus arrived to take up office, Josephus recounts that the new High Priest, Ananus, son of Ananus:

> . . . assembled the Sanhedrin of judges, and brought before them the brother of Jesus, *who was called Christ*, whose name was James, and some others; and when he had formed an accusation against them as breakers of the law, he delivered them to be stoned; but as for those who seemed the most equitable of the citizens, and such as were the most uneasy at the breach of the laws, they disliked what was done; they also sent to the king [Agrippa], desiring him to send to Ananus that he should act so no more, for that what he had already done was not to be justified; nay, some of them went also to meet Albinus, as he was upon his journey from Alexandria, and informed him that it was not lawful for Ananus to assemble a Sanhedrin without his consent; – whereupon Albinus complied with what they said, and wrote in anger to Ananus, and threatened that he would bring him to punishment for what he had done; on which, king Agrippa took the high priesthood from him, when he had ruled but three months, and made Jesus, the son of Damneus, high priest.[46] [Author's emphasis]

This is clearly a crucial passage. The argument is simple and runs like this: if James existed as per this passage, then his brother Jesus 'who was called Christ' must also have exist-

---

46 20:200-203.

ed.⁴⁷ We know from other sources, in the Bible and early Christian writers, that there certainly was a 'James', referred to often as 'the Lord's brother' or 'the brother of Jesus', who was an important figure in the early Jerusalem Church. We shall have much more to say about him later. If Josephus is referring here to that James, he would have been old – in his sixties at least – particularly if, as we have been arguing, the events of *Jesus'* life occurred a decade or more earlier than is traditionally believed. There are early traditions that James lived to a great age, but the evidence here might just be circular. But it seems to me that there is good reason to doubt that this James, and the early church leader called James, *are* really the same person. Look again at the crucial Josephus passage. If one eliminates just the four words I have placed in italics, and then re-read this passage *in the historical context we have been examining over the last few pages*, a completely different interpretation emerges, which I will now set out.

Josephus is clear that Ananus was being opportunistic. He seems to have known that the new Procurator Albinus would not approve of him killing James, so he takes the opportunity, before Albinus arrives to take up his post, to execute James. But we must ask why? According to the Gospels, Pilate had not hesitated to crucify *Jesus* at the request of a High Priest, even against his own conscience. Presumably, the argument is that James, the brother of *Jesus*, would have been guilty of whatever *Jesus* had been guilty of (and of course, we still have to establish what that might have been). So why would Ananus fear that

---

47 The issue of this 'James' is a critical one holding back many from accepting that the *Jesus* of the Gospels is a myth. Eisenman, for example, accepts that this James is the real, flesh-and-blood brother of *Jesus* and thus effectively bases his whole argument on it; he develops a theory based on *Jesus* being the founder of a sort of Christian 'caliphate', with James his brother as his successor. And Price accepts that it is the single strongest piece of evidence that Jesus was a real first-century person – yet still holds to the mythicist stance without reconciling the issue.

Albinus would not approve? Why did he behave in such an opportunistic manner? Surely Albinus would have had no problem with the execution of a troublemaker – especially in these times. Indeed, we can well imagine that he was travelling to the region with *carte blanche* from Rome to take whatever steps were necessary to calm things down in Judæa. And we know just how brutal Roman 'steps' could be. But Albinus certainly would have had a problem with an opportunistic, internecine assassination that would exacerbate an already fragile situation. The answer must be that this was *not* James, the brother of *Jesus 'who was called Christ'* – those last four words have been added by a Christian scribe who, having heard early Church traditions about James, the Lord's brother, assumed they were identical and made the connection. The James we have here in Josephus is certainly the 'brother of Jesus'; but it is Jesus ben Damneus, who is actually named at the end of the crucial passage above.[48] This Jesus ben Damneus is appointed High Priest by King Agrippa to atone for the killing of his brother James.[49] What could be more reasonable and likely in the circumstances?

This whole episode is nothing to do with Christianity. It is a playing out of the civil war within the priestly community that we saw earlier. In eliminating James, who must have been a rival priest, Ananus was taking advantage of the interregnum between procurators to carry on a priestly vendetta. That is why Josephus precedes the account of the death of James by telling us about the dynasty of the original Ananus:

> ... this elder Ananus proved a most fortunate man; for he had five sons, who had all performed the office of a high

---

48 The 'ben' in Jesus ben Damneus means 'son of'.
49 See list of High Priests, p. 162.

priest to God, and he had himself enjoyed that dignity a long time formerly . . .[50]

Josephus does not provide us with enough detail to untangle all the politics involved, but what seems clear is that for many years there had been civil war among the priesthood, and Ananus and his dynasty would have been at the forefront of this. Indeed, we now discover that it was Ananus and his dynasty that was behind the attacks on the lesser priests that Josephus regarded as so dastardly as to be the real reason why God deserted the Jews:

> . . . as for the High Priest Ananias[51] [the elder], he increased in glory every day, . . . he also had servants who were very wicked, who joined themselves to the boldest sort of people, and went to the thrashing floors, and took away the tithes that belonged to the priests by violence, and did not refrain from beating such as would not give these tithes to them. So the other high priests acted in the like manner, as did those his servants without anyone being able to prohibit them; so that [some of the] priests, that of old were wonted to be supported with those tithes, died for want of food.[52]

And surely, we have heard this story before. These lines are so close to the same story only twenty-five verses before (in verses 179–181 quoted on page 173 – I urge you to turn back and re-read them), that one wonders whether scribal interference in this whole section of Josephus has resulted in

---

50 20:198.

51 This should read 'Ananus' – the names and spellings were confusingly interchangeable. As Whiston comments in his footnote to this passage, it is the 'elder' Ananus we are dealing with here. 'This Ananais was not the son of Nebedeus . . . but he who was called . . . A[n]nanus the Elder'.

52 20:205-207.

the same narrative being repeated twice. (Remember Occam's Razor – if entities are multiplied, be very careful). Certainly, it would seem most likely that the attacks on the lesser priests back in AD 56 resulted in Ananias losing control of the priesthood until the appointment of his son, Ananus, in AD 62. Their punishment for killing James was to lose control of the priesthood again.

However, Ananus was never down for long. We learn that he was soon influencing affairs again by bribing both Albinus and Jesus ben Damneus.[53] But the strife continued. The Sicarii kidnapped Ananus' son, Eleazar, and held him ransom for the release of Sicarii prisoners. Then, Agrippa dismissed Jesus ben Damneus and replaced him with yet another Jesus, son of Gamaliel:

> ... on which account a sedition arose between the high priests, with regard to one another; for they got together bodies of the boldest sort of the people, and frequently came, from reproaches, to throwing of stones at each other; but Ananias was too hard for the rest, by his riches ... [54]

Again, I suggest that someone has been tampering with the text here. This is another parallel with the two earlier versions of this story, with several key words and phrases repeated. What is certain is that it confirms again the internecine struggles in the priesthood at this time, of which the stoning of James ben Damneus – not James, brother of the Christ – was just one result.

To summarize this chapter so far: it seems that despite passages in *Antiquities* (not the earlier *Wars*), concerning Jesus and a certain 'James', there is good reason for stating

---

53 20:205.
54 20:213.

that there is no firm evidence in Josephus to bear out the Gospel stories of Jesus' life and death. It also appears that whatever does lie behind those stories happened a decade or so earlier than the standard chronology would allow, and in particular, something momentous in terms of the evolution of Christianity seems to have happened around AD 19, soon after the arrival in Judæa of Pontius Pilate. There seems to have been no shortage of Messianic figures appearing and disappearing on the Judæan scene in the first half of the first century AD, and some of their characteristics seem to have found their way into the Gospel stories attributed to *Jesus*. And in particular, Judas the Galilean seems to have founded a new religious 'philosophy' around the time of *Jesus*' supposed birth – a philosophy that came to influence and eventually dominate events that led to the Jewish War of the sixties AD. The Jesus Movement was clearly not identical with any of the other three Jewish sects described by Josephus, although obviously influenced by two of them. On this basis, the temptation to look for correspondences between Judas the Galilean and *Jesus* the Galilean becomes irresistible.

ZECHARIAH

There are several striking parallels between *Jesus* and Judas, apart from the obvious fact that both were active in Galilee. Just as Judas' movement began in opposition to Roman taxation, so the charges put against *Jesus* at his trial included 'forbidding to give tribute to Caesar'.[55] Both men seem to have been proclaimed Messiah, and indeed, king, by their followers. The names of two of *Jesus*' disciples were Simon the Zealot and Judas Iscariot. As the movement founded by

---

55 Luke 23:2.

The Jesus Fallacy

Judas developed, his followers became known as Zealots because they were zealous for the Mosaic Law – and as we have seen, Sicarii. Many scholars believe that the name Iscariot is a corruption of this. So, if two of *Jesus'* disciples were such men of violence, what might we conclude about his movement in total?[56]

Many scholars have concluded on this sort of evidence that *Jesus* was not as meek and mild as the Gospels imply, but that he was, to some degree, a revolutionary leader. They point to other such rebel leaders catalogued by Josephus, for example the Egyptian, and suggest that *Jesus* was just another of these. The arrest of *Jesus* on the Mount of Olives is particularly interesting in this regard; whatever He and his disciples were doing there that night, they were armed with swords, and the arresting party also came armed with swords. Another indication of what was really going on in Galilee at that time is provided by the story of *Jesus* allowing his disciples to eat corn, growing in a field through which they were passing on the Sabbath. Criticized for this by some Pharisees, *Jesus* quoted the example of the Old Testament King David eating the 'shewbread' in the temple.[57] What the text in Matthew 12 does not say is that at the time David was fleeing for his life from King Saul; this extremity is what makes the violation of Mosaic Law acceptable. It seems inescapable to conclude that the real incident behind the Gospel story was Judas, the Galilean guerrilla, on the run from Roman authority. Yet despite these indications of potential violence, most Christians have had difficulty accepting that *Jesus* was anything other than a peaceful, itinerant preacher. And the parallels with Judas the Galilean are rejected on the not unreasonable grounds that he was named Judas, not

---

56 Particularly if we can equate Simon the Zealot with Simon Peter?
57 I Samuel 21:6.

Jesus. Supporters of the thesis that Judas and Jesus are historically identical argue that the name *Jesus*, which means God Saves or God's Salvation, was a Messianic title bestowed on Judas. But as we have seen, there were many characters active in the first century AD who had this name, including Jesus ben Damneus, whose brother James was murdered. Josephus mentions no less than 13 different people called Jesus, in addition to Jesus Christ, but none of these in any way matches with a crucified Messiah, and it does seem unlikely to say the least that a name as common as Jesus should also be used as a Messianic title.

So, if Judas the Galilean was not *Jesus* (albeit, the Gospel stories of *Jesus* may have drawn upon his life), and no other Jesus around at the time seems to fit the bill, we seem to be left with a simple choice; either Jesus was an historical figure after all, it is just that we can trust none of the stories about him, or he is a mythical character, invented out of thin air. I think there is a third and better alternative. As we have seen, the Gospel accounts were written relatively late and are unreliable. The letters of Paul are much earlier and do attest to a historical figure, but one about whom Paul seems to know virtually nothing, and indeed, seems to care little if anything about the details of his life, beyond his death and resurrection. Indeed, as far as Paul is concerned, Jesus could have lived and died at any time in the past; what matters to Paul is that he was raised to sit in heaven beside God and will be coming to Earth at the End of Days, to usher in the Kingdom of God. Is there then anyone in the Bible who, before the Christian era, might fit this description and is called Jesus?

The English name *Jesus* derives from the Latin name *Iesus*, which is a transliteration from the Greek name *Iēsoûs*. In the Septuagint version of the Old Testament and other Greek-language Jewish texts, (including the works of Josephus and

Philo), Iēsoûs is in turn the standard Greek form used to translate the Hebrew name Yehoshua or Yeshua, the latter being the more common way of writing the former. In the New Testament,[58] the same Greek *Iēsoûs* is also used to represent the name of Joshua ben Nun – the heroic successor to Moses who led the children of Israel into the promised land. But wherever Yeshua appears in the Old Testament it is transliterated into English as Joshua. To restate this in simple terms, the same Hebrew name Yeshua gets translated in the Bible in two ways: as Joshua for Old Testament characters and Jesus for New Testament characters. Why? Could it be because the translators did not want to draw attention to the fact that the character known as Jesus Christ had the same name as Joshua, son of Nun, who as we have seen, was regarded by many Messianic Jews as the model for the expected Messiah? Whatever the truth of this, just as devout Christians today have taken to referring to God as Yahweh rather than Jehovah, so it has become almost fashionable to refer to Christ as Yeshua rather than Jesus.

Joshua ben Nun, therefore, not only prefigures the expected Messiah, but contrary to standard biblical translation, does have the right name. His Hebrew name was Yeshua, and it would be correct to translate this as either Jesus or Joshua. But, tempting as it is to identify Joshua ben Nun as the historical figure behind the figure of *Jesus*, he just does not meet our requirements; he is reported to have died at the age of 110 and there is no suggestion of a resurrection or return.[59] But there is just one other Yeshua in the Old Testament, and excitingly, he is to be found primarily in the Book of Zechariah, which, it will be recalled, is one of the minor prophets most subjected to Messianic *Midrash*. Zechariah was said to

---

58 In Acts 7:45 and Hebrews 4:8.

59 Joshua 24:29.

have prophesied in the early sixth century BC. He lived at the time the Jews returned from Babylonian Exile, and when Yeshua ben Yehozedek was High Priest. This Yeshua ben Yehozedek, together with the civil governor at the time, Zerubbabel, was responsible for the building of the second Temple in Jerusalem – the one that Herod centuries later was to enhance. Zechariah was the name given in the Gospels to the father of John the Baptist, and Zerubbabel appears in the genealogies of Jesus in both Matthew and Luke. But it is Yeshua ben Yehozedek who figures most prominently in the Book of Zechariah. As his name implies, this Yeshua was the son of the previous High Priest, Yehozedek. That name has important overtones too; it means God's (Yahweh's) Righteousness (Zedek). The latter is the same root as Zadok, which we saw earlier corrupted to Sadduc, the co-founder with Judas the Galilean, of what Josephus calls the Fourth Philosophy. Unfortunately, we know no more about Yeshua ben Yehozedek's life than we do about Jesus Christ's earthly existence. He gets brief mentions in other minor prophets – Ezra, Nehemiah and Haggai – which confirm that he was a leading light in the restoration of the Temple and subsequently served as its High Priest. But as also with *Jesus Christ*, this Yeshua's importance was not what he did in life, but what God appointed him to after his death. These matters are dealt with in the Book of Zechariah.

Zechariah has fourteen chapters and divides broadly into two main sections. The first eight chapters contain the prophecies of Zechariah in a series of eight visions. The message of the visions is one of encouragement to the Jews in terms of a promise of imminent intervention by God on their behalf, and the introduction of a new age. A first-century practitioner of *Midrash* would have had no difficulty applying its terms to his own day. The last six chapters of Zechariah were probably written later, and according to most modern scholars, by another hand, but this would not have been evident or relevant to a first-century commentator. These last six chapters comprise passages looking forward to the triumph of God over evil, together with passages of vitriolic attack against false leaders. Much of all this is very obscure, making it a happy hunting ground for later *midrashic* and sectarian interpretation. We have already seen how passages from Zechariah provided the sources for *Jesus*' entry into Jerusalem on an ass, and for Judas Iscariot's thirty pieces of silver and death in a potter's field. But overall, one thing marks out Zechariah from most of the other prophets. Although much of his prophesying concerns the Jews as God's chosen people, nevertheless Zechariah exhibits to a remarkable degree, what the theologians call 'universalism' – that is, a concern for the Gentile races, and their salvation as part of God's plan.

For Zechariah, the role of the Jews was to be a priest nation who would minister to all God's creation in the new dispensation of God's Holy Kingdom that he prophesied was imminent. By the first century, this universalism was a widely accepted facet of popular Judaism and recognized particularly by Pharisaic interpretation of God's intent: we are told in Matthew that the Pharisees would 'compass sea and land to make one proselyte'.[60] And we know that the Alexandrian Jewish population in particular – Philo among them – produced a considerable literature to win over converts to Judaism. We saw earlier how many Gentiles became God-fearers – that is, they remained uncircumcised and therefore racially Gentile but nevertheless subscribed to Judaism as a religion. Many if not most synagogues would have Jewish members, governed by the full Mosaic Law, and God-fearers governed by the Noahic Law. This is most important when, having identified the 'real' Jesus, we come

---

60 23:15.

to consider the degree to which the Jesus Movement itself, was aimed at Gentiles as well as Jews. As we shall see, Christianity was never a solely Jewish movement that was taken to the Gentiles by the Apostle Paul; it embraced from the start a distinctive view about Gentiles and their place in the Kingdom of God. Let us take a look at Zechariah's visions in more detail.

The first and second visions reassure the Jews that God still favours them and will once again make Jerusalem his dwelling place.[61] He will punish the nations that destroyed the city and took the Jews into Exile. The second vision ends with a most tantalizing reference to 'carpenters':

> Then lifted I up mine eyes, and saw, and behold four horns . . . These are the horns that have scattered Judah, Israel and Jerusalem. And the Lord showed me four carpenters . . . these are come to . . . cast out the horns of the Gentiles, which lifted up their horn over the land of Judah to scatter it.[62]

The word translated here as 'carpenters' is much wider than this in the original Hebrew and Greek – 'smith' would probably be closer to the original meaning. Smiths and potters (remember Judas Iscariot's potter's field) were traditionally associated with a Jewish religious sect called Rechabites, and these in turn were named after Rechab, a prominent Old Testament Zealot. So, to be a carpenter or smith or potter was to be associated with Zealotry. *Jesus* was famously reported to be the son of a carpenter, Joseph. And Joseph had other sons, according to the Gospels – James, Simon, Judas and Joses, who would perhaps have been carpenters too. The Gospels also tell us that a James and a Simon (Peter) were among *Jesus*' closest disciples, and James together with John

---

[61] In Chapter 1.
[62] 1:18-21.

were known as sons of thunder – an apt nickname perhaps for sons of a black*smith*. We know of a Judas Iscariot and a Judas the Galilean. And Josephus tells us that Judas the Galilean had two sons, who led his movement after his death – and they too were called James and Simon! Strange coincidences or pointers to something more fundamental?

We shall make sense of all this eventually, but for the moment, I would argue that all this *is* beyond coincidence. I believe that here lies the reason why events surrounding the Jesus Movement have been shifted forward in time by a decade or so – to avoid the otherwise obvious identification between the movement founded by Judas the Galilean and the movement supposedly founded by *Jesus* the Galilean. Both movements were led at some point in the first half of the first century AD by characters called James and Simon. Josephus tells us that the sons of Judas with those names were killed in the forties and the traditional chronology has the Christian Simon and James still active in the fifties. My revised chronology, however, by shifting all the events back by a decade, makes identification not just possible, but extremely likely. This is not to say that Judas and *Jesus* were the same character though. The story of the *Jesus* of the Gospels has been filled out with aspects of the life of Judas, but the identity of the real Jesus is something entirely different as I shall now reveal, as we delve further into the Book of Zechariah.

The third and fourth of Zechariah's visions continue the theme of the future glory of Jerusalem and calls on all exiles to return to the city.[63] And not only Jewish exiles:

And many nations shall be joined to the Lord in that day, and shall be my people; and I will dwell in the midst of thee . . . [64]

---

63 In Chapters 2 and 3.

64 2:11.

So, the new dispensation when God sets up his kingdom on earth will embrace Gentiles as well as Jews – this is what is meant by 'universalism'. The fifth vision[65] promises that Zerubbabel will complete the Temple building; the sixth and seventh visions[66] promise a cleansing of the restored community; and the final vision[67] pictures the time of millennial peace to come. The 'universalist' promise is repeated in Chapter 8:

> Thus saith the Lord of hosts; it shall yet come to pass, that there shall come people, and the inhabitants of many cities; And the inhabitants of one city shall go to another, saying, Let us go speedily to pray before the Lord, and to seek the Lord of hosts: I will go also. Yea, many people and strong nations shall come to seek the Lord of hosts in Jerusalem, and to pray before the Lord. Thus saith the Lord of hosts; in those days it shall come to pass, that ten men shall take hold out of all languages of the nations,[68] even shall take hold of the skirt of him that is a Jew, saying, We will go with you: for we have heard that God is with you.[69]

The final lines of this passage make it clear that Zechariah here is not referring to Diaspora Jews living in other countries – it is Gentiles that he prophesies, following the example of the Jews and seeking out God in Jerusalem.

Now we can turn to Yeshua. The references to Yeshua ben Yehozedek appear in Chapters 3 to 6. Chapter 3 begins with Zechariah's fourth vision; I quote it in full here from the

---

65 In Chapter 4.
66 In Chapter 5.
67 In Chapter 6.
68 The *midrashic* source for the speaking in tongues at Pentecost?
69 8: 20-23.

King James Authorised version, with just one change – the substitution of 'Jesus' for 'Joshua' as a translation of 'Yeshua'. Please read this carefully because this crucial passage is the original source of the New Testament *Jesus*:

> And he shewed me Jesus the high priest standing before the angel of the Lord, and Satan standing at his right hand to resist him. And the Lord said unto Satan, 'The Lord rebuke thee, O Satan; even the Lord that hath chosen Jerusalem rebuke thee: is this not a brand plucked out of the fire? Now Jesus was clothed with filthy garments, and stood before the angel. And he answered and spake unto those that stood before him, saying, Take away the filthy garments from him. And unto him he said, Behold, I have caused thy iniquity to pass from thee, and I will clothe thee with change of raiment. And I said, Let them set a fair mitre [i.e. crown] upon his head. So they set a fair mitre upon his head, and clothed him with garments. And the angel of the Lord stood by. And the angel of the Lord protested unto Jesus, saying, Thus saith the Lord of hosts; if thou wilt walk in my ways, and if thou wilt keep my charge, then thou shalt also judge my house, and shalt also keep my courts, and I will give thee places to walk among these that stand by.

This passage has been in all Bibles for 2,000 years, so of course it has been noticed before. But because no one was looking for a Messianic figure before the first century AD, the passage has been interpreted as prophecy of the Christian era. But with the perspective we have gained thus far in this book we can see that this must have been the original inspiration behind the Christian movement. For the practitioner of *Midrash* in the first century AD, searching the old scriptures for indications of when God might intervene in history and bring in His Kingdom, this provided a compelling answer: this

'Jesus' had lived and died centuries before, but had been raised up by God from the burning fires of Hell and the clutches of Satan, and was now appointed by God to become judge of mankind at the End of Days. Clearly, he is not seen as the sinless Son of God at this stage – that comes later as Christian theology develops, particularly at the hands of Paul. But his sins have been forgiven, and he is given clean clothes and a crown.[70]

In the Gospels, John the Baptist is portrayed as the precursor to *Jesus* Christ, but a careful reading suggests that it is the coming of Jesus ben Yehozedek that John the Baptist preaches as imminent. The terminology 'Second Coming' is a later concept of the Christian church; John the Baptist in fact speaks nowhere in the Gospels of a *second* coming, but like Zechariah, envisages a (*first* implied) coming intervention by God to establish his Kingdom on Earth, and at that time, Jesus (ben Yehozedek) will come as judge of mankind. The Greek word used throughout the New Testament for Christ's second coming is *parousia*, but the word means merely 'arrival' – there is no implication in the word of 'second'. Here is what the Baptist says in Matthew (Luke has a similar account):

> Repent ye: for the Kingdom of heaven is at hand . . . I indeed baptize you with water unto repentance; but he that cometh after me is mightier than I; he shall baptize you with the Holy Ghost, and with fire: Whose fan is in his hand, and he will thoroughly purge his floor, and gather his wheat into the garner; but he will burn up the chaff with unquenchable fire.[71]

---

70 Clean, white clothes are a recurring theme in early Christian literature, applied to Jesus, James and others. There also seems to have been a Jewish tradition that Yeshua was in the fiery furnace with Daniel (there is no evidence of this from the Book of Daniel itself) and this is the reason for the new clothes; I suspect that this tradition arose to explain the reference to dirty clothes in Zechariah.

71 3:2-12.

Does this sound at all like the *Jesus* of the Gospel stories? Jesus is coming, not as a humble, itinerant, human preacher, but as a resurrected and anointed judge of mankind, who at the End of Days will sort out the human wheat from the chaff and consign them to heaven and hell, respectively. In the Book of Acts, the baptism with the Holy Ghost and fire takes place *after Jesus*' resurrection, not *before*. We read passages like this with the blinkers of two millennia of Christian theology. Remove the blinkers and it is immediately evident that John was not a precursor to an earthly Jesus – he was the leading figure of his day, prophesying the coming Kingdom of God, heralded by the return of Jesus ben Yehozedek as the judge of mankind, appointed to the role by God hundreds of years before.

John the Baptist's mission is actually prophesied (at least, to the *Midrash* mentality) in Zechariah:

> In that day there shall be a fountain opened to the house of David and to the inhabitants of Jerusalem for sin and uncleanness.[72]

The word translated here as fountain ('mikveh') in fact means something more like cistern or pool where water is gathered, and refers to the water cisterns created in Jerusalem, and in places like Qumran, for ritual cleansing. So, baptism by water is one of the ways in which one would be able to spot the coming of the Last Days – or to put it another way, by actively promoting baptism, one was performing 'works' that might bring on the Last Days. Of course, John baptized in the river Jordan. This too seems to be presaged in Zechariah:

---

[72] Zechariah 13:1.

And it shall be in that day, that living waters shall go out from Jerusalem; half of them toward the former sea; and half of them toward the hinder sea: in summer and in winter shall it be.[73]

John the Baptist has always been an enigmatic figure in the Christian story. In the Gospels he introduces Jesus and then obligingly disappears from the scene. But he was clearly an important figure in the first half of the first century AD. Unlike any other character that appears in the New Testament, John appears in Josephus quite unequivocally, and in a manner that all scholars seem agreed is authentic. That appearance as we have seen suggests strongly that he was such a key figure that the outcome of a battle could be ascribed to his importance. Jewish Talmudic tradition remembers him as a Pharisee rabbi called Hanan the Hidden[74] who, like *Jesus,* prayed to God as 'Abba' or 'Father'. The Gospels – particularly John – have accounts of John the Baptist as a religious leader in his own right with a powerful following in Judæa, and later the Apostle Paul finds followers of John in Ephesus.[75] Theologians have argued through the ages about the precise relationship between the Baptist and Jesus, and between their respective movements. In my view, it is inescapable that John the Baptist was identical with Judas the Galilean's associate, Sadduc, and that together they founded

---

[73] 14:8. One might also wonder whether this prophecy of 'living waters' flowing out from Jerusalem was the real reason for the Jewish protests against Pilate's new aqueduct. There is evidence that the use of temple funds (Corban) for this kind of public works was permitted under Jewish law, in which case it is hard to see any other reason except perhaps that by bringing water into the holy city, Pilate was, in effect, making God's intervention less likely.

[74] The etymology seems to be Hanan = Johanan = John. The 'Hidden' reference may refer to his career in hiding across the Jordan after the death of Judas the Galilean – see text that follows.

[75] Acts 19:3-4.

the Jesus Movement, the key belief of which was that Jesus (the son of Yehozedek) would imminently return to usher in the Kingdom of God. The Gospel writers thus had a real problem with how to portray him. He was sufficiently famous (as testified by Josephus) for them not to be able to ignore him. But his real existence left little room for their *Jesus* – so they portrayed him as 'the Precursor' and then removed him from the stage.

Is this Jesus, described in Zechariah, then to be regarded as the Messiah, and is this the philosophy that Judas the Galilean taught? Was there no human Messiah figure living in the early decades of the first century AD, and it was all an ancient myth? No, there is more to it than that. Zechariah's vision and prophecy continues:

> Hear now, O Jesus the high priest, thou, and thy fellows that sit before thee: for they are men wondered at: for behold, I will bring forth my servant the BRANCH.[76]

This strange concept of God's servant called 'Branch' appears elsewhere in the Old Testament. It is a term used for the coming Messiah, who will be descended from the Old Testament King David – effectively a branch of his lineage. The Hebrew word here is *Zemach* [the 'z' is pronounced and sometimes spelt in English 'ts']. Elsewhere, a similar concept is expressed by another word; because Ancient Hebrew was written with consonants only – the reader supplied the vowels – this word appears in Hebrew texts as N-Z-R (although written R-Z-N because Hebrew was written from right to left). This makes possible a play on words. Interpreted as 'Nazir' this word means separated and thus can mean a shoot or scion, separated from the trunk. By extension, it

---

76 3:8.

also comes to mean set apart/consecrated, and in this sense is the root of the term Nazirite that we saw earlier as a description of the Messiah, and at some stage gets confused with a place called Nazareth. But it can also be read as *Nezer* which means 'crown'. So, the Messiah is to be both consecrated and crowned. But if Jesus ben Yehozedek is the Messiah, how can the Branch also be a Messiah? What is the relationship between Jesus and the Branch? Zechariah explains thus:

> Then take silver and gold, and make crowns, and set them upon the head of Jesus [substituted as before for Joshua] the son of Josedech [i.e. ben Yehozedek], the high priest; And speak unto him, saying, Thus speaketh the Lord of hosts, saying, Behold the man whose name is The BRANCH; and he shall grow up out of his place, and he shall build the temple of the Lord: Even he [the Branch] shall build the temple of the Lord; and he shall bear the glory and he shall rule upon his throne; and he [Jesus] shall be a priest upon his throne; and the counsel of peace shall be between them both[77].

And so, at last we get to the heart of the matter. There are **two** Messiahs, as Zechariah is shown in his fifth vision:

> And the angel . . . said unto me, What seest thou? And I said . . . a candlestick all of gold, with a bowl upon the top of it, and his seven lamps thereon, and seven pipes to the seven lamps . . . And two olive trees by it . . . And I answered again, and said unto him, What be these two olive branches which through the two golden pipes empty the golden oil out of themselves? And he answered me and said . . . These are

---

77 6:11-13.

the two anointed ones, that stand by the Lord of the whole earth[78].

The first anointed Messiah is to be Jesus ben Yehozedek, who has been raised from the dead and will come back at the End of Days to judge all mankind; and the second will be a descendant of King David, who will rule the world in the new dispensation. As we have seen, the idea of twin Messiahs was current in the first century AD and features strongly in the sect behind some of the Dead Sea Scrolls. The concept is of a King-Messiah from the house of David, and a Priest-Messiah from the house of Zadok. Both become rolled into one in the Gospels and other early Christian literature, in the person of *Jesus* Christ; but originally, there were two – one waiting in heaven and the other expected to be born imminently. It had to be this way: the Priest-Messiah had to have already died and been resurrected and cleansed in order to act as a heavenly judge; but the King-Messiah needed to be a living person in order to take the throne in Jerusalem and rule the real world in real time. The question then remained, as we saw earlier: does one wait in passive faith for the apocalyptic return of the Priest-Messiah – Jesus – or does one bring about His return by crowning the King-Messiah as King of the Jews and by resisting earthly authority, bring about the End of Days? Zechariah gives no answers, and the debate between faith and works that results remains a divisive one in Christianity to this day.

But Zechariah does give some clues for the diligent pursuer of *Midrash*, as to where and when he could expect God finally to intervene in human affairs. Before the Kingdom of God can be established on Earth, God will destroy His

---

[78] Chapter 4

enemies; much of Zechariah is concerned with graphic descriptions of this apocalypse:

> Then shall the Lord go forth, and fight against those nations, as when he fought in the day of battle. And his feet shall stand in that day upon the mount of Olives . . .[79]

This explains what *Jesus* was doing, with his armed followers, on the Mount of Olives on the night he was arrested. But why did he think the time had come? Again, Zechariah is explicit:

> And it shall be, that whoso will not come up of all the families of the earth unto Jerusalem to worship the King, the Lord of hosts, even upon them shall be no rain. And if the family of Egypt go not up, and come not, that have no rain; there shall be the plague, wherewith the Lord will smite the heathen . . .[80]

Based on this text, which comes right at the end of Zechariah, the Jesus movement would have been looking for signs of famine and plague in Egypt. There were in fact two such famines in the first half of the first century AD. One took place across the Middle East in the mid-forties; it was too late for the Jesus narrative, whatever chronology you adopt, but would, as we shall see, influence events in the early Church at that time. But the famine that I believe was key to the Christian story, took place in Egypt only, and as we have already seen from Josephus' account, it occurred in AD 19 when the Roman general Germanicus visited Egypt and opened the grain stores – the very year that I have argued

---

79 14:3-4.
80 14:17-18.

Pontius Pilate arrived in Judæa, and Judas the Galilean (not *Jesus* the Galilean) was executed. Coincidence?

The second section of the Book of Zechariah opens at Chapter 9. It is here that we find the prophecy mentioned earlier in connection with the death of *Jesus* – the King-Messiah will enter Jerusalem 'riding upon an ass'.[81] He will establish peace and will rule the whole earth, not just the Jews (note the universalism again), and will raise the dead from the 'pit':

> . . . he shall speak peace unto the heathen: and his dominion shall be from sea even to sea, and from the river even to the ends of the earth. And for thee also, by the blood of thy covenant I have sent forth thy prisoners out of the pit where there is no water.[82]

A few chapters later, Zechariah renews his prophecy about the Priest-Messiah:

> . . . [the inhabitants of Jerusalem] shall look upon him whom they have pierced, and they shall mourn for him, as one mourneth for his only son . . . And one shall say unto him, What are these wounds in thine hands?[83]

These references to piercings and wounds would have referred any first-century exponent of *Midrash* straight back to Psalm 22 that we reviewed earlier as containing the essence of the Gospel crucifixion story. It would also have recalled the 'suffering servant' passages from the Book of

---

81 9:9.
82 9:10-11.
83 12:10 & 13:6.

Isaiah, Chapter 53, which has always been regarded by Christians as an 'amazing' prophecy of Jesus Christ, but which now, I hope, can be seen as yet another text, wrenched out of its historic context, to build upon these themes touched on in Zechariah:

> He is despised and rejected of men; a man of sorrows, and acquainted with grief: and we hid as it were our faces from him; he was despised and we esteemed him not. Surely he hath borne our griefs, and carried our sorrows: yet we did esteem him stricken, smitten of God and afflicted. But he was wounded for our transgressions, he was bruised for our iniquities: the chastisement of our peace was upon him: and with his stripes we are healed. And we like sheep have gone astray; we have turned every one to his own way; and the Lord hath laid on him the iniquity of us all. He was oppressed, and was afflicted, yet he opened not his mouth: he is brought as a lamb to the slaughter, and as a sheep before her shearers is dumb, so he openeth not his mouth. He was taken from prison and from judgment: and who shall declare his generation? For he was cut off out of the land of the living: for the transgression of my people was he stricken. And he made his grave with the wicked; and with the rich in his death; because he had done no violence, neither was any deceit in his mouth. Yet it pleased the Lord to bruise him; he hath put him to grief; when thou shalt make his soul an offering for sin, he shall see his seed, he shall prolong his days, and the pleasure of the Lord shall prosper in his hand. He shall see of the travail of his soul, and shall be satisfied: by his knowledge shall my righteous servant justify many; for he shall bear their iniquities. Therefore will I divide him a portion with the great, and he shall divide the spoil with the strong; because he hath poured out his soul unto death; and he was numbered with

the transgressors; and he bare the sin of many, and made intercession for the transgressors.[84]

This passage inspired the Gospel writers with such details as the imprisonment and trial of Jesus; his silence before Pilate; his physical abuse on the way to the cross; his crucifixion alongside robbers; and his burial in a rich man's tomb.

Furthermore, this passage makes the crucial link between the death of Jesus and sacrifice for the sins of the world. Yet this thought too can be found in Zechariah:

> For behold the stone that I have laid before Jesus; upon one stone shall be seven eyes: behold I will engrave the graving thereof, saith the Lord of hosts, and *I will remove the iniquity of that land in one day.*[85] [Author's emphasis]

The reference to 'the stone with seven eyes' is puzzling at first sight. Zechariah seems to offer some elucidation a little later when he says that 'those seven' are 'the eyes of the Lord, which run to and fro through the whole earth.'[86] One of the most important disciples of *Jesus* in the Gospels was Simon. *Jesus* gives him the nickname Peter. Later, in the Acts of the Apostles, we are told about this Simon Peter, and about someone called Cephas. 'Peter' and 'Cephas' are Greek and Aramaic respectively for 'stone'. We shall explore later whether Peter and Cephas are the same person, but here I would argue that this nickname refers to this passage in Zechariah and concerns the role of that individual in the early Christian movement. In my view this role was to manage the various Apostles sent forth by the movement to

---

84 53:3-12.
85 3:9.
86 4:10.

evangelize the world. The word Apostle just means 'messenger', and what were these people if not the 'eyes' of the movement, running 'to and fro through the whole earth' on behalf of the movement, and God?

Interestingly, the Catholic Church bases its mission on the 'keys' which *Jesus* metaphorically handed to Simon Peter:

> ... thou art Peter, and upon this rock I will build my church; ... And I will give unto thee the keys of the kingdom of heaven: and whatsoever thou shalt bind on earth shall be bound in heaven: and whatsoever thou shalt loose on earth shall be loosed in heaven.[87]

As the reader will by now have come to expect, this is *Midrash*, lifted from Isaiah:

> And the key of the house of David will I lay upon his shoulder; so he shall open, and none shall shut; and he shall shut, and none shall open. And I will fasten him as a nail in a sure place ...[88]

The parallels are obvious, but the one difference is significant: what in Isaiah was a nail, in Matthew becomes a rock. Both are images of steadfast surety, but Matthew changed nail to rock in order to echo Zechariah.

There is much confusion in the Bible between the disciples that followed Jesus and the Apostles that went forth into the world. The Bible does not tell us how many Apostles there were, but the number of disciples is traditionally taken to be twelve – the original twelve, less Judas Iscariot who betrayed Jesus and killed himself, plus his replacement, one Matthias.

---

87 Matthew 16:18-19.
88 Isaiah 22:22-23.

But the list of names varies between Gospels and many of the twelve names seem to exist merely to fill out an *a priori* schema that requires twelve disciples to correspond with the twelve tribes of Israel. In fact, there is some evidence to suggest that the early Church recognised only seven disciples. The Gospel of John lists seven disciples,[89] as do two early non-canonical Christian writers, Papias and Epiphanius. Three people appear in all three lists of disciples: Simon Peter, John and James. These are referred to by Paul as the three pillars of the movement and they are given prominence in the Gospel stories. However, all the other names from these lists seem to be synonyms for a consistent four characters: Matthew, Thomas, Andrew and Philip. In addition, there is a story in Acts, Chapter 6, of the selection of seven men 'of honest report, full of the Holy Ghost and wisdom' to minister to the Grecians in the congregation; presumably these are Gentile converts to the movement, watched over by the 'seven eyes'. There, 'the seven' are clearly distinct from 'the twelve', and one of these is called Philip. Also, in Acts 21:8 the writer speaks of 'Philip the evangelist, which was one of the seven'. The church traditionally teaches that the disciple Philip and this later Philip the evangelist in Acts are different people. I suspect they are in fact one and the same. Perhaps the seven were the Apostles originally sent out to the Gentiles – this would be most consonant with the Zechariah passage about 'seven eyes' running 'to and fro through the whole earth'. Note that Cephas does not appear in any of these lists; if he is not the same character as Simon Peter (and I shall argue later that he was not), then perhaps he was the first 'stone' that sent these seven 'eyes' into the world.

It will by now be apparent to the reader where I am going with all this. I am not suggesting for a moment that the

---

[89] John 1:35-51.

writer of this passage in Zechariah was describing a Messianic figure as understood in the New Testament. He is merely celebrating the re-establishment of a new high priesthood after the Babylonian Exile, and recognizing Jesus as a divinely appointed, authorized and endowed priestly leader to stand alongside the royal figure of Zerubbabel. But, whatever the intention, the language leaves open the possibility for later Messianic interpretation. The keen first-century Jew, searching for clues to the End Time through *Midrash*, would have asked, how did this man Jesus ben Yehozedek die? Why was he consigned to hell if he was God's divinely appointed High Priest? Why the filthy garments? Why Satan's resistance? Why and when is he to be a judge of mankind? He would have found the clue to all this in the references to 'piercing'. This would have led him to the 'suffering servant' of Isaiah, and this in turn would have provided the context in which to interpret all the other Messianic and End Times references that are scattered throughout Zechariah and re-emerge in the Gospel stories.

I believe that the movement founded by Judas the Galilean and Sadduc was in fact, the basis of the Christian church. But this is not at all the same as saying that Judas was the historical *Jesus*. Like the Qumran sect, the early Christian movement was founded on a belief, rooted in Zechariah, and fleshed out particularly in Psalm 22 and Isaiah 53, that there were to be two Messiahs. The first, the Priest-Messiah, had lived generations ago, when the Jerusalem Temple was founded. His name was Yeshua/Jesus and he was a High Priest, descended from Zadok the first High Priest. He had been raised from the dead by God and now sat in heaven, waiting for the End Time when he would come back to the earth as God's divine judge of mankind, destroying God's enemies and offering salvation to the devout. The precise time of that apocalyptic event was unknown, but it would coincide with a famine in Egypt and would commence with a great battle on the Mount of Olives. Judas believed that the time was right in AD 19 and endeavoured to instigate the End Times by crowning himself as the second, King-Messiah, and awaiting the return of Jesus as the Priest-Messiah on the Mount of Olives. The failure of Jesus to come led to the capture and execution of Judas in that year. The failure of this attempt to force God's hand led to a period in which the movement, now scattered outside Judæa, was content to evangelize among Jews and Gentiles alike. Presumably at that time it was led by the mysterious Sadduc. I have argued that Sadduc was, in fact, John the Baptist, who played the role of the last prophet, or *Tabeh*, bringing back the age of prophecy, and heralding the coming Kingdom of God. With Jesus, the true High Priest, in heaven, and a Temple priesthood corrupt and in league with both the Roman authorities and the Herodian fornicators, John also provided an appropriate priestly role, baptizing in water, as Zechariah's prophecy suggested, and announcing the coming of the true High Priest, Jesus. Sadduc, or Zadok, was thus his priestly title, inherited from his father (called Zechariah) in a lineage that traced its roots to the original Zadok.

CHAPTER 5

The Pauline Fallacy

I have asserted that to understand how a parochial, Jewish Messianic sect evolved into one of the most successful religions the world has ever known, we must not only dismantle the fallacy about *Jesus*, but also the fallacies surrounding the Apostle, Paul. The traditional version of Paul's life can be summarised as follows.

> Following the death of *Jesus*, the nascent Christian church underwent persecution from pious Jews who regarded the idea that *Jesus* was the son of God who died for our sins as sheer blasphemy. Paul was a zealous young man from Tarsus in eastern Asia Minor who, with the authority of the High Priest, led this persecution. He played a role in the death of the first Christian martyr, Stephen, and then left Jerusalem to carry his vendetta to the Christian community in Damascus. On the road there, he had visions from God that immediately converted him to Christianity. After justifiable initial scepticism, the Church accepted him as an Apostle at around the time that Peter, the leader of the Church in Jerusalem, was himself receiving visions from God that led him and the Church to a new understanding that the redeeming Gospel of Jesus was for Gentiles as well as Jews. The Church entrusted

The Pauline Fallacy

Paul to take the Gospel to the Gentiles, and this he did with various companions through the forties and fifties AD. His four great missionary journeys took him north, through Asia Minor, and then across the eastern Mediterranean and Greece, finally arriving in Rome itself. Quite early in his mission, Paul found he had to return to Jerusalem to sort out the detail of how Gentiles would be absorbed into an essentially Jewish movement – circumcision and dietary requirements were the key issues – but at the Council of Jerusalem these matters were amicably resolved, and he returned to the mission field until finally being arrested in Jerusalem and eventually being sent for trial to Rome. His fate thereafter is unknown, as is the date of his death.

This account derives largely from the Book of Acts and is wrong on virtually every important count. I shall show that it was Paul himself, not Peter, who had the visions to take the Gospel to Gentiles; that, as a direct result, he and the Jerusalem Church differed almost from the beginning and the so-called Council of Jerusalem was an exercise in papering over the cracks at best and that the supposed four missionary journeys are a fiction and, in fact, Paul's missionary career had ended by the mid-forties AD. I shall show that Acts, like the Gospels, is largely fiction, written by someone who knew only the barest of facts about Paul and, raiding Josephus for ideas, made up the rest to fit a Christian paradigm that was already forming by the time he wrote.

PAUL'S EPISTLES

I can assert all this because we have some contemporary documents that are authentic and which, properly understood, drive a horse and cart through the fictions of Acts. As noted previously, some of the Epistles of Paul, reputably sent by him to the early churches and individuals in them, spread throughout the Roman Empire, are the closest documents we have in time to the period when *Jesus* is said to have lived, and they paint a somewhat different picture. The letters all appear in the New Testament, after the four Gospels and the Acts of the Apostles; in order of printing they are:

- the letter to the church in Rome;
- two letters to the Church in Corinth, Greece;
- the letter to the Church in Galatia, an area of central Asia Minor;
- the letter to the Church at Ephesus, on the coast of Asia Minor;
- the letter to the Church at Philippi in Macedonia (northern Greece);
- the letter to the Church at Colossae in south west Asia Minor;
- two letters to the Church at Thessalonica in Macedonia;
- two letters to another Apostle called Timothy;
- a letter to Titus, a Christian co-worker in Crete;
- a letter to Philemon, a Church leader in Colossae; and finally,
- a letter to the 'Hebrews', written for a mixed audience of Jewish and Gentile Christians in either Rome or Jerusalem, it is not clear which.

There are two examples of letters written in Paul's name that have never been accepted in the New Testament canon because they seem clearly to be written by others:

- the Epistle to the Laodiceans and,
- a third letter to the Corinthians.

There is now a wide consensus among modern scholars on a core group of these letters that seem authentic – that is, almost certainly written by Paul, although they may contain later emendations and interpolations; these are Romans, 1 and 2

The Pauline Fallacy

Corinthians, Galatians, Philippians, 1 Thessalonians, and Philemon. Those that the scholarly jury is probably still out on are Ephesians and Colossians. The rest – 2 Thessalonians, 1 & 2 Timothy, and Titus – are regarded by the vast majority of scholars as *not* having been written by Paul, although variously intended by their authors to be read as such. Since the earliest times, there has been doubt about the anonymous letter to the Hebrews, and modern scholars do not believe it was written by Paul. In accordance with my policy in this book to avoid basing any of the argument on documents and texts about which there is any scholarly doubt or controversy, we shall draw only on the seven core authentic letters. Of course, a letter may not be written by Paul but still be relatively early, although, in general, fakes tend to come later than originals as a matter of common sense. Scholarly debate about precise dates continues to rage over these, as the other books of the New Testament. But all datings are relative in this area. If you accept, as the tradition teaches, that Jesus lived and died between AD 1 and AD 35, then you will date Paul's letters accordingly – perhaps the fifties and sixties AD. But of course, if you argue, as I have done in this book, that the foundation events of Christianity took place at least a decade earlier, this too has an implication for relative dating of other books. As we shall see, I think they were all written a decade earlier.

Of the seven core letters, the letter to the Romans contains Paul's most complete statement of his theology, and was therefore probably composed late, but there is no real evidence in the letter to say when, or indeed where, it was composed. We know from its content that at the time of writing Paul had never visited Rome, so the Church there must have been founded by others. However, it contains various salutations to people in Rome that Paul knew and had met, including a Christian couple called Priscilla and Aquila. These two also figure in the first of the letters to the Corinthians. They were with Paul in Ephesus, from whence he wrote to the Church in Corinth, which he had founded. We can assume, therefore, that the Corinthian letters were written before Romans. Galatians is the letter regarded by scholars as most unquestionably written by Paul himself and it contains most valuable information about the early Church, to which we shall return; but unfortunately, scholars are completely divided about when or where it was written, and even precisely to whom. The letter to Philippians was written from prison in Rome – Paul was taken there for trial towards the end of his career, so we can assume it was written after the letter to the Romans. The first letter to the Thessalonians seems to have been written from either Corinth or Athens, shortly after Paul had established the Church in Thessalonica, and is regarded by many scholars as the earliest of Paul's letters, so perhaps can be dated before Corinthians. And finally, the letter to Philemon, also written from prison in Rome, was roughly contemporary with Philippians.

We need now to see if the mysterious letter to the Galatians can throw any light on matters. Galatians is mysterious, not only because its origin is unknown, but because the information it provides about Paul's life is the real clue to the fictional nature of Acts. Many trees have been felled in the cause of reconciling the two, with little success. As ever, let us not seek out harmonization (although it may surprise us by occurring nonetheless) and given that no scholar seems in any doubt that Galatians is the most authentic of all the Epistles, let us approach it with some confidence that, properly understood, it will illuminate events. Although no original text has survived, and the earliest complete text, dating to around AD 200, is a bit fragmented, nevertheless, scholars are reasonably sure that the text we have in the Bible is close enough to what Paul originally wrote. And what he wrote was mainly about how Gentiles could convert to Christianity; whether they needed to be circumcised like Jews and obey the Mosaic

Law, or whether they were free of such rituals and obligations. Paul, by this stage at least, taught the latter. Just prior to the composition of the letter, the Galatian Church, founded originally by Paul himself, seems to have been visited by individuals preaching the former. Paul is appalled that they should be tempted by this 'other Gospel', and his letter sets out the arguments for his theology.

But as a preliminary, Paul seems to feel it necessary to explain his own biography and, in doing so, reveals a great deal about what was going on here. He introduces the letter and himself thus:

> Paul, an Apostle, (*not of men, neither by man*, but by Jesus Christ, and God the father, who raised him from the dead).[1]
> [Author's emphasis]

The point he seems to make here is that his Apostleship does not depend on any human authority but came directly from Jesus and God. As we saw earlier, Paul's version of Christianity knew nothing of a first-century individual called *Jesus*; he received direct visions from a risen Jesus, and these were the sole basis of his faith:

> I certify you, Brethren, that the Gospel which was preached of me is not after man. For I *neither received it of man, nor was I taught it*, but by the revelation of Jesus Christ.[2]
> [Author's emphasis]

In both these passages, he seems to make the same point twice (see the phrases in italics). We are used to this in the Bible because, in the Old Testament especially, this construction –

---

[1] Galatians 1:1.

[2] 1:11-12.

repeating the same information in a slightly different way – is used as a poetic rhetorical device. And so, the reader tends to just skate over these passages. But Galatians is a letter, not a piece of poetic literature, and I do not think that is what Paul is doing here. Why does he repeat himself? Is there a difference between 'of men' and 'by man', or between 'received it of man' and 'nor was I taught it'?

He is talking about where his authority comes from. In any walk of life, authority can only come in two ways: either by social consent, based on some perceived pre-eminent merit, or by some form of familial inheritance. In other words, it is the difference between the elected power of a prime minister or president, and the inherited power of a king. We shall call these 'authority by achievement' and 'authority by inheritance' respectively. I think this is the point he is making here. When he says 'of' men or man, he is referring to authority by inheritance. When he talks about authority that is 'by man' or 'taught', he is referring to authority by achievement. Paul's rejection of this latter kind of authority is made very clear: Paul is always insistent that his authority comes direct from God, and he receives it through his visions, not by his own efforts or because someone has bestowed it on him. But what about the authority by inheritance; what familial, inherited power could he be referring to? We shall come back to this point in a moment. Returning to the Epistle again, he now says how surprised he is to hear that so soon after he had established the Galatian Church it is being led astray by 'another Gospel', and that if anyone – another teacher, an angel, or even himself – should preach to them anything other than the Gospel with which he founded their Church, 'let him be accursed'. Then in verse 13, for some reason, he begins to relate his autobiography. Why does he feel he has to do this? Clearly, he wants to establish where his personal authority comes from, and to explain the relationship between himself and the teachers of this 'other Gospel'. But who were these other individuals, and by what authority did they contradict his teaching? Could their authority be that of familial inheritance?

He begins by relating what he says the Galatians already know – that he had been committed to the Jewish religion and 'zealous for the traditions of my fathers'. This had 'profited' him, presumably through advancement in the Temple hierarchy. And through this zeal, he had 'persecuted the church of God, and wasted it'.[3] We must assume that by this he means that he had persecuted the early Christian Church, and presumably because of his powerful position in the Temple, had succeeded to some degree in destroying it. This much is consonant with the story presented in Acts of the Apostles. Next, Paul refers to his conversion:

> But when it pleased God, who separated me from my mother's womb, and called me by his grace, to reveal his Son in me, that I might preach Him among the heathen; . . .[4]

He clearly believes he was predestined for salvation; that it is by God's grace – his free, unearned gift – that Paul is saved, and he was chosen by God for this before he was even born. This is clearly some form of Calvinism – the belief that God predestines those who are to be saved and those who are to be consigned to everlasting torment in Hell on no other basis than His Will. The concept can be found in the Dead Sea Scrolls, so it was clearly a current one when Paul was writing. The corollary of this belief is, of course, that no action by the individual can influence this one way or the other. It

---

3 1:13-14.

4 1:15-16.

clearly places Paul in the camp of those who would await God's intervention in faith, rather than seek to bring it about by works. What also seems implied by this passage is that Paul's great conviction – that God was calling him to preach to the Gentiles rather than to the Jews – was explicit in the original vision that Paul had at the time of his conversion. He was not converted to a Jewish sect and then thought his way through to his mission – it was clear to him right at the outset.

Immediately following his conversion experience he says:

> . . . I conferred not with flesh and blood: neither went I up to Jerusalem to them that were Apostles before me; but I went into Arabia, and returned again unto Damascus.[5]

This is a key passage and has always been controversial. First, it flatly contradicts the account given in Acts of the Apostles of Paul's conversion.[6] There, Paul is converted in a vision on the road to Damascus and, on specific direction from Jesus in visions, receives instruction in the Christian faith from a man called Ananias and other disciples in Damascus. Second, it flatly contradicts the subsequent account in Acts that says that from Damascus, Paul *did* go to Jerusalem and meet with the disciples there.[7] And third, the visit to Arabia seems a complete mystery. Where did he mean by 'Arabia'; why did he go there in particular; and how long did he stay there? Rather than attempt harmonization of these accounts, let us seek elucidation from close attention to the text itself, and if possible, from reliable external evidence.

---

5 1:16-17

6 9:1-22.

7 9:26-28.

The Pauline Fallacy

For example, what does Paul mean when he says that he 'conferred not with flesh and blood'? The standard interpretation of this passage is that having received some sort of direct revelation from God by means of visions, Paul is saying that he did not need human instruction. But there seems more to it than that. That interpretation covers authority by achievement, but not authority by inheritance. As a new convert, it is inconceivable that he would not want to talk with other 'Christians' (whatever might be meant by that word at that time); whether or not the Acts story of Ananias is true, he *must* have talked with others about his experience. What I believe he is saying here is that there are *specific* people he did not want to talk to – those he calls 'flesh and blood' and 'them that were Apostles before me' in Jerusalem. I believe that these were the same group of people – Apostles who were also 'flesh and blood'; those whose authority is by inheritance, not achievement. The phrase 'flesh and blood' often has a specific meaning; it is most often used in connection with relatives, as in 'my/your/his flesh and blood'. This would imply that the Apostles in Jerusalem were blood relatives of someone. Not of Paul presumably. And not of *Jesus* if one accepts that he never existed. But perhaps of Judas, the founder of the movement. And it was their inherited relationship that gave them their claimed authority. On the contrary, Paul is claiming that his authority is different. He has inherited nothing – either by bloodline or by instruction; his authority comes direct from his visions of Jesus.

But Paul is saying more even than this; not only does he owe these people nothing, but he is also actively avoiding them. Judas' family were leading the Jesus Movement after Judas' death, based naturally in Jerusalem, and it was them he wanted to avoid. In which case, why? Under this interpretation, the answer seems obvious – because Paul was not converted on the road to Damascus to join the activist branch of the Jesus Movement. After all, it was this movement, committed to violence, that he was persecuting. From the very beginning, his visions called him to something completely different: a version of the Jesus Movement that was at odds with theirs in some way. That version was the passivist, non-violent branch, still led at that time by John the Baptist – the Sadduc – not from Jerusalem, but in Exile, awaiting Jesus' triumphant descent from heaven. And this explains the mysterious 'other Gospel' that Paul is steering the Galatians away from. Having been converted by Paul to the idea of a universalist and pacifist vision of the imminent kingdom of God, the Galatians are now being contacted by Apostles from Jerusalem with a distinctly Jewish and parochial version of the same story. That is why Paul is intent on retelling his life story – to emphasize that his Gospel is different from the Jerusalem Gospel. That their Gospel is that of Judas, a Gospel focused on the Jews and on 'works', especially actions that will bring about God's intervention and the return of Jesus as judge of mankind. Whereas his Gospel, while also expectant of Jesus' return, is focused on the salvation of all nations and faith that God will bring this about without the need for Gentiles to be circumcised or to obey the Mosaic Law.

So, he was avoiding the church in Jerusalem. But then, why Arabia? Who or what was there? Traditional Christian commentators are at a loss to provide convincing answers to this. The most common view seems to be that Paul went to Arabia as a formal retreat from the world to pray and contemplate his destiny. But this seems to be ruled out by a later passage in Galatians: Paul refers again to Arabia in Chapter 4:

> . . . Abraham had two sons, the one by a bondmaid, the other by a freewoman. But he who was of the bondwoman was

born after the flesh; but he of the freewoman was by promise. Which things are an allegory: for these are the two covenants; the one from the mount Sinai, which gendereth to bondage, which is [H]agar. For this [H]agar is Mount Sinai in Arabia, and answereth to Jerusalem which now is, and is in bondage with her children. But Jerusalem which is above is free, which is the mother of us all. . ... Now we, brethren, as Isaac was, are the children of promise. *But as then he that was born after the flesh persecuted him that was born after the Spirit, even so it is now.* Nevertheless what saith the scripture? Cast out the bondwoman and her son: for the son of the bondwoman shall not be heir with the son of the freewoman. So then, brethren, we are not children of the bondwoman, but of the free. Stand fast therefore in the liberty wherewith Christ hath made us free, and be not entangled again with the yoke of bondage.[8] [Author's emphasis]

Paul then goes on to confirm that circumcision in particular is irrelevant under the new covenant of Jesus – faith alone is necessary. Some commentators regard this as clarification of the sojourn in Arabia; the reference to Mount Sinai indicating in their view that Paul went to Sinai – the Old Testament seat of God from which he gave Moses the Ten Commandments. In this interpretation, Paul's sojourn in Arabia becomes like the story of Jesus' retreat for forty days in the wilderness: Paul went to Arabia in solitary retreat from the world to contemplate his calling. But a careful reading of this passage suggests something else.

The passage is a retelling of the Old Testament story of Abraham, the founder of the Jewish people, whose wife Sarah was barren. God had promised Abraham that his descendants would be special, so it seemed that something

---

8 4:22-5.

had to be done to fulfil the prophecy. Sarah sought to solve the problem by giving her handmaid slave, Hagar, to Abraham as a second wife. Hagar subsequently gave birth to a son, Ishmael, who traditionally became the ancestor of the people we now know as Arabs. Sarah did eventually also have a son, Isaac, who became the ancestor of the Jews. Paul says these events, related in the Book of Genesis, are really an allegory; in other words, he submits them to his own version of the *Midrash* technique. In this interpretation, Paul manages to turn the traditional Jewish understanding on its head. Jews regarded their own lineage from Isaac as the legitimate people of God's promise; Paul argues that it is Christians who are the true inheritors of Isaac. His rationale goes like this:

Hagar = Ishmael = Arabia = Mount Sinai = Mosaic Law = Jerusalem = Bondage

Sarah = Isaac = 'Jerusalem above' = Freedom

Rather tortuous as this is, it confirms that Arabia in this passage is to be taken allegorically to refer to everything Paul stood against, so this is hardly evidence of a contemplative 'retreat' to Sinai. But the passage also reveals something else which is overlooked by many commentators. In the Genesis story Ishmael is portrayed as a violent man and he is expelled with his mother from Abraham's house for 'mocking' his brother Isaac.[9] This falls short of actual persecution but seems the only explanation for the words that I have italicized in the quotation above. Paul seems to suggest that just as Ishmael persecuted Isaac, someone is similarly persecuting Paul. That persecutor (or persecutors) is under bondage still to the

---

9 Chs.16 and 21.

Mosaic Law, and is, according to Paul's rationale, based in Jerusalem. Furthermore, that person is 'born after the flesh'. So, this passage reiterates the implication of Chapter 1: that Paul avoided Jerusalem after his conversion because he was avoiding 'flesh and blood'.

Which still leaves the question of why Paul went to Arabia. First, we must define where Arabia was in the Middle East of the early first century AD. Nowadays, of course, we think of Arabia as the peninsula bounded by the Persian Gulf to the east and the Red Sea to the west; the northern boundary of the peninsula merges with the Syrian Desert. But in the first century, the northern boundary was further north, indeed, Arabia was regarded as penetrating as far north as Damascus in Syria. In other words, one did not have to travel south from Judæa to reach Arabia; its northern extent lay to the east of Judæa, on the east bank of the Jordan River. Paul says he went to Arabia and Damascus, so clearly it was to this northern tip of Arabia, adjacent to Damascus that Paul travelled after his conversion. Indeed, one must ask why Paul was travelling to Damascus in the first place if he was originally pursuing Christian rebels, as Acts suggests. Acts states that he went there with 'letters of authority' from the Jewish High Priest, although it is far from clear what good such authority would have been to him in Damascus, which with the rest of Arabia was under the rule of King Aretas.

We know of this King Aretas from Book 18 of Josephus' *Antiquities of the Jews*[10] Here Josephus relates various events in the eastern Roman Empire that impacted in one way or another on Judæa. One such was the war in AD 36 between Aretas, the king of 'Arabia', and the Tetrarch, Herod Antipas. The cause of the war was that Antipas had been

---

10 From Verses 85 onwards.

married to Aretas' daughter but had cast her aside in order to marry Herodias, his own niece. Antipas was thoroughly defeated by Aretas in a decisive battle, and Josephus comments:

> Now, some of the Jews thought that the destruction of Herod's [Antipas'] army came from God, and that very justly, as a punishment of what he did against John, that was called the Baptist; for Herod slew him, who was a good man, and commanded the Jews to exercise virtue, both as to righteousness towards one another, and piety towards God, and so to come to baptism; for that the washing [with water] would be acceptable to him, if they made use of it, not in order to the putting away [or the remission] of some sins [only], but for the purification of the body; supposing still that the soul was thoroughly purified beforehand by righteousness. Now when [many] others came in crowds about him, for they were greatly moved [or pleased] by hearing his words, Herod, who feared lest the great influence John had over the people might put it into his power and inclination to raise a rebellion (for they seemed ready to do anything he should advise), thought it best, by putting him to death, to prevent any mischief he might cause, and not bring himself into any difficulties, by sparing a man who might make him repent of it when it should be too late. Accordingly, he was sent a prisoner, out of Herod's suspicious temper, to Macherus . . . and was there put to death.[11]

There seems no reason not to take this passage at face value as genuine. The story of John the Baptist in the New Testament is clearly a romance:[12] Salome dances before Herod and demands the Baptist's head on a plate as a reward. Josephus' version seems much more believable: Antipas' motive for exe-

---
11 18:116-119.
12 Mark 6:14-30.

cuting John is as a precaution against rebellion. Josephus does not portray John as protesting about Antipas' incestuous marriage as in the New Testament, but this seems implied.

John the Baptist carried out his baptisms in the River Jordan. The Bible is not clear on which side of the Jordan he based himself. It says he operated in the 'wilderness', but there are two wildernesses in the region – the Judæan and the Arabian, on the west and east banks of the Jordan, respectively. The Judæan wilderness is the one usually associated with *Jesus*' retreat and temptation; the Arabian one is associated with the Hagar/Ishmael story, Mount Sinai and the wanderings of the Jews after the Egyptian Exodus. The obvious assumption is that John was based in the Judæan wilderness. But the connection with King Aretas suggests, surely, that he operated in the Arabian wilderness – otherwise, why would he concern himself so closely with the Antipas/Aretas feud, and why would Jews draw the conclusion that the defeat of Antipas was due to his execution of John, rather than to any one of a dozen good reasons. John must have sided with Aretas – and this because the Arabian wilderness was his stamping ground.

John is not the only recognizable character that we know to have been operating in 'Arabia' at this time. The Ananias who, in Acts, instructs Paul after his conversion, is not only operating in Damascus if the Acts account is to be believed, but elsewhere in Arabia too, because Josephus also makes mention of him:

> About this time[13] it was that Helena, queen of Adiabene,[14] and her son Izates, changed their course of life, and embraced the Jewish customs, and this on the occasion following: – Monobazus, the King of Adiabene ... sent Izates ... to

---

13 i.e. the mid-forties AD.
14 A province of Assyria – modern day Iraq.

Abennerig, the king of Charax-Spasini . . . Izates abode in that country until his father's death . . . Now during the time Izates abode at Charax-Spasini, a certain Jewish merchant, whose name was Ananias, got among the women that belonged to the king, and taught them to worship God according to the Jewish religion. He, moreover, by their means became known to Izates; and persuaded him, in like manner, to embrace that religion; he also, at the earnest entreaty of Izates, accompanied him when he was sent for by his father to come to Adiabene; it also happened that Helena, about the same time, was instructed by a certain other Jew, and went over to them. . . . And when he perceived that his mother was highly pleased with the Jewish customs, he made haste to change, and to embrace them entirely; and as he supposed he that he could not be thoroughly a Jew unless he were circumcised, he was ready to have it done. But when his mother understood what he was about, she endeavoured to hinder him from doing it, and said that this would bring him into danger; and that as he were a king he would thereby bring himself into great odium among his subjects, when they would understand that he was so fond of rites that were to them strange and foreign; and that they would never bear to be ruled over by a Jew. And when he had related what she had said to Ananias . . . he [Ananias] said, that he might worship God without being circumcised, even though he did resolve to follow the Jewish law entirely; which worship of God was of a superior nature to circumcision. . . . But afterwards . . . a certain other Jew that came out of Galilee, whose name was Eleazar . . . persuaded him to do the thing; for . . . he said to him, '. . . if thou hast not yet read the law [of Moses] about circumcision, and does not know how great impiety thou art guilty of by neglecting it, read it now.'[15]

---

[15] 20:1-4.

The Pauline Fallacy

One can only sympathize with poor Izates, getting all this conflicting advice. In the end, he has a surgeon perform the operation; Ananias and his mother conspire to keep it a secret, and all is well. Whether the 'certain other Jew' that converted Helena and the 'certain other Jew' called Eleazar from Galilee are supposed to be the same person is not clear.[16] Ananias on the other hand seems to be the main instructor of Izates and Helena and can probably be identified with the Ananias of Acts who instructs Paul. The debate between Eleazar and Ananias directly reflects the debate we are seeing unfold in Galatians between two rival branches of the Jesus Movement – one that regards outward 'work' as important, for Jew and Gentile alike, and one that regards 'faith' as the supreme requirement. Josephus describes all this in terms of the Jewish religion, rather than the Jesus Movement, which, we have seen, he hardly mentions if at all. But if my interpretation is correct, this is evidence of the degree to which Christianity in these early days was still regarded as an integral part of normative Judaism.

In fact, I wonder whether John the Baptist and Ananias might even be the same person. Perhaps the original story was that someone called Sadduc or Zadok was operating in Damascus and Adiabene. And perhaps, because this was known to be a name for High Priests, a later Greek writer decided it must mean the most powerful Temple High Priest in this period – the head of the dynasty that dominated temple proceedings throughout the first half of the first century – Ananias. But, the Zadok here was the High Priest of the Jesus Movement, conducting his own rituals on the Arabian bank of the Jordan: John the Baptist. Perhaps I go too

---

16 'Eleazar' is the same name as 'Lazarus' who, of course, was raised from the dead by *Jesus* in the Gospels. It was a common name at the time so probably this is a coincidence.

far. What I do want to argue, however, is that after the death of Judas in AD 19, there was a split in the Jesus Movement. Sadduc/Zadok/John the Baptist, the co-founder with Judas of the original Jesus Movement, fled over the Jordan and for many years to come operated from there, converting both Jews and Gentiles to the new sect, and baptizing them in the Jordan. The family of Judas remained in Jerusalem, still awaiting the return of Jesus, but now looking to another member of the family, descended from King David, to become the King-Messiah. The difference between the two factions was simply, as we have identified already, whether to engage in revolutionary activity to bring about the Kingdom of God, or whether to wait patiently for God to make His move. Still one movement – but two branches. And this coincides perfectly with what seems to have been the situation with John the Baptist. Christians and scholars alike have always puzzled why, if the Gospel stories are to be believed, and John recognized *Jesus* on sight as the Son of God, he did not immediately abandon his own mission and follow *Jesus*. We know, in fact, that the Gospels are wrong. John's sect continued throughout the period; indeed, Paul refers to it as clearly part of the Jesus Movement, yet in some way separate. And we know that there were followers of the Baptist (known as Mandaeans) well into the centuries following.

So, at last we can answer the question: why did Paul go to Arabia? To see John the Baptist. Now we must turn back to those he was so anxious to avoid in Jerusalem. We know a little about the family of Judas the Galilean – the 'flesh and blood' that led the revolutionary sect of the Jesus Movement from Jerusalem. We know most about him and his Fourth Philosophy from Josephus, as we have seen. But he is also mentioned in the Book of Acts. It will be remembered that according to Josephus, Judas began his campaign in AD 6 at the time of the Quirinius Census, and Acts bears this out. The writer of Acts has Gamaliel, a member of the Sanhedrin, describe Judas as an example of a failed Messianic leader.[17] There are some real problems of chronology about this reference, which we shall examine in detail later, but the fact that Judas appears at all in the Bible seems remarkable given the argument I am developing in this book. Although we are not told by Josephus or anyone else exactly when Judas himself died, my own view is that he was executed for sedition in AD 19 or thereabouts. Josephus also tells us that his crusade was continued by his two sons, who were in their turn caught and executed by the procurator Tiberius Julius Alexander in about AD 46. But this was not the end of the family's Messianic ambition. Josephus also reports that Menahem, one of the early leaders of the Jewish Revolt in AD 66, was Judas' 'son'. This seems unlikely, but Menahem may well have been Judas' grandson. Also, Menahem's cousin, Eleazar ben Ya'ir, became a leader of the last defenders against the Roman Empire at the fortress of Masada, where he and all his compatriots were slaughtered down to the last man. We shall meet Judas' descendants in Volume III, when we come on to examine Revelation and the characters that populate its visions and judgements.

Church history, both within and without the Bible, records that a 'Christian' church existed in Jerusalem from the beginning. It has always been a puzzle how exactly this church related to the one in Rome and whether the lineage of popes should be traced back through Rome to Jerusalem, or whether the Jerusalem Church was from the beginning only a Bishopric under Roman Church authority. In particular, we know with some certainty that someone called James was

---

17 Acts 5:37.

the first leader of the Jerusalem Church, and it is a puzzle exactly how this fact sits alongside the Catholic Church's insistence that someone called Simon Peter was the first Pope – that is, the first leader of the Christian Church – and indeed, was given this role by none other than *Jesus* himself during his earthly ministry. The names of Judas' two sons are extremely resonant in this regard. They too were called James and Simon, the same names as the two most important leaders of the early Christian Church. If not for the ten-year time-slip that we have identified, surely scholars would have made the connection between the Movements of Judas and *Jesus* long ago, and recognized that the two James and Simons are almost certainly the same: Occam's Razor should at least have alerted them to the possibility. The answers to all these puzzles can all be found in Paul's Epistle to the Galatians when read correctly.

Paul says that after his visit to Arabia, he returned to Damascus:

> Then, after three years I went up to Jerusalem to see Cephas,[18] and abode with him fifteen days. But other of the Apostles saw I none, save James the Lord's brother.[19]

This 'James the Lord's brother' is clearly the leader of the Jerusalem Church, as confirmed by other early sources. We encountered him before, in our analysis of Josephus' account of the death of another James – the brother of Jesus ben Damneus. As noted then, the existence of a James who seems to be *Jesus*' brother has been the dam holding back many scholars from a final acceptance that there was no historical

---

18 Some manuscripts have 'Peter', but I believe Cephas is correct, for reasons I give below.

19 1:18-9.

The Pauline Fallacy

Jesus. Some have argued that 'brother' here just means the word in the same sense that many Christians, and especially those in monasteries, have over the centuries referred to themselves as 'brothers'.[20] And indeed, Paul sometimes uses the term in that sense. I find this argument plausible but unlikely; the reference seems too particular. In fact, the Gospels have various other references to *Jesus* having brothers, and we are even given their names – James, Simon, Jude and Joses. If all early Christians were just 'brothers', why are these four in particular singled out for mention? It does seem inescapable that there was a tradition from the beginning of a group of four 'brothers of the Lord'. A passage from 1 Corinthians that seems authentic reinforces the suspicion that we are dealing with real familial relationships here:

> Have we not power to lead about a sister, a wife, as well as other Apostles, and as the brethren of the Lord, and Cephas?[21]

This seems to indicate that for Paul, the brethren of the Lord were distinct from the other Apostles, and indeed, that James was not the only one. Must we therefore conclude after all that there was a *Jesus* and that he had brothers? I do not think so.

The idea that *Jesus* had a family usually expresses itself in two forms. The first is that explored by the authors of *The Holy Blood and the Holy Grail*, which emerged more recently in the phenomenal success of Dan Brown's *The Da Vinci Code*. In this fantasy, *Jesus* and Mary Magdalene were married, had children, and their descendants survive to this

---

20 And as I show in Volume I, the brotherly relationship between Moses and Aaron may likewise not have been familial.

21 1 Cor. 9:5.

day. I have no doubt that these books, and others like them, trace a real myth that has developed through the last two millennia, and that people throughout that time have become convinced of its reality. But since in my view *Jesus* was not a real first-century character, the story is just that – a fiction made possible by the very intriguing hints in the Bible that we are here exploring. The second form of the idea has more substance and as we have seen, is specifically endorsed by certain New Testament texts – that *Jesus* had four brothers called James, Jude, Simon and Joses. Clearly, if Jesus himself did not live in the first century, they could not be *his* brothers, but my contention will be that they could be brothers of each other and still call themselves 'brothers of the Lord' because of their belief in the *Lord Jesus* and their connection with the Lord Judas.

A word of caution here. We have noted that the Gospels were all written comparatively late. Their authors had no first-hand knowledge of the characters or the events they describe. The Gospel narratives can only be trusted to indicate what people *believed* to be the case a century later. As a result, the Gospels and Acts are full of characters with the same or similar names as each other, many or even most of whom seem to be mere ciphers with little to substantiate their reality or otherwise. We have already encountered this in the case of the twelve disciples called by Jesus to follow him. The figure twelve seems to exist in order to fulfil some symbolic reference to the twelve tribes of Israel from the Old Testament; the different Gospels ascribe different names to many of them; and about half of them seem to have no real historical existence at all, except to make up the list. We have noted the same thing happening with the three people called Mary, to the extent that we even at one point have a Mary, sister of another Mary. There are two Jameses (the Great and the Less), three Ananiases, three Simons (Peter, Cephas and

The Pauline Fallacy

Magus) and so on.[22] What we are dealing with is vague stories, tales, memories and verbal echoes of a group of characters from the early first century finding their way into romances written a hundred years later. Each Gospel writer shoehorns the names into his narrative in different ways, often self-conflicting because, at the end of the day, he has no more idea of their true existence or otherwise, than ourselves.

The scholar who has done most to try to unravel all this (what he calls the 'name game') is Robert Eisenman in his monumental book about James. We are in his debt for the way he has unpicked all the overlaps, inconsistencies and parallels, and most of the conclusions he draws seem inescapably correct. But he conducts his exhaustive analysis within a paradigm of an acceptance that the James of Josephus' narrative was indeed the brother of *Jesus* and that, therefore, there has to have been a historical character called *Jesus*. Having removed that barrier in this book, we are now free to interpret these characters within a different framework: that there was indeed a group of 'flesh and blood' brothers who led the Jesus Movement, all related to each other, but they were not blood relatives of a character called *Jesus*. They were 'brothers of the Lord' only in the sense that they were brothers committed to the work of the two Messianic Lords – Jesus and Judas. We have identified James as a historical figure. He has come down to us in Church tradition as James the Great. He led the Jerusalem Church in its early days, following the death of its first leader. We know the first leader was not someone called *Jesus*; it was someone who parallels him as he is portrayed in the Gospels – Judas the Galilean. Surely then, it is not a great leap of the imagination to see the 'brother of the Lord' who is listed as 'Jude', as being in fact, 'Judas the Galilean'.

---

22 Simon Magus will feature prominently in Volume III.

'Judas' is associated in various New Testament texts with the names Thomas and Didymus, both of which mean 'twin', and there also appears another character called 'Judas of James'. Eisenman suggests that Jude/Judas and James were twins – hence the way in which James gets singled out so often as a 'brother of the Lord'; the other twin 'brother' was Judas the Galilean. Judas led the Jesus Movement until his death in AD 19, when his brother James the Great took over. Eisenman may indeed be correct, but there is perhaps an alternative explanation for these twin references. Many commentators have suggested that Judas is the twin of Jesus, and some have regarded this as a rational explanation for the resurrection of Jesus – that whoever was crucified, it was his twin that was responsible for the appearances of a resurrected Jesus. Given the argument of this book, this can be ruled out. But if the Jesus Movement believed in 'twin' Messiahs, perhaps in a sense Judas the Galilean *was* the 'twin' of Zechariah's Jesus – the anointed King and Priest respectively of the coming Kingdom of God.

However, unravelling the name game gets even more complicated from this point because there were, apparently, *two* people called James in the early Church and *two* people called Simon. Occam's Razor would suggest that these are multiplied entities. But for once, I think this would lead us into error. And the reason I think it is legitimate in this instance to ignore the warnings of Occam's Razor, is that I think we are dealing here with two generations of the same family. The first James we have just identified – James the Great, twin brother of Judas the Galilean. The second was the man that the Church remembers as James the Less. In my view, James the Less was actually Judas' son and therefore the brother of Judas' other son, Simon. The first Simon is the 'Simon known as Cephas', one of the first generation of church leaders alongside Judas the Galilean and James the

Great. The second Simon is 'Simon known as Peter' – the son of Judas the Galilean, and brother of James the Less. We shall come back to all this presently, but for the moment let us put this complication to one side and stay with the task of unravelling the identities of the four 'brothers of the Lord'. We now know the first two – Judas the Galilean and James the Great. Who then were the remaining two of the four 'brothers'?

Paul's Epistle to the Galatians, in this as in so much else, provides the clue to identifying them all. Paul refers there to *three* 'pillars' of the Church: 'James, Cephas and John'. I believe this identifies the original *four* founders of the Jesus Movement: Judas the Galilean himself (now dead, so there are only three pillars left at the time Galatians refers to); James the Great, his 'flesh and blood' brother; Cephas, whose real name was Simon; and someone called John. The Gospels of course do describe a Galilean disciple called John, but he does not figure much in Acts and outside the Gospels. He is one of those shadowy figures that seem to have little if any real substance. He seems too lightweight a figure to be one of the founding pillars of the Church. But there is of course another John who is a heavyweight, who was there from the beginning, and who is strongly attested to in and out of the Bible – John the Baptist. In my view, it is inescapable that the John who was a pillar was actually John the Baptist, and he appears partially obscured in the Gospel list of 'brothers' as Joses.[23] The disciple John of the Gospels in my view is a write-in for the Baptist, either from confusion long after the event, or deliberate obfuscation about the relationship between John the Baptist and the Jesus Movement.

---

23 The more alert among my readers may object at this point that surely the Council of Jerusalem, that features the three pillars, took place after the Baptist's death. I would ask them to wait a little because I shall presently show that the Council took place a lot earlier than usually thought – like everything else, it needs to be shifted back by a decade or so!

These four – Judas (the Galilean), James (the Great), Simon (known as Cephas) and John (the Baptist) are the four 'carpenters' or 'smiths' from Zechariah, prophesied to drive the Roman invader from Judæa. But, you may say, these four may have been the pillars but only two of them – Judas the Galilean and James the Great – were (twin) brothers; surely Cephas and John the Baptist were not also brothers?

Indeed not. But there *were* two other brothers – the two sons of Judas the Galilean – Simon and James the Less. We parked this a couple of paragraphs ago, but now we can unravel that too. James the Less is straightforward enough. He was one of Judas's sons but as his nickname ('Less') suggests, was too young at the time of Judas's death to succeed his father, so his uncle, James the Great stood in for him. The solution to the two Simons is more complex. It will be recalled that the first Simon was called Cephas and the second was called Peter. Those who regard them as the same character argue thus: Cephas is from the Aramaic word for stone and Peter from the Latin, also for stone. Theologians however seem equally divided over the issue of whether they were the same person or different. I think the clue is in the translation. There seems real evidence to suggest that in their respective original languages, the two words are slightly different. Cephas seems to have meant more precisely 'rock' and Peter meant 'pebble'. I have already suggested that these characters were from two generations, and these translations clinch the argument. I would argue that Simon Cephas was the elder of the two, the associate of Judas the Galilean; and Simon Peter was Judas' other son, brother to James the Less. Both were really called Simon, but the two nicknames distinguished them: rock and pebble – a chip off the old block!

So, to recap our findings thus far: the original founders of the Jesus Movement were the brothers Judas the Galilean and James the Great, plus Simon Cephas and John the

Baptist. Probably all came from Galilee, and if the Gospels are to be believed, John at least was possibly the cousin of James and Judas. Judas was to be the King-Messiah, and John the last prophet and non-Temple Zadok until Jesus returned. On Judas' death in AD 19, John crossed the Jordan and there preached the coming of Jesus to judge the world – hence the emphasis he placed on repentance and baptism as a symbolic act of cleansing from sin. There he waited for God to make the first move. But Judas's 'flesh and blood' – his brother James the Great and *his* two sons Simon Peter and James the Less, plus Simon Cephas – stayed in Jerusalem, intent still on political action to place one of them on the King-Messiah throne. All this is vital to hold in mind as we now return to the subject of Paul and his relationship with the *Jesus*/Judas family. As we have seen, immediately after his 'conversion', Paul deliberately avoided them. But as time passed and as his Gentile-orientated version of Christianity began to catch on with God-fearers north of Palestine, some sort of confrontation became inevitable. Today we call this the Council of Jerusalem. As we are about to see, this indeed took place in Jerusalem, but almost everything else we thought we knew about this Council will turn out to be wrong.

The separation of the two generations of Jameses and Simons is key if we are to understand what comes next in Paul's narration of his life story in Galatians. So far, we have learnt that after the death of Judas, Paul was converted, avoided meeting with Judas's family in Jerusalem, but visited John the Baptist in Arabia and spent the next three years in Damascus.[24] Then he went to Jerusalem again.[25] It was presumably there, in the discussions with Cephas, over fifteen

---

24 1:17.
25 1:18.

days, that Paul agreed his missionary calling, because it is then that he set off for Syria and Cilicia, to the north of Judæa.[26] He says that he did this for eleven years, during which time he never returned to Jerusalem, although word of his missionary success got back there 'and they glorified God in me'.[27] However, at the end of that period, differences arose over what to do about Gentile converts. Two issues in particular sparked the controversy. First, diet. It will be recalled that the Mosaic Covenant required much of Jews by the way of dietary regulation. Gentiles on the other hand were governed only by the Noahic Covenant not to eat flesh cut from a living animal. So, when Jewish and Gentile Christians sat down to eat together, which rules applied? Second, circumcision. This was the dilemma that Izates faced. Did Gentile converts have to be circumcised – a not particularly pleasant self-mutilation in male adulthood – or were they as Gentiles excused this, and indeed, all requirements of the Mosaic Covenant and Law?

The Council of Jerusalem was called in order to determine these matters, and it is described in both the Book of Acts, which makes much of it, and in Galatians where Paul exhibits some anger over the whole affair. In short, the account in Galatians does not seem to match with that in Acts. In Galatians, Paul seems to be saying that after the Council was supposed to have settled differences between Paul and his Gentile converts and the Jewish Church based in Jerusalem, James the Great went back on his word and began to persecute Paul for erroneous teaching. Acts, on the other hand, seems to say that the Council ended in harmony, and all thereafter was sweetness and light. The puzzle is solved when one understands that the account in Galatians is not chronological. To understand this,

---

26 1:21.

27 1:24.

we need to look very carefully at Paul's actual words. Here is the Galatians account; the sectional divisions are mine:

> **Section 1** Then fourteen years after I went up again to Jerusalem with Barnabas, and took Titus with me also. And I went up by revelation, and communicated unto them that Gospel which I preach among the Gentiles, but privately to them which were of reputation, lest by any means I should run, or had run, in vain. But neither Titus, who was with me, being a Greek, was compelled to be circumcised: And that because of false brethren unawares brought in, who came in privily to spy out our liberty which we have in Christ Jesus, that they might bring us into bondage; To whom we gave place by subjection, no, not for an hour; that the truth of the Gospel might continue with you. But of these that seemed to be somewhat, (whatsoever they were, it maketh no matter to me: God accepteth no man's person:) for they who seemed to be somewhat in conference added nothing to me; But contrariwise, when they saw the Gospel of the uncircumcision was committed unto me, as the Gospel of the circumcision was unto Peter; (For he that wrought effectually in Peter to the Apostleship of the circumcision, the same was mighty in me toward the Gentiles;)
>
> **Section 2** And when James, Cephas, and John, who seemed to be pillars, perceived the grace that was given unto me, they gave to me and Barnabas the right hands of fellowship; that we should go unto the heathen, and they unto the circumcision. And they would that we should remember the poor; the same which I also was forward to do.
>
> **Section 3** But when Peter was come to Antioch, I withstood him to the face because he was to be blamed. For before that

certain came from James, he did eat with the Gentiles; but when they were come, he withdrew and separated himself, fearing them which were of the circumcision. And the other Jews dissembled likewise with him; insomuch that Barnabas also was carried away with their dissimulation[28].

These three sections, because they follow one another, have always been understood as describing events in the order in which they are written. It is this that creates the conflict with the accounts in Acts. A careful reading of the text reveals however that **the events described did not take place in the order in which they are described.** Sections 2 and 3 preceded Section 1 in time. Or – to make the point again – the events which Paul describes in Section 1 took place some years after the events which he describes in Sections 2 and 3. In other words, **Paul here is looking back in time and describing what *caused* the current events.** This is crucial but confusing so let me paraphrase Paul's meaning under the two different interpretations of these passages.

On the traditional reading, the logic of Paul's account runs like this:

> *Fourteen years after my conversion, I went to Jerusalem for a Council about Gentile converts. At that Council the three pillars – James, Cephas and John – agreed to my calling to preach to the Gentiles. They asked me to remember the poor. However, some time later, James changed his mind and when Peter was with me in Antioch, eating according to the Noahic Law, James sent representatives to stop him, which was clearly reneging on what we agreed at Jerusalem.*

---

[28] Galatians 2:1-13.

On this basis, Galatians and Acts disagree. Acts says that the Council ended in harmony; Paul says James changed his mind. The assumption, therefore, by many modern readers is that Paul and the Jerusalem Church decisively split when James reneged on his original decision and the Acts account of subsequent cooperation is a lie. Does any of this sound likely? I do not believe there *was* an outright split at Jerusalem or even soon after, because I believe the account should be read differently:

> *Fourteen years after my conversion I went to Jerusalem for a Council about Gentile converts. At that Council the Jerusalem leaders ('these that seemed to be somewhat') grudgingly accepted that I would go to the Gentiles while they to the Jews because they recognised that I had been given the authority to do so by the original three 'pillars' when I met with them years before. The only reason we had to have the Council in the first place was because James the Less was giving us a hard time about table fellowship between Jews and Gentiles.*

And importantly, there is clear evidence from Acts that this interpretation is correct. In Acts 15:1, the narrator describes how 'certain' men come down 'from Judæa' to enforce the Mosaic Law. In Acts' narrative sequence, this leads directly to the Council meeting in Jerusalem. Clearly this story is the same event as the description in Section 3 of the Galatians passage above concerning Peter in Antioch and 'certain' (note the same word used) coming 'from James'. If the visit of 'certain from Judæa' in Acts precedes the Council, then the visit of 'certain from James' in Galatians, if the same event, also precedes the Council. And thus, miraculously, the two accounts can be made to concur. There was no major bust-up at the Council. In fact, the whole matter of table fellowship was not the big issue that Acts seems to suggest.

Jews and Gentiles had always eaten together – then and now. As we have seen, nothing in the Mosaic or Noahic Covenants forbade it. The only requirement was that Jews should not eat forbidden food. So, either the menu for both would be the same and allowed under Mosaic Law or Jews and Gentiles would eat different dishes at the same table – no problem either way, except for the chef! The Council clarified the matter and there was no split at that time – as by this interpretation, Acts and Galatians agree. The real split was to come later.

A word here about likely dates. The reference at the end of Section 1 of the passage above about 'remembering the poor' may be a clue. In Judaism, just as there were seven days in the week, ending with the Sabbath day, on which God was supposed to have rested from his labours in creating the world; so, there is also a 'sabbatical' cycle of seven agricultural years and in the last year of each cycle, (*shmita*), there are strict rules restricting what can be done in the fields. Chapter 25 of the Book of Leviticus promises bountiful harvests to those who observe the *shmita*, and describes its observance as a test of religious faith. During *shmita*, the land is left to lie fallow and all agricultural activity, including ploughing, planting, pruning and harvesting, is forbidden. Other cultivation techniques (such as watering, fertilizing, weeding, spraying, trimming and mowing) may be performed as a preventative measure only, not to improve the growth of trees or other plants. Inevitably, these years were associated with much privation for the subsistence poor, who had no opportunity to store food in advance for these periods. There is some difference of opinion among scholars about historical dates for sabbatical years AD. According to Benedict Zuckermann, the years AD 19/20, AD 26/27, and AD 33/34 were sabbatical years.[29]

---

29 Benedict Zuckermann, *Treatise on the Sabbatical Cycle and the Jubilee*, trans. A Löwy (New York: Hermon, 1974).

Ben Zion Wacholder argues they should all be a year later. In my view, Zuckermann's dates look right, but either way, these sabbatical years coincide with key events in the Jesus Movement. My chronology, which I will develop more below, has Judas the Galilean executed in AD 19. *Jesus* never existed, so there was no crucifixion in the early thirties. So, Paul's conversion would have taken place soon after AD 19 – say, in AD 20 – and the Council of Jerusalem (as described in Section 1) took place 14 years later in *c*. AD 34. That is why Paul remembers the fourteen-year period between his conversion and the Jerusalem meeting: it was two sabbatical year cycles. And that is why when Paul and Barnabas were commissioned in Jerusalem, they were urged to 'remember the poor'. It took place in the sabbatical year AD 33/34. Section 2 relates the events eleven years later, after Paul's first missionary journey, and just prior to the events described in Section 1.

This chronology also makes possible my identification of the disciple John with John the Baptist. Remember that the Baptist died around AD 36. If the Council of Jerusalem came after that, then the 'pillar' John involved in that Council would have had to be someone other than the Baptist. And so it has always been held: that John the disciple and one of the three pillars was someone completely different. But the re-dating of the Council to AD 34 at last makes possible the identification that otherwise would be patently obvious: that there was only ever one John; that there is no need to multiply entities in this way; and that John the disciple was no more than a fictional write-in for the historical character we know as John the Baptist. Similarly, the 'Peter' here is Simon Peter, to be distinguished from Simon Cephas mentioned as one of the pillars in Section 1. It is thus the young son of Judas who gets into trouble about eating with Jews in Antioch. The James who he fears to upset is James the Great, the brother of Judas and leader of the Jerusalem Church. As we turn now to examine the Book of Acts in more detail, we shall see how this new, earlier chronology, also explains much else that has puzzled scholars for centuries about the Acts narrative.

THE ACTS OF THE APOSTLES: THE LIFE OF PAUL

The Acts of the Apostles is a real ragbag of texts, sewn together. The first eight chapters purport to tell the story of the early Church, immediately after the death of *Jesus*. It relates the Ascension of *Jesus*; the death of Judas Iscariot and the ballot to replace him; the day of Pentecost when the Holy Spirit descends on the disciples and they speak in tongues; travels and miracles performed by Peter, John and Philip; the communal nature of the early Church; the appointment of seven 'deacons to minister to Grecians; and the stoning of Stephen the Deacon. Chapter 8 then introduces Saul, who later becomes known as Paul (the Roman equivalent of Saul, we are told), and from Chapter 9 to the end of the Book in Chapter 28, it becomes entirely the story of Paul, his conversion, his missionary travels and his arrest and deportation to Rome. It ends with Paul in Rome where he 'dwelt for two whole years'. We are not told what then happened to him – or indeed most of the other characters from earlier in the Book, who all just recede from view. The twenty chapters dealing with Paul are clearly cobbled together from at least two entirely different texts. This is patently obvious, even to the lay reader, because while most of the narration is in the third person singular (i.e. 'Paul' did this or that), there are three sections in which, for no given reason, the text suddenly switches to first person plural (i.e. 'We' did this or that). These sections are often referred to by scholars as the 'We' sections. As we shall see, this provides an especially important clue to chronology.

As already seen, there are real question marks over the

The Pauline Fallacy

historicity of Acts. If you glance back at the list on page 65 of Books that did not 'make' the New Testament canon, you will see more than a dozen other texts also called 'Acts'. As with the Gospels, which might equally have been called the *Acts of Jesus*, such works must not be confused with history as we now understand it; they have more in common with the modern historical romance novel – i.e. based on history, but with characters, actions and speech invented to bring the narration alive. The first eight chapters of Acts are very much in this genre, with their miraculous events, long set speeches in the mouths of the heroes, and moral tales. For example, there is the story of Ananias (not to be confused with the prophet or priest of the same name – or perhaps so. Who knows?) and his wife Sapphira who embezzle church funds and drop down dead on being confronted with their crime.[30] Or the story of Philip who, having baptized a eunuch in Gaza, was 'caught away' by the Spirit of the Lord so that he literally disappears and is mysteriously transported to Azotus, some twenty miles away.[31] (This is, of course, to say nothing of the likelihood of the day of Pentecost itself when flames appear over the Apostles' heads and they are able to communicate with 'every man . . . in his own language'.) The rest of Acts sounds more like history, but it must be emphasized most strongly here – it is no more history as we understand it today, than the obviously romantic earlier chapters. The reason we might be tempted to make that mistake is because the later chapters seem to be populated with characters that we know from other more reliable sources to be historic. But as we shall see below, this is a deliberate attempt by the writer to dress up his fanciful stories with historical figures, gleaned primarily from the real

---

30 Acts 5:1-11.
31 Acts 8:39-40.

histories of Josephus. The depiction of Paul in the last twenty chapters also differs factually and theologically from what can be gleaned from Galatians and the other letters written by him. Most scholars take the same view as me: that where there is conflict, Paul's letters are always to be preferred over Acts. The only parts of Acts that seem to have the ring of historical truth are the 'We' sections referred to above. It will be my purpose in this section to examine Acts critically in the light of the letters to ascertain as far as possible, what was really going on in the early church.

Scholars are divided over the different manuscripts of Acts. Generally speaking, the versions that have survived through the western Church are a little longer than those from the eastern Church. Clearly, as with the Gospels, the very existence of these various differing manuscripts is enough to undermine any claims about scriptural infallibility. However, there are no manuscript issues that concern the arguments put forward in this chapter. Of more importance is trying to fix the date when Acts was written. The church tradition is that it was composed by the same author as the Gospel of Luke, and indeed, there are signs that the two were originally composed as one narrative (whether by someone called Luke or another, it hardly matters). Many scholars assign it to the second half of the first century AD, the main evidence being that it makes no reference to the destruction of Jerusalem in AD 70, which it is argued, would seem unlikely if the Book were written afterward. However, since the Book deals exclusively with events before AD 70, and contains no prophesies of later events, this argument is hardly compelling. In fact, as we shall see, there are very clear parallels between Acts and Josephus' *Wars* and *Antiquities,* and these parallels strongly suggest to me that Acts used material from both, which would indicate that Acts was written later: probably early in the second century AD. Certainly, I will also argue that the events in Acts took place earlier than is usually supposed, so that whatever date of composition is true, it was some considerable while after the events described.

Nothing in the first eight chapters provides any clue as to when the events described there may have taken place, except of course that they are supposed to follow the death and ascension of *Jesus*. However, as we saw earlier, it is here that we find the only reference to Judas the Galilean in the Bible. In Chapter 5, the Apostles are arrested for preaching, having previously been told to desist; but they are defended in the religious high court by an unexpected intervention:

> Then stood there up one in the council, a Pharisee, named Gamaliel, a doctor of the law . . . And said unto them, Ye men of Israel, take heed to yourselves what ye intend to do as touching these men. For before these days rose up Theudas, boasting himself to be somebody . . . and all, as many as obeyed him, were scattered, and brought to nought. After this man rose up Judas of Galilee in the days of the taxing, and drew away much people after him; he also perished; and all, even as many as obeyed him, were dispersed. And now I say unto you, Refrain from these men, and let them alone; for if this counsel or this work be of men, it will come to nought; But if it be of God, ye cannot overthrow it . . .[32]

As a result of this appeal, the Apostles are just beaten, rather than being executed. Gamaliel is an important historical figure, one of the founders of rabbinical Judaism, the only form of Judaism allowed by the Romans to continue after the Jewish Wars. Based on Pharisee teachings, it is the basis of the Judaism we know today. It seems remarkable then, that this much-revered Jewish rabbi should appear here,

---

[32] 5:34-39.

defending the Apostles. He appears again in Acts 22:3 where Paul claims to have been a pupil of Gamaliel, although interestingly for our understanding of the historical accuracy of Acts, as with Paul's birthplace of Tarsus, there is no mention of Gamaliel in the Epistles. Surely one would have expected Paul to have mentioned somewhere his pupillage to such an illustrious rabbi. Nevertheless, the defence Gamaliel makes, whether the story is true or fictional, is consonant with what we know would have been the attitude of the Pharisees to the Jesus Movement. The Pharisees are usually, though not always, presented in the Gospels as the enemy of *Jesus*. But they did believe, as do Jews today, that God will one day send his Messiah to Earth. And in that case, how would they recognize Him if, every time someone claimed to be the Messiah, He was immediately put to death? The Pharisaic approach recommended here by Gamaliel was thus entirely logical: wait and see. If *Jesus*, like Judas and Theudas before him, turns out to be a false Messiah, then it will become apparent because his followers will be scattered.

The argument is entirely logical and yet the whole scene is suspect nonetheless, because we know from Josephus that while Judas was indeed active at the time of the census taxation at the start of the century, we also know from the same source that Theudas rebelled against Rome when Fadus was procurator, *some four decades later* in AD 44–6. Whatever chronology you follow, the writer of Acts has got the two rebel leaders the wrong way round. Many have cited this as an obvious mistake, proving that the Bible is capable of error, as indeed it is. But in fact, it is easy to see how the mistake was made. The source being used here by the writer of Acts is clearly Book 20 of Josephus' *Antiquities*:

> Now it came to pass, while Fadus was procurator of Judæa,

that a certain magician, whose name was Theudas, persuaded a great part of the people to take their effects with them, and follow him to the river Jordan; for he told them he was a prophet . . . However, Fadus did not permit them . . . but . . . slew many of them and . . . took Theudas alive, and cut off his head . . . Then came Tiberius Alexander as successor to Fadus; . . . Under these procurators . . . the sons of Judas of Galilee were now slain; I mean of that Judas who caused the people to revolt, when Cyrenius came to take an account of the estates of the Jews . . . The names of those sons were James and Simon . . .[33]

The writer of Acts has missed the piece about 'the sons of' Judas in this passage and has thus got Judas after Theudas. If this is correct, then it is not only powerful evidence that Acts was written after the *Antiquities* and thus at least half a century after the events it is describing, but that the writer is cobbling together his narrative from whatever sources he can lay his hands on: this is clearly not history being written from records of what happened. It is also powerful evidence that if Acts refers to people or events also described in Josephus, it results from literary plundering rather than any historical reality.

I do not intend to dwell at all on the first eight chapters of Acts. They clearly belong to the realm of myth rather than history. Acts only becomes of interest from the point of view of this book when it introduces the figure of Paul. You could easily miss it, however, because he is introduced almost inconsequentially, and at this stage in the drama, he is called Saul; we are only told later that this was the man who became known as Paul. Saul is introduced at the beginning of Chapter 8, following on the description in the preceding chapter of the stoning to death of someone called Stephen – known in

---

[33] 20:97-102.

church history as the first Christian martyr. Stephen was apparently executed in this way by the High Priest for blasphemy. The first few verses of Chapter 8 tell us that someone called Saul 'was consenting unto his death' and then seems to have led, despite being 'a young man':

> a great persecution against the church which was at Jerusalem; and they were all scattered abroad throughout the regions of Judæa and Samaria, except the Apostles.[34]

All this seems strangely out of proportion to the claimed importance of Stephen, who was not one of the Apostles himself, but, we are told, merely one of the seven new deacons appointed by the Apostles. Perhaps Stephen is a stand-in for someone more important?

We can learn little from the Acts account of the charges against Stephen. He is accused of rejecting the Mosaic Law – a Pauline doctrine – and the speech he makes before his execution is a long rehearsal of the main Old Testament narrative. Surely not necessary as a defence before a Jewish High Priest. In fact, the trial of Stephen resembles nothing so much as the Gospel descriptions of the trial of *Jesus*. I suspect that the event this stands in for is in fact the execution of Judas the Galilean. Remember, it was Jesus ben Yehozedek, not Judas, that was believed to have been 'pierced' by crucifixion, and there is no record in Josephus of how or when Judas was killed. Stoning was a Jewish form of execution, and therefore exactly what one would expect from the High Priest's court. If Judas was executed in AD 19 for in some way cleansing the Temple as we have argued, it seems most likely that it would be the collaborationist Sadducee priesthood that would have acted on it, albeit with the

---

34 8:1.

approval of the Roman authorities. Although this is just a guess, based on its apparent importance as an event, there is perhaps another clue to this real identity of Stephen as Judas, the putative King-Messiah. The Greek name Stephen means 'the crowned one', or more simply, King!

Some modern theologians and historians have emphasized what appears to be a split in the early church after the stoning of Stephen – again, something of an over-reaction one would have thought to the death of such a minor character. On the other hand, if this is a disguised account of the death of Judas, what follows next makes much more sense. Chapter 8:1 of Acts tells us that the Jerusalem Church was 'scattered abroad throughout the regions of Judæa and Samaria, *except the Apostles* [my italics]'. The theory put forward by some commentators on this passage has it that the split between those who were scattered and the Apostles that remained in Jerusalem was between those, the Apostles, who correctly understood the Pauline Gospel, and those who wanted to retreat into a more traditional Jewish interpretation, less at variance with the authorities. These latter are usually called Judaisers. The reason why these commentators feel the need to introduce this idea is because otherwise it is inexplicable that so many branches of the early church seem to have rejected the Pauline Gospel. The Judaiser theory argues that *Jesus* taught exactly what Paul taught: that *Jesus* was the son of God who would die for the sins of the world and in doing so abolish the Mosaic Law. Given this, then the Gospels and Acts have to depict the disciples as obtuse and stupid because why else would they need to *rediscover* these truths after Jesus' death. And Acts has to show Peter rediscovering them, rather than Paul, because otherwise it might look as if Paul was responsible for introducing new ideas. Then this account in Acts 8:1 is used to establish the split between the Apostles and the Judaisers, who retreat from the truth in the face of persecution.

The reality is vastly different. The original Jesus Movement was of course Jewish, and its primary aim was to free the Jews from the Roman Empire. But its context was a universalist concept, ultimately embracing Gentiles as well as Jews in the coming establishment on earth of God's Kingdom. That is why before, during and for several years after the Council of Jerusalem, there was no split between Paul and the Jerusalem Apostles. The latter had their priorities, which for the moment did not include Gentiles; but they would have had no objection to Paul bringing Gentile God-fearers into the fold of their ultimately universalist vision. Certainly, there would be and were frictions between Paul and the Jerusalem Church; their differing priorities and perspectives would guarantee this. But provided Paul kept his head down – that is, focused on the mission field beyond Palestine and preserved the appearance of devout Judaism – there need be no open quarrel or split. The Council of Jerusalem made it clear that Gentile converts need not observe the Mosaic Covenant; they were still, as ever, bound only by the Noahic Covenant. When the split did finally happen, it would be because Paul, who was still trying to keep his head down, was 'outed' by reports from the mission field from people who knew that he was preaching that *even Jews now no longer needed to observe the Mosaic Covenant*. Once this Rubicon was crossed, a split was inevitable. But that was much later, as we shall see. Right now, the split in Acts 8:1 was between the activists who stayed in Jerusalem to continue the fight and the passivists who fled to a safety from which they could continue to proselytize quietly while they awaited the Lord's coming. The activists in Jerusalem were led by the surviving members of Judas the Galilean's family; the passivists who fled over the Jordan to Arabia were led by the man who had developed the theology behind the Jesus Movement – the Sadduc or Zadok, otherwise known as John the Baptist.

Returning now to the Acts narrative: having introduced

Paul in Chapter 8, Acts reintroduces him in Chapter 9, and gives an account of his conversion to Christianity. It will be recalled that in Paul's own account of this pivotal event in his letter to the Galatians, he gives no details of the conversion experience itself, but says very clearly that he went directly to Arabia, returned to Damascus and did not visit Jerusalem until three years had passed. Acts' account gives more detail. As part of his persecution of the Church, he is travelling to Damascus with letters of authority from the Jerusalem High Priest to arrest 'disciples of the Lord' there. Nearing the end of the journey there, he has the original Damascus Experience:

> . . . and suddenly there shined round about him a light from heaven: And he fell to the earth, and heard a voice saying unto him, Saul, Saul, why persecuteth thou me? . . . I am Jesus whom thou persecutest; it is hard for thee to kick against the pricks. . . . Arise and go into the city, and it shall be told thee what thou must do.[35]

His companions see and hear nothing, and Paul finds himself blind. He is led into Damascus and there has an encounter with Ananias. Ananias lays hands on him, he receives the Holy Spirit, is baptised and then inducted into the local church.[36]

The real problem for the authenticity of the Acts account starts in the following verses. Paul begins to preach to the Jews in the Damascus synagogues, and after 'many days', they, 'the Jews', try to kill him. He is saved by being let down the city wall in a basket.[37] Paul mentions this event himself in his second letter to the Corinthians, one of the authentic 'core' letters, so we can probably trust it. But this version is

---

35 9:3-6.
36 9:7-19.
37 9:20-25.

different; it is not 'the Jews' who try to kill him, it is 'the Governor under Aretas the King'.[38] We have, of course, met Aretas before; it was he who made war with Antipas over his daughter, an event which apparently led to the death of John the Baptist in the mid-thirties AD. If Paul says it was a Governor of the city who persecuted him, rather than 'the Jews' who the writer of Acts loves to blame for most things, we can believe him. It is much more likely that a Governor should seek to eliminate a foreign troublemaker in his city associated with the Baptist, than the Jewish inhabitants who could be expected to give Paul a hearing, as Gamaliel did the Apostles. After all, Paul had joined an existing church group in Damascus; why was *he* singled out for persecution?

And as the Acts account continues, the problems with it pile up. Having been let down in a basket, Paul goes to Jerusalem. It will be recalled that in Paul's own account of this in Galatians, he did not make this trip to Jerusalem until three years had passed after his conversion.[39] In this Acts account, only 'many days' have passed and the implication seems to be that Paul goes up to Jerusalem relatively soon after his conversion.[40] It is a moot point whether 'many days' can be interpreted as 'three years'. Either way, according to Acts, Paul is welcomed by the Apostles in Jerusalem, but again he is the target of murderous plotting, this time by 'the Grecians' (whoever they may have been), and so is sent by the Apostles to Tarsus. No explanation is given for this, although later in Acts Paul is reported to have claimed that he was born there – a claim he never makes in his own writings. Tarsus was a large and influential city in the area of Asia Minor known as Cilicia. In Galatians, Paul says he went to

---

38 2 Corinthians 11:32.
39 Galatians 1:18.
40 Acts 9:23.

Cilicia after his first visit to Jerusalem, to spend fifteen days with Peter. But then Acts enters even more confusion. Leaving Paul in Tarsus,[41] Acts says that 'Then had the churches rest',[42] presumably because Paul was no longer persecuting them. Acts therefore turns its attention now back to Peter again, who it describes as passing 'throughout all quarters'[43] – consistent with his – or Cephas' – role as the Stone with Seven Eyes. According to Acts, it is now Peter who has visions and experiences that lead him to conclude that Gentiles can be admitted to the Jesus Movement as well as Jews. He returns to Jerusalem and convinces the other Apostles of this, whereupon they agree with this important innovation, and the admission of Gentiles spreads through the Church. A particular centre for this is Antioch, which Acts tells us is where the disciples of the Jesus Movement were first called Christians. The leader of the Church at Antioch, as delegated by the Apostles in Jerusalem, was one Barnabas, who then collects Paul from Tarsus and brings him to Antioch, where they stay for a year.[44]

The writer of Acts is writing pure fiction here. The truth is that although Zechariah shows universalist tendencies, and Ananias/John the Baptist in Arabia seem to have been converting Gentiles, the Church in Jerusalem under James the Great and Cephas was focused on Jews. It was Paul who focused on Gentiles, as he says at the Council of Jerusalem in the passage above from Galatians.[45] But the writer of Acts does not want to expose this, because by the time he was writing, the tradition was that Peter was the first leader of the Church, so

---

[41] Acts 9:29
[42] 9:31.
[43] 9:32.
[44] 9:32-11:26.
[45] See p. 232.

he has Peter wander around the countryside, becoming convinced of the universalist message, and he places Paul conveniently out of the way in Tarsus until Peter's universalist credentials have been established, at which point Paul can be brought back into the story again. The writer of Acts chooses to set Paul down in Tarsus, presumably because tradition places his birth there, although we have no confirmation of this outside of Acts. The reality behind all this is that, as Paul recounts in Galatians, three years after his conversion he met with Peter (and James) in Jerusalem and then spent the next eleven years in 'Syria and Cilicia', preaching the new faith.

Let us now try our hand at refining the chronology for all this. If we accept that Judas/Stephen was killed by stoning in or around AD 19, and Paul was a young man – say, 20 years old – at that time, then Paul would have been born at the turn of the first century AD and converted to the Jesus Movement in around AD 20. The point we have reached in Acts is, as argued above, when Paul has met with the Apostles in Jerusalem, three years after his conversion – say, AD 23 – and he has been in Antioch for a year – so, c. AD 24. So far so good. But a chronological problem now arises and not for the first time. The problem is that the Acts account now tells of a famine in Judæa that we know from other historical records happened in the mid-forties AD, some 20 years later.[46] Even if we accepted the traditional dating for these events,[47] then by the same arithmetic, we would only be at this point at some time around the late thirties – still too early for the famine. Something is wrong somewhere. Events are being shifted forward again, as we saw with Josephus' accounts of these years. Let us try, as we did with Josephus, to get the chronology straight. And to do so, we

---

46 This is the famine referred to by Josephus as being a cause of the unrest leading to the first Jewish War.

47 i.e. Jesus dying in the early thirties AD.

must not be afraid to allow that perhaps the writer of Acts either did not know much or, if he did, he deliberately obfuscated his account to fit a preconceived myth about these events.

Both Acts and Galatians describe a post-conversion visit of Paul to see the Apostles in Jerusalem. Acts says this took place after 'many days'; Galatians says three years. I think we must accept that these time periods are the same. So by Acts 11:26, where we left the story above, Paul is in Antioch, about four years after conversion; in my chronology, this would be about AD 24. In Galatians at this point in the story, Paul now embarks on a decade or so of missionary activity in 'Syria and Cilicia'.[48] This same mission is also described in detail in Acts – but not following on from Acts 11:26 as you would expect, but in Chapters 13 and 14. So what happens in Acts between Chapters 11:26 and the start of Chapter 13? The story of the famine is related at the end of Chapter 11 of Acts, and Chapter 12 describes how Antipas puts James and Peter to death and then dies, 'eaten of worms'. In fact, Antipas died in AD 44 and, as we have said, the famine took place at about that time. But these events are in the wrong place. Events that we know belong to the mid-forties have been transposed to the mid-thirties under the traditional chronology and the mid-twenties under my proposed new chronology.

There is, in fact, a strong clue as to how this has happened. At the end of Chapter 11 of Acts, the famine is foretold by a prophet called Agabus.[49] The same prophet makes what appears to be a second appearance in the narrative much later in Acts Chapter 22. Here he warns Paul against going to Jerusalem because it is dangerous. Agabus is introduced in this later account as if for the first time – there is no reference to the 'earlier' prophecy about the famine. In my view (using

---

48 Galatians 1:21.

49 11:27-28.

Occam's Razor) it is highly unlikely that the two events are different. Somehow, a single prophecy by Agabus concerning both a famine and dangers in Jerusalem, has become split into two. We shall sort this out later, when we come on to discuss Acts Chapter 21 and the 'second' prophecy. For the time being, we shall simply put the passage from Acts 11:27-12:25 to one side and read the narrative without it. It will be found that all then makes perfect sense.

Here, meanwhile, is a chart showing the two chronologies side by side; as we develop the argument, it may be helpful to refer to this.

AD	Traditional Harmonized Chronology	Proposed New Chronology
1	*Jesus* Born	
6	Census Revolt by Judas the Galilean	Census Revolt by Judas the Galilean
19		Pilate arrives in Judæa Execution of Judas the Galilean (Stephen?)
20		Paul's conversion
23		Paul in Jerusalem with the three 'pillar' Apostles
26	Pilate arrives in Judæa	
28	John the Baptist killed	
30	*Jesus* begins his ministry	
33	*Jesus* is crucified	
34	Paul's conversion	Paul returns from first mission Council of Jerusalem
36		John the Baptist killed
37	Paul goes to Jerusalem	
41		Jews expelled from Rome
42		Agabus' prophecy Paul arrested in Jerusalem and sent to Rome
47	Agabus' first prophecy	
49	Council of Jerusalem	
57	Agabus' second prophecy Paul arrested in Jerusalem	
59	Paul departs for Rome	

The Pauline Fallacy

So, ignoring for the moment Acts 11:27-12:25, and having established Paul at Antioch in Acts 11:26, we jump to the start of Acts Chapter 13, where the church leaders, prompted by the Holy Spirit, commission Paul and Barnabas to go on a missionary journey to Syria and Cilicia. This has become known as Paul's first missionary journey and is equivalent to the eleven years' mission Paul himself describes in Galatians. We only know the details of this from Acts, and none of those details come from the 'We' document, so the ultimate source is unknown. According to Acts, the journey begins by them sailing to Cyprus,[50] via Seleucia, a port close to Antioch. There they meet a 'sorcerer' called 'Bar-Jesus', which Acts says means 'Elymas'. Paul, powered by the Holy Spirit, causes him to be blinded.[51] This could be true, although there is no external evidence of such an early introduction of Christianity (in any form) to Cyprus, and the blinding of Elymas parallels Paul's own blinding on the road to Damascus. The story also recalls Peter's encounter with a sorcerer called Simon in Acts Chapter 8.[52] Josephus, in *Antiquities of the Jews* Book 20, tells of a Simon who 'pretended to be a magician' who came from Cyprus and seems to have been influential in Judæa in the early fifties.[53] And early church stories feature this Simon the Sorcerer, or Simon Magus, in conflict with the early church, and responsible for a stoning of 'James, the brother of the Lord'.[54] We shall return to all these correspondences in Volume III, where we shall see that they point to something incredibly significant about Paul and about this Simon Magus.

---

50 13:1-4.

51 13:5-11.

52 8:9-24.

53 20:142.

54 In the 'Pseudo-Clementines'. See J.K. Elliott, *The Apocryphal New Testament* (Oxford: Clarendon Press, 1993).

At this point, we should merely note that these stories in Acts cannot be trusted as history; they are fictions, often derived from characters and events in Josephus, shoehorned into the story of Paul to enliven the tale and point moral lessons.

For example, I am sceptical that Paul went to Cyprus or that he travelled via Seleucia. Why would he? His mission field was north of Judæa and Arabia, into Syria and Cilicia; why would he take a difficult voyage to a Gentile island? In fact, there were several Seleucias – the name derives from the Seleucid Empire, which spawned Seleucias in the same way as the Alexandrian Empire spawned Alexandrias. This may be where the confusion has arisen. There was one Seleucia that seems a more likely candidate for Paul to journey to. It was a major city on the Tigris River in Adiabene, the kingdom of Izates and the field of activity of Ananias.[55] Whatever the truth here, as Acts relates the journey, Paul then travels from the island of Cyprus to southern Asia Minor, and his mission takes him back and forth between various towns and cities there, finally sailing from the southern coast of Asia Minor, back to Antioch in Syria. There, at the end of Chapter 14, he 'abode long time with the disciples'. In my view, therefore, the detail of this journey is unlikely to be historical, although since Paul confirms in Galatians that he was in Syria and Cilicia for eleven years, we can, I think, identify this in general terms with the Acts description of the first missionary journey.

One story in all this, however, is important. There is a long description of a missionary speech Paul makes to the Jews in the synagogue in Antioch-in-Pisidia; this is not the Syrian Antioch, but another one in Asia Minor, on the border with Galatia. The speech seems to have gone down well with the

---

55 And perhaps 'Cyprus' is a stand-in for the Herodian fortress town of the same name, near Jericho?

audience, to the extent that some Gentiles asked to hear the same speech. This makes the Jews envious, who then turn against Paul, who concludes:

> It was necessary that the word of God should first have been spoken to you (i.e. the Jews); but seeing ye put it from you, and judge yourselves unworthy of everlasting life, lo, we turn to the Gentiles.[56]

As a result, the Gentile Church becomes established there, but eventually the Jews expel Paul and Barnabas from the region. Just how true all this is we cannot say, but Acts tells this story in considerable detail (thirty-eight verses) because it is a symbolic turning point in its narrative as a whole – when Paul 'turn(s) to the Gentiles'. As we have seen, it seems likely that Paul regarded his mission to be to the Gentiles from the very start, but as with the story of Peter becoming convinced of the need to embrace Gentiles in the movement, Acts is trying to present this shift as an evolutionary one.

Following the description of the first missionary journey, Paul returns to Antioch in Syria. On my chronology, we have reached the mid-thirties AD. The next event is the Council of Jerusalem, which, it will be recalled, is also described by Paul in Galatians. We shall now review it again as described in Acts, but with the perspective gained from Paul's own account. Acts says that after a 'long time':

> ... certain men which came down from Judæa taught the brethren, and said, Except ye be circumcised after the manner of Moses, ye cannot be saved. When therefore Paul and Barnabas had no small dissension and disputation with them, they

---

56 Acts 13:46.

determined that Paul and Barnabas, and certain other of them, should go up to Jerusalem unto the Apostles and elders about this question.[57]

(As we saw in reviewing the same event in Galatians, the 'certain men' referred to here are, in my view, the same as the 'certain came from James' in Galatians 2:12; it will be recalled that this Galatians narrative, although it follows *after* the description of the Council of Jerusalem, is in fact Paul looking *back* to the event that triggered the Council in the first place.) In Acts, Paul and his companions comply[58] and what then takes place is quite clearly the Council of Jerusalem, as described in Galatians:

> And the Apostles and elders came together for to consider of this matter ... And after they had held their peace, James answered, saying ... my sentence is, that we trouble not them, which from among the Gentiles are turned to God: But that we write unto them, that they abstain from pollution of idols, and from fornication, and from things strangled, and from blood.[59]

The fact that it is James who delivers the final 'sentence' on the matter is a clear indication of his supremacy in the Church at this time. And the content of his judgement is nothing very startling. The rules he outlines as being appropriate for Gentiles are, broadly speaking, those of the Noahic Covenant. This, it will be recalled, was established after the Flood in which God destroyed all mankind except Noah and his family. God makes a Covenant with Noah that he will never wipe mankind out again as long as mankind in general

---

57 15:1-2.
58 15:3-4.
59 Acts 15:6-20.

obeys simple rules like these. This Gentile Covenant was always regarded by the Jews as separate from their own Covenant, made between God and the descendants of Abraham, which required the Jews to observe the much stricter laws set out by Moses in the Torah, including of course, circumcision. For the many Gentiles throughout the Roman Empire who were attracted to the monotheistic and moralistic religion of the Jews, this had always been the understanding, although particularly zealous converts like Izates might, if they wished, opt for a fuller commitment.

As Acts tells the story, James' 'sentence' is communicated to the churches outside Judæa both by letter and by apostolic visit, and it is received with rejoicing for its 'consolation'.[60] But matters were clearly not that simple. Two issues remained unresolved. First was the matter of 'faith'. For traditional Jews – which is what the Jerusalem Apostles were – observance of the appropriate Covenant was all that was required for *righteousness*. But Paul had a different understanding. For him, what mattered was what brought *salvation*, and that could never come from righteous observance of any covenant or law, but only through God's grace, made freely available to the believer through faith. As he explains in Galatians, Christians are now the legitimate heirs of the promise made to Abraham, and the Mosaic Law has been swept away to be replaced only by faith in Jesus:

> ... they which are of faith, the same are the children of Abraham. And the scripture, forseeing that God would justify the heathen through faith, preached before the Gospel unto Abraham, saying, In thee shall all nations be blessed ... For

---

[60] 15:22-31.

> as many as are of the works of the law are under the curse ... Christ hath redeemed us from the curse of the law ... .[61]

The second issue still unresolved was that Paul took the view that if salvation was by faith in God's grace alone, then the route to salvation must be the same for Jews as well as Gentiles. In other words, it was not just Gentiles – Jews too were no longer subject to Mosaic Law.

These two issues, if allowed to surface, would have led to a complete split between Paul and the Jesus Movement, and Paul knew that full well. The first issue – that of the role of 'faith' in salvation – could be blurred relatively easily, then as now. Most churches today still blur the issue. We are enjoined to lead a 'good' life as well as a life of faith. But the full implication of salvation by faith alone is that the believer is freed from all responsibility to *act* righteously – and indeed there have been licentious Christian sects over the centuries who have reached exactly that conclusion. So, by emphasizing faith, Paul did not necessarily have to confront head-on any issues of how to behave, and the Council's decision on the applicability of the two Covenants simply took the issue off the agenda. The Council had absolved Paul from having to get Gentile converts to observe all the Mosaic Law, and that was fine as far as it went. He was nothing if not pragmatic, and if that meant he could now go his own sweet way without interference from Jerusalem, all well and good. But the second issue – that of *Jewish* behaviour – that was a real game changer. If that was ever to surface, Paul would be in dire trouble. And in the event, although it did not surface for a number of years, when it did, as we shall see, all hell broke loose.

Acts, therefore, pictures all being sweetness and light after

---

61 3:7-13.

the Council and this was no doubt the superficial outcome. But this is not to say that relations between Paul and the Jerusalem Church were anything but cool. Clearly there must have been ongoing tensions. Some hint of this comes from subsequent events as Acts tells the story. Chapter 15 concludes with a description of a fall-out between Paul and Barnabas. The latter had been Paul's companion from the beginning of his mission. But now, back in Antioch after the Council, and as Paul proposes to revisit the churches they founded in Asia Minor, Barnabas declines to accompany him. Acts attributes this to a minor disagreement over travelling companions, but this seems highly unlikely given what we know from Galatians. Paul goes off again to Asia Minor and Barnabas heads for 'Cyprus'. We can only hypothesize that whatever the official story was, coming out of the Council, Barnabas was aware, having lived closely with Paul, that his theology and priorities were moving in a different direction and Barnabas was not comfortable with it.

As we have seen, Paul now sets off again from Antioch, without Barnabas, and Chapter 16:1 through to Chapter 18:22 describes his subsequent journeying, which has become known as his second missionary journey. This journey takes him through Asia Minor again, but also on to Macedonia and Greece, where in Corinth he meets Aquila and Priscilla. It will be remembered that Paul salutes this couple in the letter to the Romans and that prior to that, they were with Paul in Ephesus, from whence he wrote to the Church in Corinth, which he had founded and which also knew them. So, from the evidence of Paul's letters we might reasonably conclude that Paul met them in Corinth and travelled with them before they went to Rome, which at this point Paul had never visited. Yet Acts says that Aquila and Priscilla were 'lately come from Italy ... because that Claudius had commanded all Jews to depart from

Rome'.⁶² We saw earlier that there was an expulsion in AD 19, but this could not reasonably be referred to as 'lately' by this time. In addition, a few verses further on, when Paul is put on trial in Corinth we are introduced to Gallio,⁶³ described as 'the deputy of Achaia'.⁶⁴ Gallio seems to have been a historical figure, who was proconsul of Achaea at some time in the early fifties AD and as we have seen, scholars tend to use this reference as a lynchpin for calculating a chronology of Paul's life. Can these references in fact be used to date these events?

First, one must take care as ever not to regard Acts as history. One must also guard against circularity of argument since many commentators on this event use the Acts account itself as historical evidence for the timing of Claudius' expulsion. The primary reference to the expulsion comes in an oft-quoted passage from Suetonius:

> Since the Jews constantly made disturbances at the instigation of Chrestus, he expelled them from Rome.⁶⁵

Some scholars have demurred, but most seem agreed that 'Chrestus' here is a corruption of Christ, and the event described was probably civil disturbances of the sort we see often in Acts, between members of the Jesus Movement and traditional Jews. The problem lies in dating this event. Claudius' reign as Emperor began in AD 41, so Aquila and Priscilla would not have arrived in Corinth earlier than that. But Suetonius writes topically rather than chronologically, so we need to consult other texts to establish a time frame. Cassius Dio makes a comment regarding an action early in the reign of Claudius:

---

62 18:2.
63 18:12.
64 Southern Greece, where Corinth is situated.
65 Suetonius, *Lives of the Caesars*, Vol.II: Claudius 25.4.

The Pauline Fallacy

> As for the Jews, who had again increased so greatly that by reason of their multitude it would have been hard without raising a tumult to bar them from the city [Rome], he [Claudius] did not drive them out, but ordered them, while continuing their traditional mode of life, not to hold meetings.[66]

Most scholars agree that this either refers to the same event as Suetonius, or a preliminary to it. Cassius Dio *does* provide a chronological context that points to around the year AD 41. And this would fit very nicely with the chronology I have been tracking: the Council of Jerusalem took place in AD 34, so Paul probably met with Aquila and Priscilla about eight years later in around AD 42. Those eight years were spent on his missionary journeyings as described above.

However, another historian, Paulus Orosius, writing in the fifth century, provides a reference that would suggest c. AD 49 for the expulsion:

> Josephus reports, 'In his ninth year the Jews were expelled by Claudius from the city.'[67]

This quote can be found nowhere in Josephus as we now have it, and Orosius is not highly regarded by historians for his accuracy, so he was probably writing from memory. Yet despite the more solid evidence for a c. AD 42 dating, and the shaky nature of the Orosius reference, most scholars nevertheless accept this last, later dating because it fits with their preconceived chronology, and because it seems to fit with the dating of Gallio, whose tenure in Achaia can be confidently dated to between AD 51 and AD 53. Indeed, this single date

---

66 Dio Cassius, *Roman History*, Vol VII: Book 60.

67 Historiarum adversum paganos libri VII 7.6.15-16, cited in Slingerland, 'Orosius', *Jewish Quarterly Review* 83, 1 / 2 (1992), p.137.

is often regarded as the most accurately known in the life of Paul. Yet, the *c.* AD 41 dating of the expulsion – i.e. a decade or so earlier, and therefore consistent with all the other evidence we have found for a ten-year time-slip – seems to me to be irresistible and comes from a much more reliable source. And when one reads the account of Paul's Corinthian trial in Acts,[68] it has all the hallmarks of romance rather than history. Remember the writer of Acts was probably also the writer of Luke's Gospel. It is perfectly possible that, just as Luke utilized the Quirinius census as part of his nativity tale to get Jesus to Bethlehem to fulfil a prophesy, so this reference to Gallio could have been imported into the tale of Paul's life to fit with an already received chronology and provide pseudo-historical credentials. Certainly, the involvement of Gallio in the story seems to fulfil no other discernible purpose. Gallio is said to be unwilling to be drawn into theological disputes and 'cared for none of those things'.[69] He drops out of the story as soon as he has been introduced. Why then is he there if not just to bolster the historical credibility of what is, in fact, nothing more than romantic fiction? I believe that these events did take place in the very early forties AD, as Cassius Dio testifies, which means that about eight years have passed since Paul set out on this missionary journey, following the Council of Jerusalem. Aquila and Priscilla had indeed arrived in Corinth from Rome at that time. And after travelling with Paul, when he returned to Jerusalem at the end of his 'third' missionary journey (see below), they returned to Rome.

The events in Corinth are described in the first part of Acts 18, after which Paul returns to Antioch. Then, in Acts 18:23, after 'some time there', he sets off again on the third of his missionary journeys, which seems to have taken him

---

68 18:12-17.
69 18:17.

again everywhere he has ever been before. If the events in Corinth occurred towards the end of his second journey, then his third journey would have ended with a return to Jerusalem in the mid-forties. This fits well with the revised chronology we are exploring and is a decade earlier than usually reckoned. But there is more good reason to doubt the historical accuracy of these accounts. The Acts narration of the second and the third journeys contains the first three of the 'We' passages, written we must suppose by a travelling companion of Paul, and therefore perhaps more trustworthy than the rest. In the standard chronology for Paul's life, he undertook four missionary journeys over a period of about fifteen years from the mid-forties to *c.* AD 60. He had various companions with him on each. Are we to believe that one of those companions was on all the journeys and is responsible for all the 'We' passages? In that case, why is the whole narrative of these journeys not in the first person plural? Or are we to believe that the 'We' passages are by different hands? In which case again, why is so much of the narrative in first person singular? The answer to these questions lies in an interesting fact about these 'We' passages that seems to have been missed by commentators thus far.

The first such passage is in Acts 16:10-17 and describes a sea journey from Troas in Asia Minor, westwards across the northern Aegean Sea to Philippi in Macedonia. The next in Acts 20:6-15, describes a sea journey that starts in Philippi and returns to Troas, then a few miles up the coast to Assos and then on southwards through the Aegean islands to Miletus on the south-western coast of Asia Minor. The third 'We' journey is then a continuation of the second, after events in Miletus, journeying on into the Mediterranean, eastwards past Cyprus (strange not to call there, given his supposed journey there years before) to the Syrian coast at Tyre, just north of Judæa, and hence to Jerusalem. The final 'We' documents are found at the end of Acts and relate parts of Paul's supposed 'fourth journey' – from Jerusalem to Rome – by sea. So, all the 'We' documents cover the sea parts of Paul's journeys, although much of their actual content takes place following landfalls. More importantly in my view, all the 'We' passages link up; that is, where one ends, the next begins. The implications of this are far reaching. I believe there can only be one reasonable explanation for it: the 'We' passages must have originally formed a single account by a single companion of Paul, of a single missionary trip, probably towards the end of his missionary career, because it ends with his journey to Rome, which is the last part of Paul's life that we have any information about. The writer of Acts had no other source for his narrative of Paul's career, but somehow needed to describe 15 years of missionary activity to fit a preconceived chronology. The rest of Paul's journeys in Acts have been inserted into this single document to stretch out the limited scope of that document to cover the whole of Paul's career. Some of this infill material may well be based on other sources, reliable or otherwise, and some of it may well be purely mythical or fictional. Certainly, Paul himself provides a fertile source in a listing in Galatians of all the trials he has undergone for his faith:

> Of the Jews five times received I forty stripes save one. Thrice was I beaten with rods, once was I stoned, thrice I suffered shipwreck, a night and a day I have been in the deep; In journeyings often, in perils of waters, in perils of robbers, in perils of my own countrymen, in perils by the heathen, in perils in the city, in perils in the wilderness, in perils in the sea, in perils among false brethren; In weariness and painfulness, in watchings often, in hunger and thirst, in fastings often, in cold and nakedness.[70]

---

70 2 Corinthians 11:24-27.

The Pauline Fallacy

We do not in reality know exactly when or how all these trials took place, but it seems highly likely that the writer of Acts used them as a template to fill out the 'We' document.

Even if the details of Paul's travels cannot be relied upon, we have seen good evidence to suggest that he was in Corinth at the beginning of the forties, (rather than the traditional early fifties), and that he had finally returned to Jerusalem in the mid-forties (rather than the traditional mid-fifties). Just to drive the point home – all of this evidence for a revised chronology for Paul also reinforces the evidence for a revised chronology for *Jesus* – or to be more accurate, for the historic events that subsequently were subsumed in the fictitious narratives about *Jesus*. And this is where we must return to the misplaced passage concerning the 'Agabus' prophecy of the famine, the deaths of James and Peter, and the death of Antipas, that we put to one side earlier on; that is, Acts 11:27 to 12:24. It can now be seen that since both the famine and the death of Antipas can be reliably dated to the mid-forties, so this misplaced passage is actually chronologically parallel to the events described in Acts 21:10 onwards, also dated to the early forties rather than the fifties. It will be recalled that this is where the prophet Agabus makes his second appearance and, as I argued earlier, it parallels his appearance in Acts 11:28. This is the same event. It is Paul's final visit to Jerusalem after his conversion – a decade or so after the Council of Jerusalem. John the Baptist is now dead, beheaded in AD 36 or thereabouts. And as Acts 12:1-17 describes, the early forties were a time when 'Herod the king (i.e. Antipas) stretched forth his hands to vex certain of the church'. He beheads James the Great and although Peter's fate is not defined, he is arrested, escapes, and goes 'into another place' from whence, wherever it is, we hear no more of him. In my view, this story disposes of the first Simon – not Peter, but Cephas: the two are constantly confused in the Bible. This is also the time of the famine in Judæa, forecast by Agabus, and for which Paul brings 'relief' from abroad for the Church in Jerusalem. So, we can identify this period, described in the misplaced passage in Acts 11 and 12, when Paul goes to Jerusalem, as characterized by famine; renewed persecution of the Church in Jerusalem, and the deaths of the two remaining pillars, James the Great and Simon Cephas.

Paul's visit to Jerusalem in Acts 21:11 ff – the point we have reached in our analysis – has all the same characteristics. In previous passages, Paul has been intimating that he must go to Jerusalem but fears to do so. Then, when he arrives in Caesarea on his way south to Jerusalem, Agabus comes to him and prophesies that he will be arrested by 'the Jews' and handed over to 'the Gentiles'.[71] This prophecy, confirming Paul's own fears fits perfectly with the early forties as described in Acts 12. I suggest that at this point James the Great and Cephas are both dead or on the run, and the leadership that is left now in Jerusalem is the two sons of Judas – James the Less and Simon Peter. In addition to worries about King Herod Antipas, Paul would also have been worried about the attitude of these revolutionary Christians towards his own version of Christianity. So why does he nevertheless go to Jerusalem? He explains his motivation in Acts 24:16:

> And herein do I exercise myself, to have always a conscience void of offence toward God, and toward men. Now after many years I came to bring alms to my nation . . .

The alms he refers to here clinches the identification of this visit with the earlier account; both visits are preceded by a

---

[71] 21:11.

prophecy by Agabus, and both are necessitated by the need to bring alms to the Jerusalem Church which is suffering from the famine in Judæa. And both, therefore, take place in the mid-forties. If this were not the case, why would he collect for the home church in Jerusalem? Nowadays churches in England collect for the mission field, not vice versa. The only reason the mission field would collect alms for Jerusalem would be if there was a famine specific to that area, which, as we have seen, there was in the forties, *and at no other time*.

THE ACTS OF THE APOSTLES: PAUL'S ARREST

The assertion that Paul's final visit to Jerusalem takes place in the forties AD of course flies in the face of the normal chronology which sets it in the late fifties. The standard chronology is based on the Acts account, which as I shall now show is almost entirely fictitious. Paul is now in Jerusalem with alms for the famine. As events unfold in Acts, Paul's belief that Jews are free from the Mosaic Law is finally made manifest to all in Jerusalem; a riot ensues across the city, as a result of which Paul is arrested. At this point, the action *could* be taking place in the late fifties, or a decade earlier as I have argued. However, Acts now describes over several chapters, Paul being brought sequentially before the two Roman Governors of Caesarea in the late fifties and early sixties – Felix and Festus – whose existence and dates are confirmed by Josephus as well as other Roman sources. Game, set and match you might think; this proves the traditional chronology is correct. But as with Gallio in Achaia, the stories in Acts about Paul's encounters with these characters reads like romantic fiction, not history. I believe that, like Gallio, they have been introduced from Josephus into the narrative to give it pseudo-historical credentials, and to anchor it to a period – determined by the supposed life and death of a mythical *Jesus* – a decade later than is warranted by the real chronology of events. Everything about this narrative is unbelievable, not just because it involves supernatural events, but because the events themselves are not credible.

Paul is shown in a series of set pieces being interviewed by Felix and his wife Drusilla, then Agrippa II the Judæan king and his sister Drusilla, and then Festus. All these characters are historical, but they also all feature prominently in Josephus. In each set piece, Paul is given the opportunity to preach his Gospel and in each, the Romans are shown as unwilling to pass judgement on him. In the final interview, Agrippa is even pictured as being on the verge of conversion himself:

Almost thou persuadest me to be a Christian[72]

These interviews parallel the interview of *Jesus* by Pilate, who was also unwilling to pass judgement, famously washing his hands of the affair. Just like the original trials of *Jesus*, Paul's trials are characterized by a total disregard of legal protocol, unstated, vague or trumped-up charges, Jews baying for his blood, and weak, sympathetic Romans. Another reference in these passages is telling. When Paul is first arrested by the Romans, he is mistaken for someone else:

Art not thou that Egyptian, which before these days madest an uproar, and leddest out into the wilderness four thousand men that were murderers?[73]

---

72 26:28.
73 Acts 21:38.

The Pauline Fallacy

This too is lifted straight from Josephus' *Antiquities*; we saw his reference to the Egyptian in our discussion above about the stoning of James ben Damneus, confused at some early stage in the development of the story with James the brother of Jesus. Why would the unpopular Paul, who has caused a riot by suggesting that Jews should abandon their Mosaic heritage, be mistaken for a Messianic figure who led a popular uprising? All of these historical characters feature prominently in Josephus, and in my view have been lifted by Luke to populate his tale about Paul, just as he had done in his tale about *Jesus*; the reality was that he knew very little about the lives of either. One might well ask why, if Paul's life intersected so closely with all these characters from Josephus, Josephus nowhere makes any mention of Paul! This is an important issue for my chronology, so let us examine these narratives more closely to see whether they operate as history or fiction.

The Roman commander Lysias allows Paul to address the rioting Jewish crowd. Surely not the most sensible way to quieten things down. But then, this is not history; it is a Hellenistic romance in which the hero always makes such set speeches. Paul then reveals to Lysias that he is a Roman citizen,[74] which is very strange because a few verses later Lysias writes to Felix that he originally rescued Paul from the crowd having already 'understood that he was a Roman'.[75] And while contemplating Paul's Roman citizenship, which here spares him from being flogged, one must wonder why he did not use this to escape on the other occasions when, according to Acts and 2 Corinthians he was flogged. In fact, Paul says in his second letter to the Corinthians that he had

---

74 22:27.

75 23:27.

been flogged three times with 'rods'.[76] Why did Roman citizenship spare him from Roman punishment by Roman methods on this occasion, but not those? Paul then appears before the Sanhedrin. To read this account one would never guess that this was in fact a dignified, legal court with procedures going back centuries. Instead, we are asked to believe that the High Priest has Paul beaten 'on the mouth', and this is followed by a riot from which Paul has to be rescued by Lysias.

Lysias then sends Paul to Caesarea for trial. He travels there by night on horseback, escorted by two centurions, 200 soldiers, 70 horsemen and 200 spearmen. That is 472 Roman soldiers for just one Jewish preacher. The foot soldiers only accompany Paul as far as the town of Antipatris, which was about forty-five miles from Jerusalem. According to Acts, they made this trip overnight. The distance the legions could march in a day of course varies according to the kit they are carrying and the terrain they are covering. But a good day's march would be about 20 miles; a forced march might achieve 25 miles; and an average march, under no time pressure, would probably achieve 15–18 miles per day. A forty-five-mile march then, and achieved overnight, seems highly unlikely to say the least. The trial is postponed for five days until 'Ananias the high priest' arrives to accuse him. There is, of course, a problem with this. Ananias ben Nebedeus could be the High Priest intended here. But he held office from AD 46–52 and Felix did not arrive in Judæa until AD 52. According to Acts, Paul's trial was later than this because Felix did not marry Drusilla until *c.* AD 54, and Paul says to Felix 'that thou hast been of many years a judge unto this nation'. This Ananias was succeeded by Jonathan, who Felix had ordered murdered in AD 46, who in turn was succeeded by Ishmael ben Fabus, who officiated for the rest

---

76 11:25. 'rods' refers to the Roman 'lictors' used for floggings.

of Felix' tenure. Neither of these can be confused with Ananias. It could be argued that the Ananias intended here was Ananus ben Seth, who had been High Priest from AD 6 to AD 15 and whose family, as we have seen, had dominated Temple affairs for decades after. But this was the period when they lost control of the high priesthood, not to regain it again until AD 63 when Ananus ben Ananus became High Priest (only then to blot his copybook by killing James ben Damneus). And if this was the original Ananus, why does Paul say he does not recognize him (23:5), given that prior to his conversion this was Paul's employer in persecuting the Church?[77] There is a simple answer to all this. Ananias is named here, not because it is a historical description but because he is the 'bad guy' of Luke, who persecutes not only the Church, but also *Jesus* and has him crucified. What we have here is a replay of that story, with Paul standing in for *Jesus* – or perhaps it was the other way round? Either way, with the mention of Ananias as High Priest at this point, the whole narrative betrays its fictional origins.

Paul's case is then deferred, apparently to await the arrival of Lysias from Jerusalem with more evidence, although in fact that never occurs and Lysias disappears from the story. Strangely, Paul is not kept in prison but put into the custody of a centurion and is allowed visitors, though we are informed of none such. Note how, by contrast to the bloodthirsty 'Jews', who have already tried three times to kill him since he arrived in Jerusalem, the Romans throughout treat Paul with extreme courtesy and respect – almost kindness. This of course is typical of the writer of Luke and Acts, who writing in Greek for a Roman Gentile audience, and for

---

[77] There may be another reason Paul does not recognize him, as we shall see in Volume III.

whom 'the Jews' were the wicked people that crucified *Jesus* and were now persecuting his loyal servant, Paul.

After 'certain days', Paul is brought before the Roman Governor:

> Felix came with his wife Drusilla, which was a Jewess ... and heard him concerning the faith in Christ. And as he reasoned of righteousness, temperance, and judgment to come, Felix trembled, and answered, Go thy way for this time; when I have a convenient season, I will call for thee.[78]

Why Felix' wife gets involved in all this is a complete mystery — except, of course, that she appears prominently in Josephus so has to be dragged in here too. In fact, it was Drusilla who by Josephus' account, was persuaded by Simon Magus to leave her husband, deny her Jewish heritage, and marry Felix. Presumably that is why Acts makes special reference to her as a Jewess.

And then we are asked to picture Felix 'trembling' with fear and treating Paul with incredible decency. Let us just remind ourselves of how Josephus describes Felix: he caught and put to death 'robbers' (i.e. revolutionaries) and 'imposters' (i.e. Messianic leaders like the Egyptian, but apparently not Paul) 'every day'; he feuds with Jonathan the High Priest, so bribes one of Jonathan's friends to have him killed; deals with a stone-throwing civil disturbance by sending in the troops to slaughter the participants and pillage their homes.[79] This same Felix, we are then told, in hope of a bribe from Paul, 'sent for him the oftener, and communed with him'.[80] We can only wonder where Paul was keeping the money for the bribe,

---

78 24:24-25.

79 *Antiquities* 20:160-178.

80 Acts 24:26.

The Pauline Fallacy

since presumably he was searched; and indeed, if it were a bribe he wanted, surely it would have been quicker and easier to look for one from the High Priest? *He* would have had no religious or moral scruples about supplying one since, after all, he had no such scruples about trying to *kill* Paul on several occasions. We must also wonder what Paul and Felix 'communed' about at their frequent meetings since, apparently according to Acts, this continued for two whole years.

Then, the Acts narrative suddenly tells us that Festus replaced Felix, which indeed, we know from Josephus, he did. Acts tells us that three days into his tenure, Festus travels from Caesarea to Jerusalem, where 'the Jews' ask him to fetch Paul for trial there. Festus declines, quite reasonably one might think, and delays the trial for twelve days until he is back in Caesarea. So, having waited two years under Felix for no believable reason, Paul is now on trial before Festus only fourteen days after his arrival on the scene. Presumably, Felix had nothing more pressing, even though, as we have seen, he inherited a society rife with both civil war and rebellion. But no, he clearly has the leisure to debate theology with an itinerant Jewish preacher. And if the trial before Felix bore a resemblance to the trial of Jesus, the trial before Festus is yet another replay. Festus, like Pilate, sits on the judgement seat.[81] Paul's defence, like that of Jesus, is effectively a simple 'not guilty'. And then, mystifyingly, having before refused to hold the trial in Jerusalem, Festus now suggests moving the trial back to Jerusalem again. He does this apparently, 'to do the Jews a pleasure', although he is not proposing to hand Paul over to a Jewish religious court: the trial, he says, will still be 'before me'.

Yet Paul seems to understand the opposite, because he now pulls his trump card, and as a Roman citizen (apparently),

---

81 Acts 25.6. cf Matthew 27.19 and John 19.13.

declines to be judged in Jerusalem, and makes an 'appeal unto Caesar'. It is hard to see what this is all about. It has been known from the outset (either before or after his original arrest a couple of years before, depending on which verse you read, that he is a Roman citizen). He is already before Caesar's appointed court and although the charges against him seem to be religious, no one seems to be suggesting that he be handed over to a religious court. And remember who Caesar is at this time: the notorious and mad Nero who reputedly had Christians burnt to illuminate his games. The truth is that the whole narrative of Paul's various trials has just two aims: to fill out the ten-year chronological gap and to get him to Rome, the seat of the empire, and the future home of the Christian Church. Indeed, on the very night of his arrest, Paul has one of his visions of Jesus, prophesying this future:

> ... the Lord stood by him, and said, Be of good cheer, Paul; for as thou hast testified of me in Jerusalem, so must thou bear witness also at Rome.[82]

This may be great mythmaking, but it is terrible history. Then, before Paul is despatched to Rome yet another, 'trial' is convened, this time before Agrippa. Why this third trial? Because it is designed to follow the same pattern as the trials of *Jesus* who was brought before Pilate, then before Antipas, and then before Pilate again. Agrippa, parallelling Antipas in Luke's Gospel is keen to meet Paul.[83] In this whole section, we are treated to verbatim accounts of intimate conversations between the Roman Governor and his client king.[84] It

---

82 Acts 23:11.

83 23:8.

84 Luke also seems to know what was said in Antipas' apartments when he questioned Jesus! See Luke 23:7-11.

is hard to conceive what source the writer could have had for these descriptions: divine inspiration or novelistic imagination? As with *Jesus*, 'the Jews' are after Paul's blood again. Paul's defence is interesting:

> Having therefore obtained help of God, I continue unto this day, ... saying none other things than those which the prophets and Moses did say should come: That Christ should suffer, and that he should be the first that should rise from the dead, and should shew light unto the people, and to the Gentiles.[85]

He makes no reference here to the *Jesus* of the Gospels; 'Christ should suffer' is just the 'suffering servant' of Isaiah, and 'the first that should rise from the dead' is of course, the Jesus of Zechariah. There is nothing said of a recently executed historical person called *Jesus*, nor of the amazing signs and wonders that accompanied his crucifixion. Paul makes no request for witness testimony from the 'above five hundred' who apparently saw the resurrected Jesus, 'many of whom', supposedly, 'were still alive'[86]" and living in the area. He does not call on the testimony of any of the Apostles, still actively working miracles and converting whole towns to the new faith, or even on the recent convert, Cornelius, who was apparently a Roman centurion, resident in Jerusalem.[87] Instead, he just invokes 'the prophets and Moses'. Why? Because it is all fiction.

Agrippa tells Festus that he would like to set Paul free, but since he has appealed to Caesar, so it must be. One is

---

85 Acts 26.22-23.

86 1 Corinthians 15:6.

87 Acts: 10.

tempted to ask yet again, why? But of course, we know the reason: Paul's destiny is Rome. And so:

> ... it was determined that we should sail into Italy.[88]

At this point, the narrative becomes 'We' again. Paul is put into the care of 'one named Julius, a Centurion of Augustus' band'.[89] Another telling detail, you might think, indicative that we are dealing with real history here. Not so I am afraid. This detail, like all the others in the trial narrative, is lifted straight from Josephus; just before the arrival of Felix in Judæa, there is a civil disturbance in Samaria:

> When Cumanus heard of this action of theirs, he took the band of Sebaste, with four regiments of footmen, and armed the Samaritans, and marched out against the Jews, and caught them, and slew many of them, and took a great number of them alive.[90]

Easy to miss, but *Sebaste* is Greek for Augustus; the 'band of Sebaste' is one and the same as 'Augustus' band'. Writing in Greek, Luke would have made the connection easily. And so the tale continues – and as ever, apart from the 'We' sections, the fictions come thick and fast. When the ship to Rome hits storms, it is Paul who, with divine guidance, saves the day. Nevertheless, they are shipwrecked on Malta, where Paul is bitten by a venomous snake but miraculously comes to no harm, so miraculously, in fact, that the ship's crew conclude he must be some kind of god. Today, there are indeed snakes

---

88 27:1.
89 27:1.
90 *Antiquities of the Jews*, 20.122.

on Malta: the cat snake, the leopard snake, the Algerian whip snake and the black whip snake. The only problem is there are no (and as far as we can tell, have never been) *venomous* snakes on Malta. Eventually, Paul arrives in Rome where his treatment continues to be unfeasibly courteous. He is supposed to be under arrest and transported to Rome for trial before Caesar, yet the last we hear of him in Acts, and indeed, anywhere else, is in the last two verses:

> And Paul dwelt two whole years [as he had in Caesarea under Felix] in his own hired house, and received all that came in unto him, Preaching the kingdom of God, and teaching those things which concern the Lord Jesus Christ, with all confidence, no man forbidding him.[91]

One must conclude that the whole narrative has little if any basis in history. The only things we can be sure of, I think, borne out by the 'We' passages, is that Paul did land up in Jerusalem, get arrested, and was sent to Rome. All the references to governors and kings mean nothing, and certainly cannot be taken as dating evidence. My contention is that Paul arrived in Jerusalem with alms for famine relief in the forties AD and walked into the turmoil created by Agrippa II's persecution of the Church at that time. Let us now look at the reasons for his arrest.

Paul's problem arises first, not with the Romans, but with the Church. It will be recalled that according to my chronology, Judas the Galilean and the three pillars – John the Baptist, James the Great and Simon Cephas – are now all dead or missing in action. The movement is now led by the two sons of Judas the Galilean – James the Less and his brother Simon Peter. They are wary of Paul, whose mission was sanctioned a

---

91 28:30-31.

decade before by the pillars, but who seems to have developed a theological stance that goes beyond what they feel comfortable with. But one can imagine that they are nevertheless at this point tolerant of Paul, because he is bringing Gentiles to the movement, and that in itself brings nearer the Kingdom of God, because Zechariah indicates this as a sign of the End of Days. But they need reassurance that Paul, as a Jew, still observes the Mosaic Law. 'Believing Gentiles' can be exempt, as they have always been, and as James' letter following the Council of Jerusalem confirmed, but Jews are still God's chosen race and must keep to their own, stricter covenant.

At some point in the previous decade, according to Acts,[92] Paul had made a 'Nazirite vow' (which usually lasted for 30 days) and shaved his head, so we know that, until recently, he had been keen to give at least an outward show of compliance.[93] But rumours had reached Jerusalem that he had now gone one step further:

> He [Paul] declared particularly what things God had wrought among the Gentiles by his ministry. And when they heard it, they glorified the Lord, and said unto him, Thou seest, brother, how many thousands of Jews there are which believe; and they are all zealous of the law; And they are informed of thee, that thou teachest all the Jews which are among the Gentiles to forsake Moses, saying that they ought not to circumcise *their* children, neither to walk after the customs.[94]

We know from the Epistles that this was exactly what Paul

---

[92] 18:18.

[93] The requirements for the Nazirite vow were set out in Numbers 6:1-21. It required a period of separation and abstinence, followed by sacrifices and shaving of the head, the latter being the visible evidence that someone had undertaken such a vow.

[94] 21:19-21.

had begun at some point to preach. Christ had brought freedom from the curse of the law to *all* that have faith in Him – Jew and Gentile alike. The church leaders therefore ask Paul to (again) take a Nazirite vow and shave his head as visible reassurance to the Jewish converts to the movement that he was not guilty of advocating abandonment of the Mosaic Law *for Jews as well as Gentiles*. They say that there are four other Jews who are about to take the vow, and they suggest that Paul joins them. Paul complies. Hypocritical as this clearly was, we know that Paul saw things differently:

> For though I am free from all men, I have made myself a servant to all, that I might win the more; and to the Jews I became as a Jew, that I might win Jews; to those who are under the law, as under the law, that I might win those who are under the law; to those who are without law, as without law (not being without law toward God, but under law toward Christ), that I might win those who are without law; to the weak I became as weak, that I might win the weak. I have become all things to all men, that I might by all means save some. Now this I do for the Gospel's sake, that I may be partaker of it with you.[95]

He was not about to create unnecessary tension. Remember, he is not in Jerusalem this time to get theological matters resolved, as with the Council of Jerusalem. He is just there to deliver food aid. So, he shaves his head, carries out purification rituals, and observes Temple disciplines for a week.

But some at least were not fooled. Apparently, it was some 'Jews which were of Asia' who called his bluff; presumably because they came from Paul's own mission field, they had

---

[95] 1 Corinthians 9:19.

first-hand experience of Paul's preaching and they knew he was dissembling:

> This is the man, that teacheth all men every where against the people [i.e. the Jews], and the law, and this place [i.e. the Temple]; and further brought Greeks also into the temple, and hath polluted this holy place. (For they had seen before with him in the city Trophimus an Ephesian, whom they supposed Paul had brought into the temple).[96]

Apparently, this sets the whole city in uproar. Paul is thrown out of the Temple and is about to be beaten to death by an angry mob when the Roman authorities intervene to restore order. In doing so, they put Paul in chains and drag him off to be whipped. He escapes this by claiming Roman citizenship, as he was to do two years later before Festus. There are indications that Paul was indeed well connected, irrespective of whether he actually held Roman citizenship. At the end of the Epistle to the Romans, for example, he sends a long list of salutations to people in Rome, including 'Herodion my kinsman'.[97] There are several other possible parallels between people Paul claims connection with and notables in the Roman and Herodian world who get mentions in Josephus. So, Paul does seem to have had some pull with the Roman authorities. Remember that John the Baptist was executed simply as a *precaution* against the *possibility* of an uprising. Why would Paul be treated any differently unless he pulled some sort of influence?

As we have seen, his arrest leads eventually to Paul being shipped to Rome, sometime in the late forties AD according to my revised chronology. And we know from Josephus that

---

96 Acts 21:28-29.
97 16:11.

around that time Judas's sons – James and Simon – are caught by the Roman authorities and executed. This probably has implications for the whole story of Paul's arrest. Acts presents it as the fault of 'the Jews' and goes to great lengths to exonerate the Romans – in Caesarea and then in Rome itself – of anything but courteous treatment of Paul. Luke and the other Gospel writers play the same trick in the story of *Jesus*' arrest, trial and execution: it was all the fault of 'the Jews' and the Romans were just unwilling tools of divine intent. It all had to be presented this way if Christianity was to survive in a Roman Empire that had just had to put down a bloody revolution in Judæa and was heartily sick and tired of Jews of whatever sect causing disturbances across the eastern Empire, and even in Rome itself. But the truth is different.

Christianity grew out of the Jesus Movement, which was created by a group of Messianic, revolutionary Jews led by Judas the Galilean, and later by his sons. The Roman Empire had done what it always did – it had ruthlessly hunted down these leaders and killed them: Judas in AD 19; John the Baptist in AD 36; James the Great and Simon Cephas in AD 44; and James the Less and Simon Peter in AD 48. Under the old chronology, it was impossible to make the connection between the sons of Judas – James and Simon – with the people of the same name in the New Testament. But with everything shifted back in time by a decade, it is immediately possible to identify Judas' sons with James the Less and Simon Peter. Paul could not escape being tarred with the same brush. Ironically, he was actively trying to turn the movement from a Jewish Messianic sect into a universal religion of love that would eventually, under Constantine, become the state religion of the Empire. But whatever happened to him eventually in Rome, he seems to have disappeared from the scene at that point.

There is a line of argument that regards Paul negatively and to some degree duplicitous. The Ebionites, an early Christian sect whose writings were suppressed by the Church, give a most unflattering account of Paul. They denied that he was a Pharisee, trained by Gamaliel as claimed in the Book of Acts; instead, by their account he was a Gentile convert to Judaism who worked for the Jerusalem High Priest until lack of advancement (rather than a Damascus Road revelation) led him to found a breakaway religion. In fact, Paul never claims a connection with Gamaliel in his own writings, and he says explicitly that he *did* receive advancement when he worked for the High Priest, so as with all these early documents, the question is who one chooses to believe. The Ebionites wanted to preserve a Judaic, human version of Jesus. They rejected Paul's teaching that Jesus was divine and had done away with the need to follow the Jewish religious laws, so they had a giant axe to grind with Paul.

But their view was highlighted again by Baur and the Tübingen School in the nineteenth century and has been influential ever since. As we have seen, under this view, Paul and the Jerusalem Church irrevocably split at the Council of Jerusalem as Paul's own theology grew increasingly inconsistent with that of the original Jesus Movement. We have shown how, in fact, when properly understood, the narratives in Acts and Galatians can be reconciled – albeit within a different chronological framework, and how the relationship over time between Paul and the Jerusalem Apostles can be understood in a way that is psychologically convincing. Certainly, Paul was in no hurry to create a split, and when it finally came it resulted in his immediate removal to Rome; there never was a period of decades in which Paul and Jerusalem were at odds with one another. However, the Tübingen School and its intellectual descendants in the twentieth century have adduced evidence outside of Acts and Galatians to support the view that there was a history of outright enmity between Paul and Jerusalem Church.

Some of the most recent exponents of this version of scepticism go so far as to present Paul as a Roman sympathizer and fifth columnist who infiltrates the early Church to emasculate its Messianic roots and convert it to a harmless mystery religion. His motive is seen as either to please his friends and masters in the Roman Empire and its allies, and/or to steal the alms collected by the churches outside Judæa for the famine relief and support of the Jerusalem Church. Paul's Roman connections, adverted to above in the context of his claim to Roman justice, are thus adduced in support of this view. On this basis, Paul is then sometimes identified with an unprincipled, contemporary character called Saulus, who appears in Josephus' *Antiquities of the Jews*:

> And now Jesus, the son of Gamaliel, became the successor of Jesus, the son of Damneus, in the high priesthood, which the king had taken from the other; on which account a sedition arose between the high priests, with regard to one another; for they got together bodies of the boldest sort of people, and frequently came, from reproaches, to throwing of stones at each other; but Ananias was too hard for the rest, by his riches, – which enabled him to gain those that were most ready to receive. Costobarus also, and Saulus, did themselves get together a multitude of wicked wretches, and this because they were of the royal family; and so they obtained favour among them, because of their kindred to Agrippa: but still they used violence with the people, and were very ready to plunder those that were weaker than themselves. And from that time it principally came to pass, that our city was greatly disordered, and that all things grew worse and worse among us.[98]

---

98 20:213-214.

It will be recalled that this was the period, leading up to the Jewish War in the sixties AD, in which internecine strife between powerful High Priest families was rampant and a certain 'James, brother of Jesus' was stoned to death. If this Saulus were to be identified with the Apostle Paul, then he by implication would seem to have been involved in some way in James' death, and if this James were the brother of *Jesus* Christ, this could be taken as evidence that the enmity between Paul and the Jerusalem Church under James' leadership reached the level of actual physical violence. But of course, we have shown that this is another James entirely, and since we have argued that Paul was shipped off to Rome in the mid-forties, it is hard to see how this Saulus figure, part of Agrippa's royal family, could be the same person.

And so we come full circle. We began by arguing that most of the New Testament cannot be trusted because, among other things, it was written well after the events it describes. By treating the relevant texts with caution, and with a minimum of adjustment, we have arrived at a New Paradigm – one that places all the events even further back in time; that allows a complete identification between key leaders of the Jesus Movement and key leaders of Judas the Galilean's movement; and removes all these key players from the scene by the end of the forties AD. Is it any wonder then that the writers of the Gospels and Acts, writing at the end of the first century at the earliest, with at least half a century and a devastating war between them and the events they describe, get things muddled up? There may or may not have been later, well-meaning alterations and/or interpolations to the key texts as they have come down to us. And certainly, throughout the history of the later Christian Church, there has been what can only be described as conspiracy to maintain the laity in unquestioning ignorance of anything but the party line, and the ruling church elite in power. But unlike some writers, I see little or no evidence of conspiracy to deceive in the early Church. As with most conspiracy theories, the eternal ability of fallible human beings, as opposed to infallible divine ones, to make mistakes, ignore uncomfortable facts, and smooth things over wherever possible, seems to me to be the best explanation for the matters that have been the subject of this book. Luke – whoever he was, as he plundered his various sources to fabricate his tales of *Jesus*, the Apostles and Paul – was not setting out to deceive anybody. Unfortunately, for more than 2,000 years, that is what he did.

And with this final piece of the jigsaw in place, we can now move to attempt a summary of the New Paradigm in its entirety.

CHAPTER 6

The New Paradigm

It seems incredible that the whole of western civilization for 2,000 years should have been based on such a succession of fallacies. Now that we can see that the whole of Christian belief is a house of cards, it is fascinating to reflect what might have been. Without all the Pauline nonsense – of predestined sin, judgement and hell – it is hard to believe that the equally nonsensical tales of a Jewish preacher who was the divine in human form and who was crucified for the sake of us all, would ever have taken root. The Church has always known its trump card and it has played it deftly all down the years: believe and repent they say or you are doomed to eternal punishment; don't worry about social injustice in this life, they say, because it doesn't matter – your reward will be in heaven; and in the meantime they say, give generously to the Church because in making us rich you glorify God and make extra sure of your own eternal destiny; and don't concern yourself with worries about a greedy, paedophile, ambitious, misogynist priesthood they cry, because God will right all wrongs in His Kingdom – a Kingdom that Paul believed was just round the corner. No wonder he cared little for the things of this life. But we have been waiting for two millennia now, with no sign of it. Isn't it about time we woke up and smelt the coffee?

The New Paradigm

I said in my Preface that I cannot prove there is no God, but the odds of me being wrong are vanishingly small. I am happy to admit too that I cannot prove a word of my New Paradigm. Perhaps I am wrong. Perhaps John the Baptist met his longed-for Messiah and did then walk away to do his own thing. Perhaps the disciples really were stupid and did not properly understand the man they followed for three years. Perhaps Jesus really was a peaceful itinerant preacher who wandered with impunity in a countryside ravaged by civil war and brutal Roman oppression. Perhaps it is just a coincidence that the sons of Judas and the successors of Jesus had the same names. Perhaps Josephus just forgot to write about Jesus, even though he lived at the same time and in the same place while Jesus was astounding thousands with his miracles. Perhaps Paul did tell Jesus' family that they were related to the Son of God and they did not call for the men in white suits. I could go on. I believe that the paradigm I have developed in this book, while ultimately unprovable, fits what we know better than any other and does so in a way that seems psychologically credible.

John the Baptist never met his Messiah; he died still waiting for his coming. The early leaders of the Jesus Movement weren't stupid; they never believed the things the Church ascribes to them in the first place. There was no *Jesus* 'meek and mild'; just a revolutionary whose memory was transmuted into something different. The revolutionary sons of Judas and the first two candidates for Pope amazingly *were* the same people; you just need to adjust chronology by a decade. Josephus forgot nothing; despite being a contemporary and a countryman, he had never heard of a *Jesus*. And Paul's private visions were never exposed to the derision of *Jesus*' family; they never existed. Just because he lived 2,000 years ago does not change the reality: what Dawkins called the God Delusion, in the case of Christianity, was based on the tragic delusions of the Apostle Paul. We really do not need this nonsense anymore, if indeed we ever did. And here are eleven[1] reasons why:

1. **The Bible is not the inerrant, inspired word of God; it cannot be because it contains historical errors and internal inconsistencies.** I have provided a few examples of these in the text; for more, the reader need only refer to books such as Dawkins' *The God Delusion* and Hitchens' *God is Not Great*, or less polemical, Lane Fox's excellent *The Unauthorised Version*.[2] It was no part of my purpose in writing this book to provide a more thorough demolition of the principle of 'inerrancy', or the infallibility of scripture, but I do recognize that without an acceptance that the texts examined here are the product of human inspiration rather than divine, then my arguments will not convince. To maintain a belief in the inerrancy of scripture in the face of the facts requires some supreme step of faith. It requires a belief that the errors and inconsistencies will turn out to be apparent rather than real – that they are the result of human error in interpretation rather than genuine mistakes. But as I also point out in this book, it requires a belief that somehow God guides not just the writers of scripture, but all the various copyists, editors and translators over the millennia. The ancient belief that the Septuagint translation of the Old Testament from Hebrew to Greek was produced miraculously by seventy translators who discovered they had all produced the same translated text rather proves the point; without stupendous suspensions of common sense of this sort, faith in inerrancy is impossible. Of course, many Christians today accept that the Bible is not inerrant but

---

[1] It was so tempting to make them twelve!
[2] See Select Bibliography.

maintain nevertheless that it contains general truths about God and the moral life. Fair enough, but this is a slippery slope that allows for the kind of radical reappraisal contained in this trilogy.

2. **Prophecies are, therefore, not true; when they appear to be true, it is because they reflect later fictional accounts based on earlier texts.** This, of course, follows on naturally once one accepts that inerrancy is untrue. But it also fails the test of Occam's Razor: that the more unlikely assumptions you have to make in order to believe something, the less true it is likely to be; or in other words, the simplest explanations are usually the right ones. This is a perception that has fallen out of favour with many today, particularly the legions of people, fed by a free and unfettered internet, who believe all manner of conspiracy theories, from the idea that governments are drugging populations through chemicals in aeroplane vapour trails, to the faking of the moon landings and putting microchips in COVID-19 vaccines. Unfortunately, many such people will be attracted to the thesis I put forward in this book, because it will reinforce their beliefs that the Church (and particularly established churches) are collaborators with governments in conspiracy. For this reason, I said earlier that in my judgement the writers of the New Testament were sincere in what they were doing; to criticize their fictions by the standards of modern historical method is to misunderstand their purposes. But nonetheless, much of what they wrote was 'untrue' by modern standards. The simple fact is that they took ancient prophecies and, by a process of imaginative allegorization, reshaped their perception of contemporary people and events to reflect them. The ancient prophets were deluded about their abilities to see the future, just as some modern-day

spiritualists are deluded about their ability to contact the dead. They were sincere but wrong, as were their interpreters in later times. Prophecies about a future Messiah were not fulfilled by a person called *Jesus*; the Gospel writers invented a person called *Jesus* to 'fulfil' those prophecies.

3. **The prophet Zechariah had visions in the sixth century BC of a decisive intervention by God to establish his Kingdom on Earth. This would embrace Gentiles as well as Jews.** This is perhaps the most extraordinary facet of my thesis in this book. The key passages from Zechariah have been in Christian Bibles from the beginning. Given the perspective of points 1 and 2 above, it seems inescapable to me that this is the catalyst for what I have called the Jesus Movement of the first century. Yet readers and Christian commentators for centuries have gone into raptures when considering this 'amazing' prophecy of *Jesus*. Zechariah is the key source for the Christian story – for the coming of the two Messiahs, the triumphal entry to Jerusalem, the role of the Mount of Olives, the fate of Judas Iscariot, the crucifixion, the descent to hell and the resurrection. And unlike other Old Testament sources, its universalist tenor marks it out as the key document for Pauline Christianity, with its focus on Gentiles. In this context, it seems clearer than ever that neither branch of the Jesus Movement – the passivist nor the activist – ever envisaged the foundation of a religion that would last for two millennia. They believed that they were living in the Last Days and that God's final intervention was at hand. New Testament teachings about how to live one's life were never intended as anything but temporary – the world was about to end so making long-term plans was pointless. Of course, many other sects in Judæa at the

time had similar beliefs – the 'signs' were there for all to see. The Essenes for example, seem to have lived life in the expectation of an imminent apocalypse. But if the thesis of this book is accepted, they were a different sect from the Jesus Movement.

4. **Zechariah prophesied that there would be two Messiahs in the Last Days.** The Priest-Messiah would be the High Priest of his own time, Yeshua/Joshua/Jesus ben Yehozedek, who with Zerubbabel commenced the rebuilding of the Jerusalem Temple in the sixth century BC, following the return from Babylonian captivity. He would be raised from the dead, cleansed and act as judge of mankind in the Last Days. Under Pauline theology, this concept developed into Jesus as the eternal Son of God, member of the Holy Trinity, existent for all time with God. But this was not the original stance of Judas the Galilean and John the Baptist, the founders of the Jesus Movement. For them, as for Zechariah, Jesus was a special human being, descended from Zadok, the first High Priest of Israel, and chosen by God to be his judge of mankind. The Jesus Movement believed that they were living in the Last Days when Jesus would come from heaven in glory. There was no earthly *Jesus* of the first century and no *Second Coming* – just the belief that the Jesus who had lived 500 years before was returning at any moment. The reasons for that belief were partly because of the sense that Pilate's outrages were the last straw, and partly because a famine in Egypt in AD 19 seemed to fulfil Zechariah's prophecy.

The King-Messiah also prophesied by Zechariah, known as the 'Branch', was to be God's representative on Earth when He established his Kingdom. This seemed entirely logical. Of course, God himself would not actually rule in person. When He had set the Jews apart to be His people, He had ordained that they should be ruled by kings, and it was that model that would determine the political structure of His new Kingdom on Earth. This King-Messiah had yet to live, but according to Zechariah he would be a descendant of David and he would lead the forces of good in the final battle against evil on the Mount of Olives. As Christianity developed in the Gentile world under the influence of Paul and following the death of Judas the Galilean who had declared himself King, the idea of two Messiahs was merged into one, the Kingdom of God became increasingly spiritualized, and the 'return' of Jesus endlessly delayed.

5. **John the Baptist, known as Zadok (or Sadduc), an anti-establishment Pharisee, interpreted the Zechariah prophecy as applying to his own time: the first half of the first century.** I have made some leaps in my thesis to identify the disciple/Apostle John of the Gospels and Acts with John the Baptist. Many will find this baffling since they have always been regarded in the Church as different – indeed, the Gospels portray John the disciple as having originally been a disciple of John the Baptist before coming over to be a follower of *Jesus*. We have been at pains to establish that the Gospel stories and Acts are fictions, and the authorship attributions are late and tenuous. And certainly, there is little about the way John the Apostle is described in the New Testament to establish an identity separate from John the Baptist who, on the other hand, is well attested in Josephus and Jewish tradition as well as the Bible. I believe that although the Gospel writers wrote the Baptist out of their narratives as quickly as they decently could, they were nonetheless uncomfortably aware that, nevertheless, 'John' continued to be a major player in the Jesus Movement – so they invented another

John, one who had originally followed the Baptist but now switched his allegiance to *Jesus*. Using Occam's Razor, which discourages the multiplying of entities, we can conclude that there was only ever one John – the founder of the Jesus Movement and a key player in it until his death in the thirties AD.

6. **John the Baptist identified Judas the Galilean as the King-Messiah.** My identification of John the Baptist with Josephus' 'Sadduc' or Zadok is perhaps less contentious. Other candidates that have been suggested for Sadduc are Peter and James, on the basis that both seem to have been early Christian leaders in Jerusalem. But if I am right in regarding these early leaders as James the Less and Simon Peter (as opposed to James the Great and Simon Cephas), then these first two individuals are of the second generation of leaders of the Movement, which leaves only John the Baptist as a candidate for the first-generation founder. John the Baptist certainly founded a movement of his own, and the relationship of that with the Jesus Movement has always been problematical; my solution sees the Baptist as the founder of the Jesus Movement which then split after the death of Judas the Galilean into two branches, after which John led the passivist branch from exile in Arabia. That branch remained essentially Jewish in orientation, but its passivist nature enabled it to survive in exile while the activist branch in Jerusalem was eventually wiped out in the Jewish War. Pauline Christianity – also passivist, but Gentile rather than Jew orientated – flourished in Rome and eventually supplanted John's movement.

The implication of Josephus is that the Jesus Movement was founded by Judas, and 'Sadduc' was his accomplice. But I suspect that the Gospels' account of *Jesus*' baptism and endorsement by John is a garbled memory of John's endorsement of Judas as the King-Messiah. Convinced that they were living in the Last Days and about to witness the coming of Jesus as the Priest-Messiah, they then led the Jesus Movement together. Judas' role in the Movement was to build an armed rebellion that itself would finally trigger God's intervention. John's role was to act as the High Priest of the Movement until Jesus did return to Earth as Priest-Messiah. His baptismal rite, foreshadowed in Zechariah, inducted people into the Movement until that day. Judas began his rebellion in AD 6 when Roman taxation became the rallying issue. We know from Josephus that the rebellion was put down, but Josephus does not tell us what happened to Judas. My belief is that if he had been killed at that time, Josephus would have said so. We do know on the other hand from Josephus, that the revolt he started fizzled on over the next decade, to be reignited again with the atrocities of Pilate. The contention of this book is that it was Pilate who eventually caught, tried and killed Judas by stoning in AD 19 as an integral part of the events at that time described by Josephus. This stoning appears in Acts as the stoning of Stephen, but the memory of it as a crucial point in the history of the Jesus Movement informs the Gospel stories of the death of Jesus.

7. **Key events in the history of early Christianity took place at least a decade before commonly supposed.** I have presented considerable evidence that there are significant and suspicious gaps in Josephus' narrative of the early decades of the first century. Perhaps he genuinely did not know or perhaps he has been edited – we do not know. But the evidence is clear that someone has tampered with Josephus to make his story fit with the story and chronology of *Jesus*, as it became established within the Church in the early years of the second century. When this perception

The New Paradigm

is combined with the realization that most or all the 'historical' references in Acts are suspect because they were lifted wholesale from Josephus, a completely new chronology begins to emerge. Standard chronology has *Jesus* born at the start of the first century and crucified early in the thirties AD. Paul is then active over the next three decades arriving in Rome in the early sixties. My revised chronology of course assumes there was no first century *Jesus* but that Judas the Galilean was killed in AD 19 with the connivance of Paul, and that Paul's own activities took place from soon after that date until he arrived in Rome in the mid-forties. It also makes possible the identification of the Christian leaders James the Less and Simon Peter with the two sons of Judas the Galilean, also called James and Simon. Such an identification has tempted many commentators in the past, but without the time shift outlined in this book it has until now been impossible to substantiate. In other words, the whole story shifts back in time by a decade or so. This means that by the end of the forties, all the early leaders of the Jesus Movement – both branches, and two generations of them – were dead, except for Paul who was in Rome. Twenty years then passed, followed by a devastating war that saw Jerusalem destroyed and its inhabitants scattered. Only then – and probably some decades even after this – did Gentile Christians in Rome begin to write down stories about *Jesus* and his Apostles. This alone is capable of explaining why so much of what they wrote now appears to us as fiction. There was no one left who knew what really happened.

8. **After Judas' death, there was a split in the Jesus Movement into two branches.** Judas' brother James (the Great) became leader of the activist section in Jerusalem, until

Judas' successor, his son, also called James (the Less), was of age. The family continued to believe that Jesus was coming as Priest-Messiah, and that one of their number would be the King-Messiah, and they maintained that belief right up until their deaths in the forties, and on until the second and last Jewish War in the second century. Simon, called Cephas, the 'stone with seven eyes' of Zechariah's prophecy, was probably another family member and acted as chief evangelist for the activists. They focused their efforts on recruiting Jews in Judæa and the Diaspora to their cause. John the Baptist, however, became leader of the passivist branch, operating on the east bank of the River Jordan until he was killed sometime around AD 36. His branch also held to the original beliefs of the Movement, and remained an essentially Jewish phenomenon, but following the failure of Judas, ceased to seek to precipitate God's intervention but were content to await his Kingdom in faith. As time went by, and increasingly after John's death, the activists of the movement came to see the passivists as traitors to the cause, and as Josephus testifies, internecine strife broke out sporadically between the two branches until the Jewish War finally united all Jews in what they believed would be the apocalyptic battle at the End of Days.

9. **Understanding events in the early Church requires reconciliation between the accounts in Acts and Galatians.** I have radically reinterpreted the Book of Acts, especially where it seems to be contradicted by Galatians. I have been able to show that properly interpreted, Galatians' and Acts' accounts of the Council of Jerusalem do in fact tie up together, and that although tensions existed at that time between Paul and the first generation of Judas' family, there was no outright split at the Council in the

mid-thirties. The real split only occurred about a decade later when it became apparent that Paul had taken the final step of asserting that even Jews were now free of the Mosaic Law; no matter how universalist the early Church was, and how much they welcomed Gentile God-fearers, they could not countenance a theology that removed in effect the special position of the Jews as God's chosen people with their own special Covenant, and their own special role as priests to the world in God's coming Kingdom. As my reinterpretation shows, this understanding of events has been obscured by a failure to understand the order of events as described by Paul in Galatians, and a confusion in Acts about the prophet Agabus whose intervention only took place once at the time of the famine in the forties. Once these points are understood, all falls naturally into place.

10. **Christianity as we know it was developed by Paul as a Gentile, spiritualized version of John's passivist branch of the Jesus Movement.** The Apostle Paul participated in the death of Judas and subsequently persecuted the Jerusalem Church, as narrated in Acts and Galatians. He was converted by visions of Jesus, probably around AD 20, to the passivist section of the Jesus Movement, and from the beginning saw his calling as to convert Gentiles to a belief in the imminent coming of Jesus and the Kingdom of God. He had minimal contact with the activist section – especially Judas' family – in Jerusalem, except to attend the Council of Jerusalem in *c.* AD 34, when it was agreed that Gentile converts were required only to observe the Noahic Covenant. Paul developed the essentials of Christian doctrine as we know it today over the ten years following the Council, and eventually taught that even Jews were now freed from Mosaic Law. There was a

famine in Jerusalem in the early forties, which coincided with renewed persecution of the Jerusalem Church, leading to the death of James the Great and the exile or death of Cephas. James the Less took over as leader in Jerusalem and as King-Messiah. His brother Simon Peter took over as 'stone with seven eyes' from Cephas. Paul returned to Jerusalem at the time of the famine, bringing aid, but by this time news that Paul was preaching that Jews were no longer subject to the Mosaic Covenant had reached James the Less and Simon Peter. Despite Paul's willingness to dissemble, matters got out of hand, and in the ensuing riot Paul was arrested and eventually deported to Rome in the mid-forties. Meanwhile, persecution of the Church in Jerusalem continued and both James the Less and Simon Peter were killed in the late forties. So, all the leaders of both sections of the Jesus Movement have been killed or exiled from Judæa by the late forties.

11. **The activist section continued in Judæa and was instrumental in the uprisings that led eventually to the Jewish War of the sixties. The passivist section continued outside Judæa and evolved over time into the Christian Church as we know it.** In the seventies, Josephus in Rome wrote his history of the events leading to the war. He gave Judas a central role but knew nothing of the philosophy of Zadok or about *Jesus*. Later, in the nineties, he wrote his *Antiquities* and mentioned Zadok but still knew little about him, even spelling his name wrong. He *perhaps* had heard something of *Jesus* and gave him a mention, not really knowing anything about him. Sometime in the early second century AD, Christians in Rome – descendants of the passivist section, but now nearly a century after the death of Judas – know only Paul's theology. All they know of *Jesus* is what Paul

knew and believed. The catastrophic Jewish war had destroyed all record of events in Judæa in the first half of the first century – except for Josephus' histories. They wrote the Gospels and Acts as purely imaginative creations, based on Josephus and Old Testament prophecies.

Finally, even if you do not accept most of the arguments of this book, the undeniable truth is that the *Jesus Movement* of the first half of the 1st century AD had its roots in messianic belief. And the *Jesus Movement* was a *movement* rather than just a set of someone's beliefs; they really believed the Messiah was imminent and that frightening expectation required action, not discussion. The scriptural signs were clear and events in the real world bore them out – Jesus was coming. So, everywhere in the New Testament we are enjoined to take no heed of earthly needs, to throw off familial ties, and to turn the other cheek because there was no time for revenge or anything else. But Jesus didn't come and two thousand years later he still hasn't come – that's sixty-five generations that have lived their lives and died without God calling Time on it all. The *Jesus Movement* was wrong; it is as simple as that. In the 1840s in New York, a man called William Miller predicted that Jesus would return on 22 October, 1844. It didn't happen then either of course, yet today, the Seventh Day Adventist Church that Miller founded is the twelfth largest religious organisation in the world. They call the 22 October 1844 the *Great Disappointment*. We shall meet Mr. Miller again, and many more like him, in Volume III when we look into Jesus' return and the apocalyptic events that are supposed to accompany it. But we can conclude for now that the *whole* of Christianity – in all its inane varieties – is a 'great disappointment'. Jesus is never coming back because he never existed in the first place. It is all based on a fallacy and the time is long overdue when we put it behind us.

Select Bibliography

PRIMARY SOURCES

The Bible, The Authorised King James Version, www.kingjamesbibleon line.org.
Whiston, William (Trans.) *Josephus: The Complete Works* (Nashville, TN: Thomas Nelson, 1998).
The Loeb Classical Library translations into English of:
Philo.
Pliny.
Tacitus.
Cassius Dio.
Suetonius.
Paulus Orosius.
Charlesworth, James H., (ed.), *The Apocrypha and Pseudepigrapha of the Old Testament, 2 vols.,* (Oxford: Oxford University Press, 1913).
Elliott, J. K., *The Apocryphal New Testament* (Oxford: Clarendon Press, 1993).
Vermes, Geza, *The Complete Dead Sea Scrolls in English* (London: Allen Lane, Penguin, 1997).
Eisenman, Robert and Wise, Michael, *The Dead Sea Scrolls Uncovered* (Shaftesbury: Element Books, 1992).
Robinson, J.M. (ed.), *The Nag Hammadi Library in English: Revised Edition* (San Francisco: Harper & Row, 1988).

SECONDARY SOURCES

Allegro, John M., *The Dead Sea Scrolls* (London: Penguin, 1956).
Allegro, John M., *The Sacred Mushroom and the Cross* (London: Hodder & Stoughton, 1970).
Aune, David, *The New Testament in its Literary Environment* (Philadelphia, PA: Westminster Press, 1987).
Baigent, M., Leigh, R. and Lincoln, H., *The Holy Blood and the Holy Grail* (London: Jonathan Cape, 1982).
Baigent, M and Leigh, R., *The Dead Sea Scrolls Deception* (London: Jonathan Cape, 1991).
Baldwin, Joyce G., *Haggai, Zechariah, Malachi* (London: Tyndale, 1972).
Bammel, E. and Moule, C. F. D., (eds.), *Jesus and the Politics of His Day* (Cambridge: Cambridge University Press, 1984).
Barnstone, W., *The Other Bible* (London: Harper Collins, 1984).
Barrett, C. K., *The New Testament Background: Selected Documents* (New York: Harper & Row, 1961).
Baur, F.C., *Church History of the First Three Centuries* (London: Williams & Norgate, 1878). [Translation by Allan Menzies of the original *Kirchengeschichte* (Tübingen, 1853)].
Bickerman, E. J., *The Jews in the Greek Age* (Cambridge, MA: Harvard University Press, 1988).
Black, Matthew, *The Scrolls and Christian Origins* (London: Nelson, 1961).
Brandon, S.G.F., *The Fall of Jerusalem and the Christian Church* (London: SPCK, 1951).
Brandon, S.G.F., *Myth, Ritual and Kingship* (Oxford: Oxford University Press, 1958).
Brandon, S.G.F., *Jesus and the Zealots* (Manchester: Manchester University Press, 1967).
Brandon, S.G.F., *The Trial of Jesus of Nazareth* (London: B.T. Batsford, 1968).
Brandon, S.G.F., *Religion in Ancient History* (London: George Allen & Unwin, 1969).
Boardman, J., Griffin, J. and Murray, O., *The Oxford History of the Classical World* (Oxford: Oxford University Press, 1986).
Bockmuehl, Markus, *This Jesus* (Edinburgh: T. & T. Clark, 1994).
Borg, M., *Conflict, Holiness and Politics in the Teachings of Jesus* (New York: Edwin Mullen, 1984).
Borg, M., *Jesus: A New Vision* (San Francisco: Harper & Row, 1987).

Select Bibliography

Borg, M., *Jesus in Contemporary Scholarship* (Valley Forge: Trinity Press, 1994).

Brown, Raymond, *An Introduction to New Testament Christology* (London: Chapman, 1994).

Bruce, F. F., *Jesus and Christian Origins Outside the New Testament* (London: Hodder & Stoughton, 1974).

Bultmann, Rudolf, *Jesus and the Word* (New York: Scribner, 1958).

Bultmann, Rudolf, *History of the Synoptic Tradition* (Oxford: Blackwell, 1963). [Translation by John Marsh of the original Die *Geschichter der Synoptischen Tradition*, (Gottingen, 1921)].

Burkert, W., *Ancient Mystery Cults* (Cambridge, MA: Harvard University Press, 1987).

Burridge, R. A., *Four Gospels, One Jesus?* (London: SPCK, 1994).

Burtchaell, J. T., *From Synagogue to Church* (Cambridge: Cambridge University Press, 1992).

Carroll, R. P., *The Bible as a Problem for Christianity* (Philadelphia, PA: Trinity, 1991).

Casey, Maurice, *From Jewish Prophet to Gentile God* (Cambridge: James Clarke, 1991).

Charlesworth, J., *Jesus Within Judaism* (New York: Doubleday, 1988).

Charlesworth, J., (ed.), *The Messiah: Developments in Earliest Judaism and Christianity* (Minneapolis, MN: Fortress Press, 1992).

Cohen, Stuart, *The Three Crowns* (Cambridge: Cambridge University Press, 1990).

Cohn, Norman, *Cosmos, Chaos, and the World to Come: The Ancient Roots of Apocalyptic Faith* (New Haven, CT: Yale University Press, 1993).

Cohn, Norman, *The Pursuit of the Millennium* (Oxford: Oxford University Press, 1970).

Collins, J. J., *The Apocalyptic Imagination* (New York: Crossroad, 1984).

Collins, J.J., *The Scepter and the Star* (New York: Doubleday, 1995).

Crossan, J. D., *The Historical Jesus* (Edinburgh: T. & T. Clark, 1991).

Cupitt, D. and Armstrong, P., *Who Was Jesus?* (London: BBC, 1977).

Cupitt, D., *The Debate About Christ* (London: SCM Press, 1979).

Dawkins, Richard, *The God Fallacy* (London: Bantam Press, 2006).

Dennett, Daniel C., *Breaking the Spell* (London: Penguin, 2006).

Downing, F. G., *Cynics and Christian Origins* (Edinburgh: T. & T. Clark, 1992).

Dunn, J. D. G., *The Parting of the Ways Between Christianity and Judaism* (London: SCM Press, 1991).

Ehrman, B. D., *The Orthodox Corruption of Scripture* (Oxford: Oxford University Press, 1993).

Eisenman, Robert, *The Dead Sea Scrolls and the First Christians* (Shaftesbury: Element, 1996).

Eisenman, Robert, *James the Brother of Jesus: Recovering the True History of Early Christianity* (London: Faber, 1997).

Eisenman, Robert, *The New Testament Code* (London: Watkins, 2006).

Eisler, Robert, *The Messiah Jesus and John the Baptist* (London: Methuen, 1931).

Ellegård, Alvar, *Jesus: One Hundred Years Before Christ* (London: Century, 1999).

Farmer, W. R., *The Synoptic Problem* (London: Macmillan, 1964).

Faulkner, Neil, *Apocalypse: The Great Jewish Revolt Against Rome, AD 66–73* (Stroud: Tempus, 2002).

Feldman, L. H., *Jew and Gentile in the Ancient World* (Princeton, NJ: Princeton University Press, 1993).

Finegan, J., *Handbook of Biblical Chronology* (Princeton, NJ: Princeton University Press, 1964).

Fishbane, M., *Biblical Interpretation in Ancient Israel* (Oxford: Oxford University Press, 1988).

Fitzmyer, J.A., *Essays on the Semitic Background of the New Testament* (London: Chapman, 1971).

Fredrickson, Paula, *From Jesus to Christ* (New Haven, CT: Yale University Press, 1988).

Friedman, R. E., *Who Wrote the Bible?* (London: Jonathan Cape, 1988).

Fox, Robin Lane, *Pagans and Christians* (London: Penguin, 1986).

Fox, Robin Lane, *The Unauthorised Version* (London: Viking, 1991).

Fox, Robin Lane, *The Classical World* (London: Penguin, 2005).

Freke, Timothy and Gandy, Peter, *The Jesus Mysteries* (London: Thorsons, 1999).

Funk, Robert W., Hoover, Roy W., and the Jesus Seminar, (eds.), *The Five Gospels: The Search for the Authentic Words of Jesus* (New York: Polebridge Press, 1993).

Glasson, T. Francis, *Jesus and the End of the World* (Edinburgh: St. Andrew Press, 1980).

Godwin, J., *Mystery Religions in the Ancient World* (London: Thames & Hudson, 1981).

Golb, Norman, *Who Wrote the Dead Sea Scrolls?* (New York: Scribner, 1995).

Select Bibliography

Graves, Robert, *The Greek Myths: Combined Edition* (London: Penguin, 1992).

Hanson, A. T., *Jesus in the Old Testament* (London: SPCK, 1965).

Harris, H., *The Tübingen School* (Oxford: Clarendon Press, 1975).

Harvey, A. E., *Jesus and the Constraints of History* (London: Duckworth, 1982).

Hengel, M., *Judaism and Hellenism* (Philadelphia, PA: Fortress Press, 1974).

Hengel, M., *The Zealots* (Edinburgh: T. & T. Clark, 1989).

Herford, R. T., *Christianity in Talmud and Midrash* (London: Williams & Norgate, 1903).

Hitchens, Christopher, *God is Not Great* (London: Atlantic Books, 2007).

Hodge, Stephen, *The Dead Sea Scrolls: An Introductory Guide* (London: Piatkus, 2001).

Horsley, R. & Hanson, J. S., *Bandits, Prophets, and Messiahs: Popular Movements in the Time of Jesus* (Minneapolis, MN: Winston Press, 1985).

Jaspers, Karl & Bultmann, Rudolf, *Myth and Christianity* (New York: Noonday Press, 1958). [Translation of the original *Die Frage der Entmythologisierung*].

Kennedy, H. A. A., *St Paul and the Mystery Religions* (London: Hodder & Stoughton, 1969).

Kersten, Holger, *Jesus Lived in India* (Shaftesbury: Element Books, 1994).

Kersten, Holger, and Gruber, Elmar R., *The Jesus Conspiracy: The Turin Shroud and the Truth About the Resurrection* (Shaftesbury: Element Books, 1994).

Kingsley, P., *Ancient Philosophy, Mystery and Magic* (Oxford: Oxford University Press, 1995).

Kinane, Karolyn and Ryan, Michael A., [eds.], *End of Days: Essays on the Apocalypse from Antiquity to Modernity* (Jefferson: McFarland, 2009).

Klausner, J., *The Messianic Idea in Israel* (London: Allen & Unwin, 1956).

Krosney, Herbert, *The Lost Gospel: The Quest for the Gospel of Judas Iscariot* (Washington, D.C.: National Geographic, 2006).

Kümmel, W.G., *The New Testament: The History of the Investigation of Its Problems* (London: SCM Press, 1975).

Leaney, A.R.C., *The Jewish and Christian World: 200 BC to 200 AD* (Cambridge: Cambridge University Press, 1984).

Maccoby, Hyam, *The Mythmaker: Paul and the Invention of Christianity* (New York: Harper & Row, 1986).

Maccoby, Hyam, *Judaism in the First Century* (London: Sheldon Press, 1989).

Maccoby, Hyam, *Judas Iscariot and the Myth of Jewish Evil* (London: Peter Halban, 1992).

Maccoby, Hyam, *Jesus the Pharisee* (London: SCM Press, 2003).
Mack, Burton L., The *Lost Gospel: The Book of Q and Christian Origins* (Shaftesbury: Element Books, 1993).
Mack, Burton L., *Who Wrote the New Testament? The Making of the Christian Myth* (New York: Harper One, 1995).
Mackey, J. P., *Jesus, the Man and the Myth* (London: SCM Press, 1979).
Meeks, W. A., *The First Urban Christians: The Social World of the Apostle Paul* (New Haven, CT: Yale University Press, 1983).
Metzger, Bruce M., *The Canon of the New Testament* (Oxford: Oxford University Press, 1987).
Metzger, Bruce M. and Coogan, Michael D., (eds.), *The Oxford Companion to the Bible* (Oxford: Oxford University Press, 1993).
Mowri, Lucetta, *The Dead Sea Scrolls and the Early Church* (Chicago, IL: Chicago University Press, 1962).
Neusner, J., Green, W.S. and Fredrichs, E., *Judaisms and their Messiahs at the Turn of the Christian Era* (Cambridge: Cambridge University Press, 1987).
Osman, Ahmed, *Out of Egypt: The Roots of Christianity Revealed* (London: Century, 1998).
Pagels, Elaine, *The Gnostic Gospels* (London: Weidenfeld & Nicolson, 1979).
Powell, Enoch, *The Evolution of the Gospel* (New Haven, CT: Yale University Press, 1994).
Price, Robert M., *The Case Against the Case for Christ* (Cranford: American Atheist Press, 2011).
Price, Robert M., *The Christ-Myth Theory and its Problems* (Cranford, NJ: American Atheist Press, 2011).
Price, Robert M., *The Amazing Colossal Apostle: The Search for the Historical Paul* (Salt Lake City, UT: Signature Books, 2012).
Pritchard, James B. (ed.), *The Times Concise Atlas of the Bible* (London: Times Books, 1991).
Riddle, Donald W., 'The Cephas-Peter Problem', *Journal of Biblical Literature*, 59, 1940, pp. 169–80.
Robertson, J. M., *Pagan Christs* 2nd ed. (London: Watts & Co., 1911)
Robertson, J.M., *Jesus and Judas* (London: Watts & Co., 1927).
Robinson, James, *A New Quest of the Historical Jesus* (London: SCM Press, 1961).
Romer, John, *Testament: The Bible and History* (London: Michael O'Mara, 1988).
Rowland, Christopher, *The Open Heaven: A Study of Apocalyptic in Judaism and Early Christianity* (London: SPCK, 1982)

Select Bibliography

Rowland, Christopher, *Christian Origins* (London: SPCK, 1985).
Safrai, S. and Stern, M., *The Jewish People in the First Century* (2 vols., Philadelphia, PA: Van Gorcum, 1974).
Salibi, Kamal, *Who Was Jesus? A Conspiracy in Jerusalem* (London: I.B. Tauris, 1992).
Sanders, E. P., *The Historical Figure of Jesus* (London: Allen Lane, 1993).
Sanders, Jack T., *The Jews in Luke-Acts* (London: SCM Press, 1987).
Scarrow, Simon, *The Eagle in the Sand* (London: Headline, 2006).
Scholem, G., *The Messianic Idea in Judaism* (New York: Schocken Books, 1971).
Schonfield, Hugh, *The Passover Plot* (Shaftesbury: Element, 1965).
Schonfield, Hugh, *Those Incredible Christians* (London: Hutchinson, 1968).
Schonfield, Hugh, *The Essene Odyssey* (Shaftesbury: Element, 1984).
Schürer, E., *History of the Jewish People in the Age of Jesus Christ*. rev. ed. (Edinburgh: T. & T. Clark, 1973).
Schweitzer, Albert, *The Quest of the Historical Jesus* (London: Macmillan, 1968).
Shanks, H., *Understanding the Dead Sea Scrolls* (London: SPCK, 1992).
Sheehan, T., *The First Coming: How the Kingdom of God became Christianity* (New York: Random House, 1986).
Sherwin-White, A.N., *Roman Society and Roman Law in the New Testament* (Oxford: Clarendon Press, 1963).
Shorto, Russell, *Gospel Truth* (London: Hodder & Stoughton, 1997).
Silberman, Neil Asher, *The Hidden Scrolls* (London: Heinemann, 1995).
Silver, A. H., *A History of Messianic Speculation in Israel* (New York: Macmillan, 1927).
Smallwood, E. M., *The Jews Under Roman Rule* (Leiden: Brill, 1976).
Smith, Morton, *Palestinian Parties and Politics that Shaped the Old Testament* (New York: Columbia University Press, 1971).
Smith, Morton, *Jesus the Magician* (New York: Harper & Row, 1978).
Spong, J. S., *Rescuing the Bible From Fundamentalism* (San Francisco: Harper, 1991).
Stanton, Graham, *The Gospels and Jesus* (Oxford: Oxford University Press, 1989).
Stanton, Graham, *Gospel Truth? Today's Quest for Jesus of Nazareth* (London: Fount, 1995).
Stendahl, K., *Paul Among Jews and Gentiles* (Philadelphia, PA: Fortress Press, 1976).
Stone, Michael E., *Scriptures, Sects, and Visions: A Profile of Judaism from Ezra to the Jewish Revolts* (Philadelphia, PA: Fortress Press, 1980).

Strauss, D. F., *The Life of Jesus Critically Examined*. [Trans. George Eliot] (London: Chapman, 1846).
Streeter, B. H., *The Four Gospels. A Study of Origins* (London: Macmillan, 1927).
Theissen, G., *The Shadow of the Galilean; The Quest of the Historical in Narrative Form* (London: SCM Press, 1987).
Thiering, Barbara, *Jesus the Man* (London: Doubleday, 1992).
Unterbrink, Daniel T., *Judas the Galilean: The Flesh and Blood Jesus* (Lincoln, NE: iUniverse, 2004).
Unterbrink, Daniel T., *New Testament Lies: The Greatest Challenge to Traditional Christianity* (Lincoln, NE: iUniverse, 2006).
Unterbrink, Daniel T., *The Three Messiahs: The Historical Judas the Galilean, The Revelatory Christ Jesus, and The Mythical Jesus of Nazareth* (Lincoln, NE: iUniverse, 2010).
Vaganay, L. & Amphoux, C.-B., *An Introduction to New Testament Textual Criticism* (Cambridge: Cambridge University Press, 1991).
Vermes, Geza, *Jesus the Jew* (London: Collins, 1973).
Vermes, Geza, *Jesus and the World of Judaism* (London: SCM Press, 1983).
Vermes, Geza, *The Religion of Jesus the Jew* (London: SCM Press, 1993).
Webb, Robert, *John the Baptizer and Prophet: A Socio-Historical Study* (Sheffield: JSOT, 1991).
Wells, G. A., *The Jesus of the Early Christians* (London: Pemberton Books, 1971).
Wells, G.A., *Did Jesus Exist?* (London: Pemberton Books, 1975).
Wells, G.A., *The Historical Evidence for Jesus* (New York: Prometheus, 1982).
Wells, G.A., *The Jesus Legend* (Chicago, IL: Open Court Publishing Co., 1996)
Wilken, R. L., *The Christians as the Romans Saw Them* (New Haven, CT: Yale University Press, 1984).
Wilson, A. N., *Jesus* (London: Sinclair-Stevenson, 1992).
Wilson, A.N., *Paul: The Mind of the Apostle* (London: Pimlico, 1998).
Wilson, Edmund, *The Dead Sea Scrolls 1947–1969* (Oxford: Oxford University Press, 1969).
Wilson, Ian, *Jesus: The Evidence* (London: Weidenfeld & Nicolson, 1984).
Wink, W., *John the Baptist in the Gospel Tradition* (Cambridge: Cambridge University Press, 1968).
Wright, N. T., *Who Was Jesus?* (London: SPCK, 1992).
Zuckermann, Benedict, *Treatise on the Sabbatical Cycle and the Jubilee*, Trans. A Löwy (New York: Hermon, 1974).

A Bonfire of Inanities: The Bible Dismantled offers, in three volumes, a revolutionary new understanding of the roots of Judaism and Christianity by way of a complete, rationalistic re-interpretation of the Bible, from Genesis to Revelation. There has never been anything like this – in scope, in approach, and in findings. It may be possible to continue in Jewish or Christian belief in the light of this trilogy, but it would be a very different kind of religious faith from the one normally espoused. Each volume has been written to stand alone, but there is a natural sequence to the arguments developed which is facilitated if they are read in order.

VOLUME ONE

Ancestral Tales analyses the various source texts that make up the so-called Books of Moses in the Old Testament in conjunction with non-Biblical records, and separates history from myth. It traces the true ancestral and religious history of the Israelites and in particular, it identifies among much else, the Pharoah of the Exodus, and the historical figures behind Joseph and Moses.

A Bonfire of Inanities: The Bible Dismantled offers, in three volumes, a revolutionary new understanding of the roots of Judaism and Christianity by way of a complete, rationalistic re-interpretation of the Bible, from Genesis to Revelation. There has never been anything like this – in scope, in approach, and in findings. It may be possible to continue in Jewish or Christian belief in the light of this trilogy, but it would be a very different kind of religious faith from the one normally espoused. Each volume has been written to stand alone, but there is a natural sequence to the arguments developed which is facilitated if they are read in order.

VOLUME THREE

Apocalypse Postponed focusses on the Christian belief in imminent apocalypse and traces how thoroughgoing misunderstanding of the relevant Old and New Testament texts has led to two centuries of fallacious expectation. It identifies the key apocalyptic themes and locates them, not in our future, but in people and events contemporary with the writer of Revelation.

www.ingramcontent.com/pod-product-compliance
Lightning Source LLC
Chambersburg PA
CBHW052131070526
44585CB00017B/1788